A-O volume 5

experiment CENTRAL

understanding scientific principles through projects

M. Rae Nelson

Allison McNeill, Project Editor

Detroit • New York • San Diego • San Francisco • Cleveland • New Haven, Conn. • Waterville, Maine • London • Munich

THOMSON
™
GALE

Experiment Central, Volumes 5 and 6
M. Rae Nelson

Project Editor
Allison McNeill

Permissions
Margaret Chamberlain

Imaging and Multimedia
Kelly A. Quin, Christine O'Bryan

Product Design
Eric Johnson, Tracey Rowens, Cynthia Baldwin

Composition
Evi Seoud

Manufacturing
Rita Wimberley

LIBRARY OF CONGRESS CATALOGING-IN-PUBLICATION DATA

Loret, John.
Experiment central: understanding scientific principles through projects / John Loret, John T. Tanacredi.
   p. cm.
Includes bibliographical references and index.
Contents: v. 1. A-Ec – v. 2. El-L – v. 3. M-Sc – v. 4. So-Z
Summary: Demonstrates scientific concepts by means of experiments, including step-by-step instructions, lists of materials, troubleshooter's guide, and interpretation and explanation of results.
ISBN 0-7876-2892-1 (set). – ISBN 0-7876-2893-X (v. 1) – ISBN 0-7876-2894-8 (v.2)– ISBN 0-7876-2895-6 (v.3) – ISBN 0-7876-2896-4 (v. 4)
1. Science-Experiments-Juvenile literature. [1. Science-Experiments. 2. Experiments.] I. Tanacredi, John T. II. Title.
Q164 .L57 2000   199-054142
507'.8-dc2

ISBN 0-7876-7735-3 (set); ISBN 0-7876-7615-2 (volume 5); ISBN 0-7876-7622-5 (volume 6)

Printed in the United States of America
10 9 8 7 6 5 4 3 2 1

contents

Volume 5: A–O

experiment
CENTRAL

Volume 6: P–Z

contents

experiment
CENTRAL

reader's guide

Experiment Central: Understanding Scientific Principles Through Projects provides in one resource a wide variety of science experiments covering nine key science curriculum fields—Astronomy, Biology, Botany, Chemistry, Ecology, Food Science, Geology, Meteorology, and Physics—spanning the earth sciences, life sciences, and physical sciences.

Experiment Central, Volumes 5 and 6, a continuation of U•X•L's four-volume base set, presents fifty-four new experiments and projects for students in twenty-seven subject-specific chapters. Chapters, each devoted to a scientific concept, include: Air and Water Pollution, Caves, DNA, Fungi, Periodic Table, Storms, and Time. Two experiments or projects are provided in each chapter.

Entry format

Chapters are arranged alphabetically by scientific concept and are presented in a standard, easy-to-follow format. All chapters open with an explanatory overview section designed to introduce students to the scientific concept and provide the background behind a concept's discovery or important figures who helped advance the study of the field.

Each experiment is divided into eight standard sections designed to help students follow the experimental process clearly from beginning to end. Sections are:

- Purpose/Hypothesis
- Level of Difficulty
- Materials Needed
- Approximate Budget
- Timetable
- Step-by-Step Instructions
- Summary of Results
- Change the Variables

Each chapter also includes a "Design Your Own Experiment" section that allows students to apply what they have learned about a particular concept and to create their own experiments. This section is divided into:

- How to Select a Topic Relating to this Concept
- Steps in the Scientific Method
- Recording Data and Summarizing the Results
- Related Projects

Concluding all chapters is a "For More Information" section that provides students with a list of books and Web sites with further information about that particular topic.

Special Features

- A **"Words to Know"** section runs in the margin of each chapter providing definitions of terms used in that chapter. Terms in this list are bolded in the text upon first usage. A cumulative glossary collected from all "Words to Know" sections in the twenty-seven chapters is included in the beginning of each volume.
- **Experiments by Scientific Field** index categorizes experiments by scientific curriculum area. This index cumulates all 154 experiments across the six-volume series.
- **Parent's and Teacher's Guide** recommends that a responsible adult always oversees a student's experiment and provides several safety guidelines for all students to follow.
- Standard sidebar boxes accompany experiments and projects:

  "What Are the Variables?" explains the factors that may have an impact on the outcome of a particular experiment.

  "How to Experiment Safely" clearly explains any risks involved with the experiment and how to avoid them. While all experiments have been constructed with safety in mind, it is always recommended to proceed with caution and work under adult supervision while performing any experiment (please refer to the Parent's and Teacher's Guide on page xv).

  "Troubleshooter's Guide" presents problems that a student might encounter with an experiment, possible causes of the problem, and ways to remedy the problem.
- Approximately **80 photographs** enhance Volumes 5 and 6.

- Approximately **170 drawings** illustrate scientific concepts and specific steps in the experiments, helping students follow the experimental procedure.

Four indexes, which cumulate all 154 experiments across the six-volume series, conclude each volume:

- **Budget Index** categorizes experiments by approximate cost. Budgets may vary depending on what materials are readily available in the average household.
- **Level of Difficulty Index** lists experiments according to "Easy," "Moderate," "Difficult," or a combination thereof. Level of difficulty is determined by such factors as the time necessary to complete the experiment, level of adult supervision recommended, and skill level of the average student. Level of difficulty will vary depending on the student. A teacher or parent should always be consulted before any experiment is attempted.
- **Timetable Index** categorizes each experiment by the time needed to complete it, including setup and followthrough time. Times given are approximate.
- **General Subject Index** provides access to all major terms, people, places, and topics covered in *Experiment Central*.

Acknowledgments

A note of appreciation is extended to the *Experiment Central* advisors, who provided their input when this work was in its formative stages:

Teresa F. Bettac
Middle School Advanced Science Teacher
Delaware, Ohio

Linda Leuzzi
Writer, Trustee of The Science Museum of Long Island

David J. Miller
Director of Education

The Science Museum of Long Island

The author also wishes to acknowledge and thank Joyce Katz, Cindy O'Neil, and Alana Brette Nelson for their contributions to the experiments in Volumes 5 and 6, as well as science copyeditor Chris Cavette and illustrator Temah Nelson for their contributions to *Experiment Central*, Volumes 5 and 6.

Comments and Suggestions

We welcome your comments on *Experiment Central.* Please write: Editors, *Experiment Central,* U•X•L, 27500 Drake Rd., Farmington Hills, Michigan, 48331–3535; call toll free: 1–800–877–4253; fax: 248–699–8097; or send e-mail via http://www.gale.com.

parent's and teacher's guide

The experiments and projects in *Experiment Central* have been carefully constructed with issues of safety in mind, but your guidance and supervision are still required. Following the safety guidelines that accompany each experiment and project (found in the "How to Experiment Safely" sidebar box), as well as putting to work the safe practices listed below, will help your child or student avoid accidents. Oversee your child or student during experiments, and make sure he or she follows these safety guidelines:

- Always wear safety goggles if there is any possibility of sharp objects, small particles, splashes of liquid, or gas fumes getting in someone's eyes.

- Always wear protective gloves when handling materials that could irritate the skin.

- Never leave an open flame, such as a lit candle, unattended. Never wear loose clothing around an open flame.

- Follow instructions carefully when using electrical equipment, including batteries, to avoid getting shocked.

- Be cautious when handling sharp objects or glass equipment that might break. Point scissors away from you and use them carefully.

- Always ask for help in cleaning up spills, broken glass, or other hazardous materials.

- Always use protective gloves when handling hot objects. Set them down only on a protected surface that will not be damaged by heat.

parent's and teacher's guide

- Always wash your hands thoroughly after handling material that might contain harmful microorganisms, such as soil and pond water.
- Do not substitute materials in an experiment without asking a knowledgeable adult about possible reactions.
- Do not use or mix unidentified liquids or powders. The result might be an explosion or poisonous fumes.
- Never taste or eat any substances being used in an experiment.
- Always wear old clothing or a protective apron to avoid staining your clothes.

experiment
CENTRAL

experiments by scientific field

Chapter name in brackets, followed by experiment name; *italic* type indicates volume number, followed by page number; **boldface** volume numbers indicate main entries in *Experiment Central*, Volumes 5 and 6.

Astronomy

Biology

experiment
CENTRAL

Botany

Chemistry

**experiments
by scientific
field**

Ecology

Food Science

Geology

experiment CENTRAL

experiments by scientific field

All Subjects

words to know

A

Absolute dating: The age of an object correlated to a specific fixed time, as established by some precise dating method.

Acceleration: The rate at which the velocity and/or direction of an object is changing with respect to time.

Additive: A chemical compound that is added to foods to give them some desirable quality, such as preventing them from spoiling.

Air: Gaseous mixture that envelopes Earth, composed mainly of nitrogen (about 78 percent) and oxygen (about 21 percent) with lesser amounts of argon, carbon dioxide, and other gases.

Air density: The ratio of the mass of a substance to the volume it occupies.

Air mass: A large body of air that has similar characteristics.

Air pressure: The force exerted by the weight of the atmosphere above a point on or above Earth's surface.

Alkali metals: The first group of elements in the periodic table, these metals have a single electron in the outermost shell.

Alkaline: A substance that is capable of neutralizing an acid, or basic. In soil, soil with a pH of more than 7.0, which is neutral.

Amino acids: The building blocks of proteins.

Angiosperm: A flowering plant, which has its seeds produced within an ovary.

Anther: The male reproductive organs of the plant, located on the tip of a flower's stamen.

Antibiotic resistance: The ability of microorganisms to change so that they are not killed by antibiotics.

Antibiotics: A substance produced by or derived from certain fungi, bacteria, and other organisms that can destroy or inhibit the growth of other microorganisms; widely used in the prevention and treatment of infectious diseases.

Antioxidants Used as a food additive, these substances can prevent food spoilage by reducing the foods exposure to air.

Atmosphere: Layers of air that surround Earth.

Atom: The smallest unit of an element, made up of protons and neutrons in its center, surrounded by moving electrons.

Atomic mass: Also known as atomic weight, the average mass of the atoms in an element; the number that appears under the element symbol in the periodic table.

Atomic number: The number of protons (or electrons) in an atom; the number that appears over the element symbol in the periodic table.

Atomic symbol: The one- or two-letter abbreviation for a chemical element.

Axis: An imaginary straight line around which an object, like a planet, spins or turns. Earth's axis is a line that goes through the North and South Poles.

B

Bacteria: Single-celled microorganisms that live in soil, water, plants, and animals that play a key role in the decay of organic matter and the cycling of nutrients. Some are agents of disease. (Singular: bacterium.)

Barometer: An instrument for measuring atmospheric pressure, used especially in weather forecasting.

Base: Substance that when dissolved in water is capable of reacting with an acid to form salts and release hydrogen ions; has a pH of more than 7.

Base pairs: In DNA, the pairing of two nucleotides with each other: adenine (A) with thymine (T), and guanine (G) with cytosine (C).

experiment
CENTRAL

Bedrock: Solid layer of rock lying beneath the soil and other loose material.

Biodegradable: Capable of being decomposed by biological agents.

Bioluminescence: The chemical phenomenon in which an organism can produce its own light.

Biopesticide: Pesticide produced from substances found in nature.

Blueshift: The shortening of the frequency of light waves toward the blue end of the visible light spectrum as they travel towards an observer; most commonly used to describe movement of stars towards Earth.

Boiling point: The temperature at which a substance changes from a liquid to a gas or vapor.

Bone joint: A place in the body where two or more bones are connected.

Bone marrow: The spongy center of many bones in which blood cells are manufactured.

Bone tissue: A group of similar cells in the bone with a common function.

C

Cancellous bone: Also called spongy bone, the inner layer of a bone that has cells with large spaces in between them filled with marrow.

Canning: A method of preserving food using airtight, vacuum-sealed containers and heat processing.

Carbonic acid: A weak acid that forms from the mixture of water and carbon dioxide.

Cartilage: The connective tissue that covers and protects the bones.

Cast: In paleontology, the fossil formed when a mold is later filled in by mud or mineral matter.

Cave: Also called cavern, a hollow or natural passage under or into the ground large enough for a person to enter.

Cell membrane: The layer that surrounds the cell, but is inside the cell wall, allowing some molecules to enter and keeping others out of the cell.

Cell wall: A tough outer covering that overlies the cell membrane of bacteria and plant cells.

Centrifugal force: The apparent force pushing a rotating body away from the center of rotation.

Centripetal force: A force that pushes an object inward, which causes the object to move in a circular path.

Chemosense: A sense stimulated by specific chemicals that cause the sensory cell to transmit a signal to the brain. The senses of taste and smell.

Chromatography: A method for separating mixtures into their component parts (into their "ingredients") by flowing the mixture over another substance and noting the differences in attraction between the substance and each component of the mixture.

Cilia: Hairlike structures on olfactory receptor cells that sense odor molecules.

Circumference: The distance around a circle.

Clay: Type of soil comprising the smallest soil particles.

Collagen: A protein in bone that gives the bone elasticity.

Colony: A visible growth of microorganisms, containing millions of bacterial cells.

Coma: Glowing cloud of gas surrounding the nucleus of a comet.

Comet: An icy body orbiting in the solar system, which partially vaporizes when it nears the Sun and develops a diffuse envelope of dust and gas as well as one or more tails.

Comet head: The nucleus and the coma of a comet.

Comet nucleus: The core or center of a comet. (Plural: Comet nuclei.)

Comet tail: The most distinctive feature of comets; comets can display two basic types of tails: one gaseous and the other largely composed of dust.

Compact bone: The outer, hard layer of the bone.

Concave lens: A lens that is thinner in the middle than at the edges.

Condense: When a gas or vapor changes to a liquid.

experiment
CENTRAL

Conservation of energy: The law of physics that states that energy can be transformed from one form to another, but can be neither created nor destroyed.

Contract: To shorten, pull together.

Control experiment: A setup that is identical to the experiment, but is not affected by the variable that acts on the experimental group.

Convection current: Also called density-driven current, a cycle of warm water rising and cooler water sinking. Also a circular movement of a gas in response to alternating heating and cooling.

Convex lens: A lens that is thicker in the middle than at the edges.

Coprolites: The fossilized droppings of animals.

Coriolis force: A force that makes a moving object appear to travel in a curved path over the surface of a spinning body.

Crater: An indentation caused by an object hitting the surface of a planet or moon.

Crest: The highest point of a wave.

Cross-pollination: The process by which pollen from one plant pollinates another plant of the same species.

Crystal: Naturally occurring solid composed of atoms or molecules arranged in an orderly pattern that repeats at regular intervals.

Crystal faces: The flat, smooth surfaces of a crystal.

Crystal lattice: The regular and repeating pattern of the atoms in a crystal.

Cumulonimbus cloud: The parent cloud of a thunderstorm; a tall, vertically developed cloud capable of producing heavy rain, high winds, and lightning.

Currents: The horizontal and vertical circulation of ocean waters.

Cytoplasm: The semifluid substance inside a cell that surrounds the nucleus and other membrane-enclosed organelles.

D

Deficiency disease: A disease marked by a lack of an essential nutrient in the diet.

Degrade: Break down.

Dehydration: The removal of water from a material.

Density: The mass of a substance compared to its volume.

Deoxyribonucleic acid (DNA): (Pronounced DEE-ox-see-rye-bo-noo-klay-ick acid) Large, complex molecules found in the nuclei of cells that carry genetic information for an organism's development.

DNA replication: The process by which one DNA strand unwinds and duplicates all its information, creating two new DNA strands that are identical to each other and to the original strand.

Doppler effect: The change in wavelength and frequency (number of vibrations per second) of either light or sound as the source is moving either towards or away from the observer.

Dormant: A state of inactivity in an organism.

Double helix: The shape taken by DNA (deoxyribonucleic acid) molecules in a nucleus.

Dust tail: One of two types of tails a comet may have, it is composed mainly of dust and it points away from the Sun.

E

Effort: The force applied to move a load using a simple machine.

Elastomers: Any of various polymers having rubbery properties.

Electron: A subatomic particle with a mass of about one atomic mass unit and a single electrical charge that orbits the center of an atom.

Element: A pure substance composed of just one type of atom that cannot be broken down into anything simpler by ordinary chemical means.

Elongation: The percentage increase in length that occurs before a material breaks under tension.

Enzyme: Any of numerous complex proteins produced by living cells that act as catalysts, speeding up the rate of chemical reactions in living organisms.

Eukaryotic: Multicellular organism whose cells contain distinct nuclei, which contain the genetic material. (Pronounced yoo-KAR-ee-ah-tic)

Eutrophication: The process by which high nutrient concentrations in a body of water eventually cause the natural wildlife to die

Extremophiles: Bacteria that thrive in environments too harsh to support most life forms.

F

Family: A group of elements in the same column of the periodic table or in closely related columns of the table. A family of chemical compounds share similar structures and properties.

Fat-soluble vitamins: Vitamins such as A, D, E, and K that can be dissolved in the fat of plants and animals.

Fermentation: A chemical reaction in which enzymes break down complex organic compounds (for example, carbohydrates and sugars) into simpler ones (for example, ethyl alcohol).

Filament: In a flower, stalk of the stamen that bears the anther.

Filtration: The mechanical separation of a liquid from the undissolved particles floating in it

Fireball: Meteors that create an intense, bright light and, sometimes, an explosion.

First law of motion (Newton's): An object at rest or moving in a certain direction and speed will remain at rest or moving in the same motion and speed unless acted upon by a force.

Flagella: Whiplike structures used by some organisms for movement. (Singular: flagellum.)

Flower: The reproductive part of a flowering plant.

Focal length: The distance from the lens to the point where the light rays come together to a focus.

Force: A physical interaction (pushing or pulling) tending to change the state of motion (velocity) of an object.

Fortified: The addition of nutrients, such as vitamins or minerals, to food.

Fossil: The remains, trace, or impressions of a living organism that inhabited Earth more than ten thousand years ago.

Fossil record: The documentation of fossils placed in relationship to one another; a key source to understanding the evolution of life on Earth.

Frequency: The rate at which vibrations take place (number of times per second the motion is repeated), given in cycles per second or in hertz (Hz). Also, the number of waves that pass a given point in a given period of time.

Friction: A force that resists the motion of an object, resulting when two objects rub against one another.

Front: The area between air masses of different temperatures or densities.

Fulcrum: The point at which a lever arm pivots.

Fungi: Kingdom of various single-celled or multicellular organisms, including mushrooms, molds, yeasts, and mildews, that do not manufacture their own food.

Funnel cloud: A fully developed tornado vortex before it has touched the ground.

G

Germ theory of disease: The theory that disease is caused by microorganisms or germs, and not by spontaneous generation.

Gnomon: The perpendicular piece of the sundial that casts the shadow.

Gravity: Force of attraction between objects, the strength of which depends on the mass of each object and the distance between them.

Greenhouse effect: The warming of Earth's atmosphere due to water vapor, carbon dioxide, and other gases in the atmosphere that trap heat radiated from Earth's surface.

Greenwich Mean Time (GMT): The time at an imaginary line that runs north and south through Greenwich, England, used as the standard for time throughout the world.

Group: A vertical column of the periodic table that contains elements possessing similar chemical characteristics.

H

Heterogeneous: Different throughout; made up of different parts.

Homogenous: The same throughout; made up of similar parts.

Humus: Fragrant, spongy, nutrient-rich decayed plant or animal matter.

Hypha: Slender, cottony filaments making up the body of multicellular fungi. (Plural: hyphae)

Hypothesis: An idea in the form of a statement that can be tested by observation and/or experiment.

I

Imperfect flower: Flowers that have only the male reproductive organ (stamen) or the female reproductive organs (pistil)

Inclined plane: A simple machine with no moving parts; a slanted surface.

Inertia: The tendency of an object to continue in its state of motion.

Inorganic: Made of or coming from nonliving matter.

Insoluble: A substance that cannot be dissolved in some other substance.

Ion: An atom or groups of atoms that carries an electrical charge—either positive or negative—as a result of losing or gaining one or more electrons.

Ion tail: One of two types of tails a comet may have; it is composed mainly of charged particles and it points away from the Sun.

words to know

K

Kingdom: One of the five classifications in the widely accepted classification system that designates all living organisms into animals, plants, fungi, protists, and monerans.

L

Lava cave: A cave formed from the flow of lava streaming over solid matter.

Leaching: The movement of dissolved chemicals with water that percolates, or oozes, downward through the soil.

Ligaments: Tough, fibrous tissue connecting bones.

M

Machine: Any device that makes work easier by providing a mechanical advantage.

Macrominerals: Minerals needed in relatively large quantities.

Melting point: The temperature at which a substance changes from a solid to a liquid.

Meteor: An object from space that becomes glowing hot when it passes into Earth's atmosphere; also called shooting star.

Meteorites: A meteor that is large enough to survive its passage through the atmosphere and hit the ground.

Meteoroid: A piece of debris that is traveling in space.

Meteorologists: Professionals who study Earth's atmosphere and its phenomena, including weather and weather forecasting.

Meteor shower: A group of meteors that occurs when Earth's orbit intersects the orbit of a meteor stream.

Microvilli: The extension of each taste cell that pokes through the taste pore and first senses the chemicals.

Mineral: A nonorganic substance found in nature that originates in the ground; has a definite chemical composition and structure.

Mixture: A combination of two or more substances that are not chemically combined with each other and that can exist in any proportion.

Mold: In paleontology, the fossil formed when acidic water dissolves a shell or bone around which sand or mud has already hardened.

Molecule: The smallest particle of a substance that retains all the properties of the substance and is composed of one or more atoms.

Monomer: A small molecule that can be combined with itself many times over to make a large molecule, the polymer.

Mucus: A thick, slippery substance that serves as a protective lubricant coating in passages of the body that communicate with the air.

Muscle fibers: Stacks of long, thin cells that makeup muscle; there are three types of muscle fiber: skeletal, cardiac, and smooth.

Mycelium: In fungi, the mass of threadlike, branching hyphae.

N

Nectar: A sweet liquid found inside a flower that attracts pollinators.

Neutron: A particle that has no electrical charge and is found in the center of an atom.

Noble gases: Also known as inert or rare gases; the elements argon, helium, krypton, neon, radon, and xenon, which are unreactive gases and form few compounds with other elements.

Nucleation: The process by which crystals start growing.

Nucleotide: The basic unit of a nucleic acid. It consists of a simple sugar, a phosphate group, and a nitrogen-containing base. (Pronounced noo-KLEE-uh-tide.)

Nucleus, cell: Membrane-enclosed structure within a cell that contains the cell's genetic material and controls its growth and reproduction. (Plural: nuclei.)

O

Objective lens: In a refracting telescope, the lens farthest away from the eye that collects the light.

Oceanographer: A person who studies the chemistry of the oceans, as well as their currents, marine life, and the ocean floor.

Olfactory: Relating to the sense of smell.

Olfactory bulb: The part of the brain that processes olfactory (smell) information.

Olfactory epithelium: The patch of mucous membrane at the top of the nasal cavity that contains the olfactory (smell) nerve cells.

Olfactory receptor cells: Nerve cells in the olfactory epithelium that detect odors and transmit the information to the brain.

Oort cloud: Region of space beyond Earth's solar system that theoretically contains about one trillion inactive comets.

Orbit: The path followed by a body (such as a planet) in its travel around another body (such as the Sun).

Organelle: A membrane-enclosed structure that performs a specific function within a cell.

Organic: Made of, or coming from, living matter.

Oscillation: A repeated back-and-forth movement.

Osmosis: The movement of fluids and substances dissolved in liquids across a semi-permeable membrane from an area of greater concentration to an area of lesser concentration until all substances involved reach a balance.

Ovary: In a plant, the base part of the pistil that bears ovules and develops into a fruit.

Ovule: Structure within the ovary that develops into a seed after fertilization.

P

Paleontologist: Scientist who studies the life of past geological periods as known from fossil remains.

Papillae: The raised bumps on the tongue that contain the taste buds.

Parent material: The underlying rock from which soil forms.

Particulate matter: Solid matter in the form of tiny particles in the atmosphere. (Pronounced par-TIK-you-let.)

Pasteurization: The process of slow heating that kills bacteria and other microorganisms.

Pendulum: A free-swinging weight, usually consisting of a heavy object attached to the end of a long rod or string, suspended from a fixed point.

Perfect flower: Flowers that have both male and female reproductive organs.

Period: A horizontal row in the periodic table.

Periodic table: A chart organizing elements by atomic number and chemical properties into groups and periods.

Permineralization: A form of preservation in which mineral matter has filled in the inner and outer spaces of the cell.

Pest: Any living thing that is unwanted by humans or causes injury and disease to crops and other growth.

Pesticide: Substance used to reduce the abundance of pests.

Petal: Leafy structure of a flower just inside the sepals; they are often brightly colored and have many different shapes.

Petrifaction: Process of turning organic material into rock by the replacement of that material with minerals.

pH: A measure of a solution's acidity. The pH scale ranges from 0 (most acidic) to 14 (least acidic), with 7 representing a neutral solution, such as pure water.

Photosynthesis: Chemical process by which plants containing chlorophyll use sunlight to manufacture their own food by converting carbon dioxide and water into carbohydrates, releasing oxygen as a by-product.

Pili: Short projections that assist bacteria in attaching to tissues.

Pistil: Female reproductive organ of flowers that is composed of the stigma, style, and ovary.

Plasmolysis: Occurs in walled cells in which cytoplasm, the semifluid substance inside a cell, shrivels and the membrane pulls away from the cell wall when the vacuole loses water.

Pollen: Dustlike grains or particles produced by a plant that contain male sex cells.

Pollination: Transfer of pollen from the male reproductive organs to the female reproductive organs of plants.

Pollinator: Any animal, such as an insect or bird, who transfers the pollen from one flower to another.

Pollution: The contamination of the natural environment, usually through human activity.

Polymer: Chemical compound formed of simple molecules (known as monomers) linked with themselves many times over.

Polymerization: The bonding of two or more monomers to form a polymer.

Preservative: An additive used to keep food from spoiling.

Prokaryote: A cell without a true nucleus, such as a bacterium.

Protein: A complex chemical compound consisting of many amino acids attached to each other that are essential to the structure and functioning of all living cells.

Proton: A positively charged particle in the center of an atom.

Pulley: A simple machine made of a cord wrapped around a wheel.

R

Radioisotope dating: A technique used to date fossils, based on the decay rate of known radioactive elements.

Radon: A radioactive gas located in the ground; invisible and odorless, radon is a health hazard when it accumulates to high levels inside homes and other structures where it is breathed.

Rancidity: Having the condition when food has a disagreeable odor or taste from decomposing oils or fats.

Redshift: The lengthening of the frequency of light waves toward the red end of the visible light spectrum as they travel away from an observer; most commonly used to describe movement of stars away from Earth.

Reflector telescope: A telescope that directs light from an opening at one end to a concave mirror at the far end, which reflects the light back to a smaller mirror that directs it to an eyepiece on the side of the tube.

Refractor telescope: A telescope that directs light through a glass lens, which bends the light waves and brings them to a focus at an eyepiece that acts as a magnifying glass.

Relative age: The age of an object expressed in relation to another like object, such as earlier or later.

Ribosome: A protein composed of two subunits that functions in protein synthesis (creation).

Rock: Naturally occurring solid mixture of minerals.

Root hairs: Fine, hairlike extensions from the plant's root.

Rotate: To turn around on an axis or center.

Runoff: Water not absorbed by the soil; moves downward and picks up particles along the way.

s

Salinity: A measure of the amount of dissolved salt in seawater.

Saliva: Watery mixture with chemicals in the mouth that lubricates chewed food.

Sand: Granular portion of soil composed of the largest soil particles.

Saturated: In referring to solutions, a solution that contains the maximum amount of solute for a given amount of solvent at a given temperature.

Screw: A simple machine; an inclined plane wrapped around a cylinder.

Scurvy: A disease caused by a deficiency of vitamin C, which causes a weakening of connective tissue in bone and muscle.

Sea cave: A cave in sea cliffs, formed most commonly by waves eroding the rock.

Second law of motion (Newton's): The force exerted on an object is proportional to the mass of the object times the acceleration produced by the force.

Sediment: Sand, silt, clay, rock, gravel, mud, or other matter that has been transported by flowing water.

Sedimentary rock: Rock formed from compressed and solidified layers of organic or inorganic matter.

Seed crystal: Small form of a crystalline structure that has all the facets of a complete new crystal contained in it.

Self-pollination: The process in which pollen from one part of a plant fertilizes ovules on another part of the same plant.

Sepal: The outermost part of a flower; typically leaflike and green.

Shell: A region of space around the center of the atom in which electrons are located.

Sidereal day: The system of time to measure a day based on the time it takes for a particular star to travel around and reach the same position in the sky; about four minutes shorter than the average solar day.

Silt: Medium-sized soil particles.

Simple machine: Any of the basic structures that provide a mechanical advantage and have none or few moving parts.

Smog: A form of air pollution produced when moisture in the air combines and reacts with the products of fossil fuel combustion. Smog is characterized by hazy skies and a tendency to cause respiratory problems among humans.

Soil: The upper layer of Earth that contains nutrients for plants and organisms; a mixture of mineral matter, organic matter, air, and water.

Soil horizon: An identifiable soil layer due to color, structure, and/or texture.

Soil profile: Combined soil horizons or layers.

Solar day: Called a day, the time between each arrival of the Sun at its highest point.

Solubility: The tendency of a substance to dissolve in some other substance.

Soluble: A substance that can be dissolved in some other substance.

Solute: The substance that is dissolved to make a solution and exists in the least amount in a solution, for example sugar in sugar water.

Solution: A mixture of two or more substances that appears to be uniform throughout, except on a molecular level.

Solvent: The major component of a solution or the liquid in which some other component is dissolved, for example water in sugar water.

Speleologist: One who studies caves.

Speleology: Scientific study of caves and their plant and animal life.

Spelunkers: Also called cavers, people who explore caves for a hobby.

Spoilage: The condition when food has taken on an undesirable color, odor, or texture.

Spore: A small, usually one-celled reproductive body that is capable of growing into a new organism.

Stalactite: Cylindrical or icicle-shaped mineral deposit projecting downward from the roof of a cave. (Pronounced sta-LACK-tite.)

Stalagmite: Cylindrical or icicle-shaped mineral deposit projecting upward from the floor of a cave. (Pronounced sta-LAG-mite.)

Stamen: Male reproductive organ of flowers that is composed of the anther and filament.

Stigma: Top part of the pistil upon which pollen lands and receives the male pollen grains during fertilization.

Stomata: Pores in the epidermis (surface) of leaves.

Storm: An extreme atmospheric disturbance, associated with strong damaging winds, and often by thunder and lightning.

Storm chasers: People who track and seek out storms, often tornadoes.

Stratification: Layers according to density; applies to fluids.

Style: Stalk of the pistil that connects the stigma to the ovary.

Sublime: The process of changing a solid into a vapor without passing through the liquid phase.

Sundial: A device that uses the position of the Sun to indicate time.

Supersaturated: Solution that is more highly concentrated than is normally possible under given conditions of temperature and pressure.

Supertaster: A person who is extremely sensitive to specific tastes due to a greater number of taste buds.

Supplements: A substance intended to enhance the diet.

Synthesized: Prepared by humans in a laboratory; not a naturally occurring process.

Synthetic: Something that is made artificially, in a laboratory or chemical plant, but is generally not found in nature.

Synthetic crystals: Artificial or manmade crystals.

T

Taste buds: Groups of taste cells located on the papillae that recognize the different tastes.

Taste pore: The opening at the top of the taste bud from which chemicals reach the taste cells.

Telescope: A tube with lenses or mirrors that collect, transmit, and focus light.

Tendon: Tough, fibrous, connective tissue that attaches muscle to bone.

Tensile strength: The force needed to stretch a material until it breaks.

Theory of Special Relativity: Theory put forth by Albert Einstein that time is not absolute, but it is relative according to the speed of the observer's frame of reference.

Thermal inversion: A region in which the warmer air lies above the colder air; can cause smog to worsen.

Thermal pollution: The discharge of heated water from industrial processes that can kill or injure water life.

Third law of motion (Newton's): For every action there is an equal and opposite reaction.

Tides: The cyclic rise and fall of seawater.

Topsoil: Uppermost layer of soil that contains high levels of organic matter.

Tornado: A violently rotating, narrow column of air in contact with the ground and usually extending from a cumulonimbus cloud.

Toxic: Poisonous.

Trace minerals: Minerals needed in relatively small quantities.

Transpiration: Evaporation of water in the form of water vapor from the stomata on the surfaces of leaves and stems of plants.

Troglobites: An animal that lives in a cave and is unable to live outside of one.

Troglophiles: An animal that lives the majority of its life cycle in a cave but is also able to live outside of the cave.

Trogloxenes: An animal that spends only part of its life cycle in a cave and returns periodically to the cave.

Troposphere: The lowest layer of Earth's atmosphere, ranging to an altitude of about 9 miles (15 kilometers) above Earth's surface.

Trough: The lowest point of a wave. (Pronounced trawf.)

Turgor pressure: The force that is exerted on a plant's cell wall by the water within the cell.

U

Unit cell: The basic unit of the crystalline structure.

Updraft: Warm, moist air that moves away from the ground.

Upwelling: The process by which lower-level, nutrient-rich waters rise upward to the ocean's surface.

V

Vacuole: An enclosed, space-filling sac within plant cells containing mostly water and providing structural support for the cell.

Variable: Something that can affect the results of an experiment.

Velocity: The rate at which the position of an object changes with time, including both the speed and the direction.

Vitamins: Organic substance that are essential for people's good health; most of them are not manufactured in the body.

Volatilization: The process by which a liquid changes (volatilizes) to a gas.

Vortex: A rotating column of a fluid such as air or water.

W

Water clock: A device that uses the flow of water to measure time.

Water-soluble vitamins: Vitamins such as C and the B-complex vitamins that dissolve in the watery parts of plant and animal tissues.

experiment
CENTRAL

Water vapor: The change of water from a liquid to a gas.

Wave: The rise and fall of the ocean water; also, a motion in which energy and momentum is carried away from some source; a wave repeats itself in space and time with little or no change.

Wavelength: The distance between the crest of a wave of light, heat, or energy and the next corresponding crest.

Weathered: Natural process that breaks down rocks and minerals at Earth's surface into simpler materials by physical (mechanical) or chemical means.

Wedge: A simple machine; a form of inclined plane.

Wheel and axle: A simple machine; a larger wheel(s) fastened to a smaller cylinder, an axle, so that they turn together.

Work: Force applied over a distance.

X

Xylem: Plant tissue consisting of elongated, thick-walled cells that transport water and mineral nutrients. (Pronounced ZY-lem.)

experiment
CENTRAL

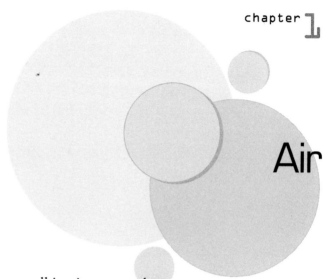

chapter 1

Air

Even though you cannot feel it, see it, or smell it, air surrounds you and extends far upward for miles. **Air** is a mixture of gases, mainly nitrogen and oxygen, with about four times as much nitrogen. With few exceptions, all living things on Earth need air to survive. It is what makes all flight possible, from airplanes to birds. It allows fuels to burn and it shields Earth from the Sun's harmful rays. Air is also what gives us our weather patterns. Air's temperature, pressure, density, and volume all create the weather.

Surrounded by air

All the air that covers Earth is called the **atmosphere.** Earth's gravity holds the atmosphere in place around our planet. The atmosphere is a blanket of air over 600 miles (1,000 kilometers) high. Scientists have divided the atmosphere into five layers, according to differences in the temperature of the air. The layer closest to Earth is called the **troposphere.** The troposphere extends about 9 miles upward (15 kilometers). It contains almost all of what makes up Earth's weather, including clouds, rain, and snow.

Like any gas, air has pressure, mass, and a temperature. Air is composed of 78 percent nitrogen, 21 percent oxygen, 0.9 percent argon, and the remaining 0.1 percent a handful of other gases, including carbon dioxide. The molecules in air's gases are constantly flying around at high speeds. This air can feel completely still because there are billions of individual molecules zipping in all directions. When the molecules travel in one direction it results in wind.

Words to Know

Air:
Gaseous mixture that covers Earth, composed mainly of nitrogen (about 78 percent) and oxygen (about 21 percent) with lesser amounts of argon, carbon dioxide, and other gases.

Air density:
The ratio of the mass of a substance to the volume it occupies.

Air mass:
A large body of air that has similar characteristics.

Words to Know

Air pressure:
The force exerted by the weight of the atmosphere above a point on or above Earth's surface.

Atmosphere:
Layers of air that surround Earth.

Barometer:
An instrument for measuring atmospheric pressure, used especially in weather forecasting.

Control experiment:
A setup that is identical to the experiment, but is not affected by the variable that acts on the experimental group.

Convection currents:
Circular movement of a gas in response to alternating heating and cooling.

Front:
The area between air masses of different temperatures or densities.

Oh, the pressure

Winds begin with differences in **air pressure.** Air always moves from areas of high pressure to low pressure. The greater the difference in pressures, the stronger the wind's force.

Air's pressure is caused by the weight of the air in Earth's atmosphere pushing down on the air below. Air in the troposphere has the highest pressure of all the layers. The air at the top of the atmosphere has little weight above it to push it down, so its pressure is less. The air at the bottom of the atmosphere is being pushed down by the hundreds of miles of air above it. This results in air low to the ground having more pressure than air high in the atmosphere. The air pressing down on you weighs about 1 ton (0.9 metric ton). You cannot feel this pressure because you are supported by equal air pressure on all sides, and your body is filled with gases and liquid that push back with equal pressure.

Meteorologists, or people who study weather, measure air pressure with a **barometer.** Changes in the air pressure or barometric pressure occur during changes in the weather. The mercury barometer uses the heavy liquid metal mercury, which is about fourteen times heavier or denser than water. An empty glass tube with the upper end closed is inserted into a dish of mercury. The height of the column of mercury in the glass tube is controlled by the air pressing down on the mercury in the dish. Normal air pressure lifts the mercury to a height of about 30 inches (760 millimeters). When air

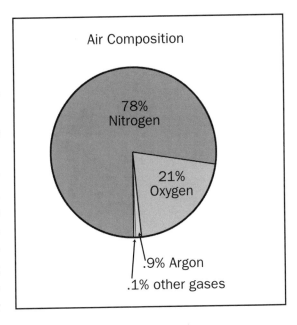

Air Composition

78% Nitrogen

21% Oxygen

.9% Argon

.1% other gases

The air on Earth is composed of several different gases.

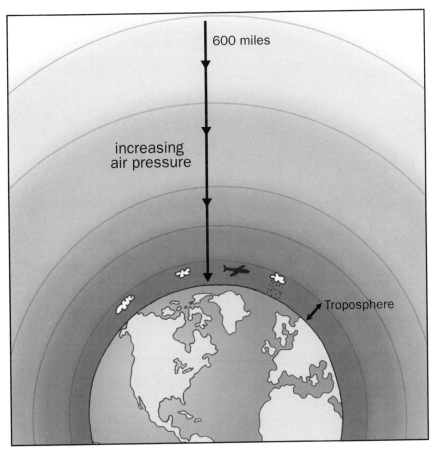

600 miles

increasing air pressure

Troposphere

Air presses down from the upper atmosphere, causing more pressure in the layer closest to Earth, the troposphere.

pressure falls, the air does not push on the mercury in the dish as much, and the column of mercury falls. When air pressure increases, the column of mercury will rise. In general, falling air pressure means that clouds and rains or snow are likely. Rising air pressure signals that clear weather is likely.

In the mid 1600s Italian mathematician Evangelista Torricelli (1608–47) designed the first barometer to prove that air had weight and pressure. Then in 1648 French philosopher and mathematician Blaise Pascal (1632–62) hypothesized that air pressure decreased with altitude. He sent his brother-in-law up to the peak of a mountain in France with a barometer. The column of mercury dropped lower and lower the higher he went. Today, the international unit of pressure is called the Pascal, in his honor.

Changing densities

Quick changes in the weather are caused by movements of large bodies of air called **air masses.** Air masses usually cover very large areas. All the air in an air mass has nearly the same properties. When two air masses that have different densities meet, they mix slowly and form an area between them called a **front.**

The density of an air mass is related to its pressure and temperature. **Air density** is the amount of matter or mass in a specific volume. Increasing the temperature of a gas pushes its molecules farther apart. When the Sun heats up the air, the space between the molecules increases and the hot air expands. The air becomes less dense and has less pressure. When the temperature of air decreases its molecules move closer together and the air contracts. The air becomes more dense and has greater pressure.

There are three main types of fronts: cold fronts, warm fronts, and occluded fronts. A cold front forms when a cold air mass meets and pushes under a warm air mass. Violent storms are associated with a cold front. Fair, cool weather usually follows. A warm front forms when a mass of warm air moves into a cold air mass. Rain and showers usually accompany a warm front. Hot, humid weather usually follows. An occluded front happens when a cold front catches up and merges with a warm front. An occluded front often brings heavy rain.

The closer air lies to the surface of Earth, the denser it is because there are more molecules of air compressed into a smaller volume.

Words to Know

Hypothesis:
An idea in the form of a statement that can be tested by observation and/or experiment.

Meteorologists:
Professionals who study Earth's atmosphere and its phenomena, including weather and weather forecasting.

Troposphere:
The lowest layer of Earth's atmosphere, ranging to an altitude of about 9 miles (15 kilometers) above Earth's surface.

Variable:
Something that can affect the results of an experiment.

experiment
CENTRAL

The troposphere layer is so compressed that it contains about 80 percent of the air found in the entire atmosphere by mass. The higher up in the atmosphere someone goes, the less dense the air. When mountain climbers trek up high mountains, they often need to bring tanks of oxygen with them because the air is less dense and contains less oxygen for them to breathe.

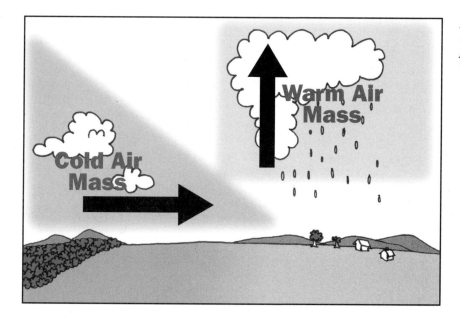

A cold front occurs when a cold air mass meets and pushes under a warm air mass.

When mountain climbers trek up high mountains, they often need to bring tanks of oxygen with them because the air is less dense and contains less oxygen for them to breathe. (Reproduced by permission of AP/Wide World Photos.)

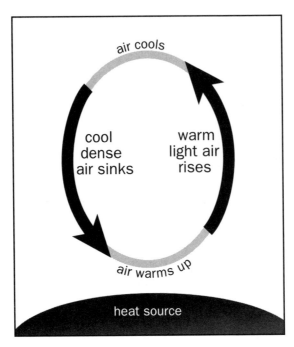

air cools

cool
dense
air sinks

warm
light air
rises

air warms up

heat source

The up-and-down movement of air due to different densities is called convection currents.

The up-and-down movement of air due to different densities is called **convection currents.** When the air becomes less dense it rises upward through the denser, cool air above it. As this warm air moves through the cold air it cools off, becomes more dense again, and eventually sinks back to the bottom.

Experiment 1
Air Density: Does warm air take up less room than cool air?

Purpose/Hypothesis

Density is the mass of anything divided by the volume it occupies. As the temperature of a given mass of air increases, its volume expands and the air gets less dense as a result—same mass, but larger volume, means less dense. As the temperature of a given mass of air decreases, its volume contracts and the air gets more dense. In this experiment, you will examine the density of air by causing a mass of air in a closed container to become both more and less dense by changing the temperature. To see these changes you will place a balloon over the open end of a bottle. When the trapped air expands, the balloon should get bigger; when the air contracts, the balloon should get smaller.

Before you begin, make an educated guess about the outcome of this experiment based on your knowledge of air density. This educated guess, or prediction, is your **hypothesis.** A hypothesis should explain these things:

* the topic of the experiment
* the **variable** you will change

experiment
CENTRAL

 What Are the Variables?

Variables are anything that might affect the results of an experiment. Here are the main variables in this experiment:

- Thickness of the plastic bottles
- Material the balloons are made from

In other words, the variables in this experiment are everything that might affect the density of the air. If you change more than one variable at the same time, you will not be able to tell which variable had the most effect on air density.

- the variable you will measure
- what you expect to happen

A hypothesis should be brief, specific, and measurable. It must be something you can test through further investigation. Your experiment will prove or disprove whether your hypothesis is correct. Here is one possible hypothesis for this experiment: "As the air gets warmer and less dense it will cause the the balloon to get larger; as the air gets cooler and less dense it will cause the balloon to get smaller."

In this case, the variable you will change is the temperature of the air inside the bottle by warming and cooling the outside of the bottle. The variable you will measure is the balloon's circumference.

Conducting a **control experiment** will help you isolate each variable and measure the changes in the dependent variable. Only one variable will change between the control and the experimental trials. Your control experiment will not heat or cool the air in the bottles.

Level of Difficulty

Easy.

Materials Needed

- two rubber balloons
- ice
- hot water
- two plastic bottles, such as plastic soda bottles

How to Experiment Safely
Have an adult present when working with the hot water.

- two containers that go at least midway up the sides of the bottles (one should be heatproof)

Approximate Budget
$2.

Timetable
15 minutes.

Step-by-Step Instructions
1. Place a balloon over the mouth of each plastic bottle. Leave one bottle out as your control.
2. Fill up one container with very hot water. Fill up the other container with a little ice and some cold water.
3. Place the experimental bottle in the container of cold water and hold it there for roughly 1 minute. (Another option is to place the bottle in a freezer for 1 minute.) Note the size of the balloon compared to the control balloon.
4. Place the experimental bottle in the container of hot water for 1 minute. (Another option is to carefully hold the bottle under running hot tap water.) Note the size of the balloon compared to the control balloon.

Steps 3 and 4: Heat causes the air in the bottle to warm; ice causes the air in the bottle to cool.

experiment
CENTRAL

Troubleshooter's Guide

Below is a problem that may arise during this experiment, some possible causes, and some ways to remedy the problems.

Problem: Nothing happened to the balloon.

Possible cause: Your water may not have been hot or cold enough. You may also not given enough time to allow the air temperature to change. Try the experiment again, placing your bottles deeper into the hot and cold water.

Possible cause: Your balloon may have a slight leak. Try the experiment again with a new balloon.

5. Again, place the experimental bottle in the pan of cold water and hold for 30 seconds.

Summary of Results

Examine how much the balloon grew or shrunk in your experiment. Was your hypothesis correct? How did the size of the experimental balloon compare to the control balloon? Did the experimental balloon shrink more or at a different rate the second time you placed it in the cold water? Draw a picture of the results of your experiment and write a brief summary.

Experiment 2
Convection Currents: How can rising air cause weather changes?

Purpose/Hypothesis

Convection currents occur as rising gas carries heat upward and the cooler gas is brought downward. In the atmosphere, convection currents rise above warm areas on Earth's surface. These rising air currents produce differences in air pressure, which cause changes in the weather. Small convection currents can produce winds and rain. Larger convection currents can cause severe thunderstorms and hurricanes.

What Are the Variables?

Variables are anything that might affect the results of an experiment. Here are the main variables in this experiment:

- The amount of smoke
- The temperature of the warm air
- The temperature of the cold air

In other words, the variables in this experiment are everything that might affect the movement of the smoke. If you change more than one variable at the same time, you will not be able to tell which variable had the most effect on the convection currents.

When convection occurs in an enclosed container, the currents help distribute the heat throughout the container. The entire process is driven by the differences in air density. In this experiment, you will create a convection current in a closed container and look at the air's actions. You will cool the air in one glass jar and warm the air in another. Visible smoke from an incense stick will go into the warm jar. Then you will observe what occurs to the movements of the smoke.

Before you begin, make an educated guess about the outcome of this experiment based on your knowledge of air convection. This educated guess, or prediction, is your **hypothesis.** A hypothesis should explain these things:

- the topic of the experiment
- the **variable** you will change
- the variable you will measure
- what you expect to happen

A hypothesis should be brief, specific, and measurable. It must be something you can test through further investigation. Your experiment will prove or disprove whether your hypothesis is correct. Here is one possible hypothesis for this experiment: "Air in the warmer container will rise, pushing the cold air above it downward, and creating movement of the smoke."

In this case, the variable you will change is the temperature of the air in the glass jar. The variable you will measure is the visible movement of the smoke.

Conducting a **control experiment** will help you isolate each variable and measure the changes in the dependent variable. Only one variable will change between the control and the experimental trial. Your control experiment will use jars that have not been heated or cooled.

Level of Difficulty
Easy/Moderate (the experiment is simple, but working with burning incense increases the difficulty level).

Materials Needed
- four glass jars of equal size with equal-sized openings (mayonnaise jars work well; you do not need the lids)
- incense stick (do not use smokeless incense)
- matches
- small piece of thick paper (big enough to cover the opening of the jars)
- lamp with at least a 100-watt bulb
- black piece of paper or cardstock about the size of the jars
- access to freezer or cold-water bath

Approximate Budget
$5.

Timetable
20 minutes.

Step-by-Step Instructions
1. Place one jar in the freezer or cold-water bath for about 5 minutes.

2. While the first jar is cooling, run hot water over the outside of the second jar.

3. When about 3 minutes have passed, turn on the lamp and position the warm jar upside down in front it. Fold the black paper in half and lean it closely against the side of the jar opposite the lamp to help heat the air.

4. After 5 minutes, take the jar out of the freezer or cold-water bath and have the small piece of thick paper nearby. (You may need to wipe off the outside of the jar so that you can see inside it.)

5. Light the stick of incense, lift up the warm jar (with the opening still facing downward), and hold the burning incense underneath the opening of the warm jar. The incense stick should give off black smoke. Blow out the incense stick and capture any remaining black smoke inside the warm jar.

6. Quickly place the small piece of thick paper firmly over the opening in the warm jar to hold the smoke inside. Turn the warm jar

Step 6: Turn the warm jar right side up while you hold the thick paper in place. Turn the cold jar upside down and set it directly on top of the warm jar so their openings line up exactly and the thick piece of paper is between them.

experiment
CENTRAL

Troubleshooter's Guide

Below is a problem that may arise during this experiment, a possible cause, and a way to remedy the problem.

Problem: No black smoke was visible.

Possible cause: You may have used a smokeless incense stick. Try purchasing another type and repeating the experiment.

right side up while you hold the thick paper in place. Turn the cold jar upside down and set it directly on top of the warm jar so their openings line up exactly and the thick piece of paper is between them.

7. Lift the cold jar slightly and pull the paper out from between the jars. Observe what happens to the smoke.

8. For the control experiment, repeat Steps 5 through 7 with two room-temperature glass jars. Note the results.

Summary of Results

Was your hypothesis correct? Compare the results between the movement in the air of the control jars and the cold and warm jars. Use arrows to draw what was happening to both the cold and warm air in the jars. What do you hypothesize would occur if the cold jar was placed on the bottom and the warm jar was placed on top of it. Write a brief description of how air of different temperatures causes weather change.

Design Your Own Experiment

How to Select a Topic Relating to this Concept

Whenever you step outside you are feeling the effects of air's properties and movement. Consider what types of weather-related topics are of interest to you. Watch the weather forecast carefully and write down what terms and pictures look interesting to you.

Check the For More Information section and talk with your science teacher to learn more about air properties and weather. As you

consider possible experiments, make sure to discuss them with your science teacher or another adult before trying them.

Steps in the Scientific Method

To do an original experiment, you need to plan carefully and think things through. Otherwise, you might not be sure what question you are answering, what you are or should be measuring, or what your findings prove or disprove.

Here are the steps in designing an experiment:

- State the purpose of—and the underlying question behind—the experiment you propose to do.
- Recognize the variables involved and select one that will help you answer the question at hand.
- State your hypothesis, an educated guess about the answer to your question.
- Decide how to change the variable you selected.
- Decide how to measure your results.

Recording Data and Summarizing the Results

In any experiment you conduct, you should look for ways to clearly convey your data. You can do this by including charts and graphs for the experiments. They should be clearly labeled and easy to read. You may also want to include photographs and drawings of your experimental setup and results, which will help others visualize the steps in the experiment. You might decide to conduct an experiment that lasts several months. In this case, include pictures or drawings of the results taken at regular intervals.

If you are preparing an exhibit, you may want to display your results, such as any experimental setup you designed. If you have completed a nonexperimental project, explain clearly what your research question was and illustrate your findings.

Related Projects

There are many related projects you can undertake related to air and the weather. Because air is not visible to the naked eye, there are instruments that enable people to "see" how the air reacts. To explore air temperature, you could make a radiometer, an instrument that uses reflection and absorption to measure the Sun's rays. A radiometer will allow you to see how the Sun's energy causes the warm air to

OPPOSITE PAGE:
The less-dense hot air in a hot air balloon allows it to rise high above the ground. (© Duomo/CORBIS. Reproduced by permission.)

move. You could also make a barometer to measure air pressure. By watching changes in the barometer, you can observe how varying air pressures result in changes in the weather.

To further explore convection, you can make a convection box as another way to see how air currents with clashing temperatures act. The cyclical process of convection currents also occurs in liquids, which follow the same density rules as gases. Warm water, less dense than cold water, rises to the surface as the cooler water sinks to the bottom. The results cause currents in the water. You can examine convection currents in bodies of water by adding drops of different food colorings to the hot and cold water.

For More Information

Dixon, Dougal. *Macmillan Revised Encyclopedia of Science: The Earth*. New York: Macmillan Reference USA, 1997. ❖ Brief, clear description of the atmosphere.

Elsom, Derek. *Weather Explained*. New York: Henry Holt and Company, 1997. ❖ From basic weather and air questions to weather extremes, this book answers how weather forms, with lots of colorful pictures.

"Guide to the Science of the Atmosphere." *USA Today*. December 19, 2001. http://www.usatoday.com/weather/wworks0.htm#pressure (accessed August 24, 2003). ❖ Graphics and clear text that explains various weather phenomena.

Met Office. http://www.met-office.gov.uk/education/training/air.html (accessed August 24, 2003). ❖ Information on air masses and fronts.

The Weather Classroom. http://www.weather.com/education/student/index.html (accessed August 24, 2003). ❖ Articles on various weather-related phenomena, including an encyclopedia and information on weather careers.

Wright, David. "How Much Does the Sky Weigh?" *Chain Reaction*. http://chainreaction.asu.edu/weather/digin/wright.htm (accessed August 24, 2003). ❖ Article on air and its pressure.

chapter 2

Air and Water Pollution

Air or water that is contaminated with impurities is described as **polluted.** The contamination is the **pollution.** Directly or indirectly, the overwhelming majority of pollution results from human activity, yet nature can also release pollutants. Pollution usually is in the form of gas, liquid, and solid materials; it results from anything that alters the natural environment, such as a temperature shift and noise. Air and water pollution has become a significant problem since the growth of cities, industry, and travel in the late nineteenth century.

All life on Earth depends on air and water to live and grow. Pollution of these substances harms and destroys plants, animals, and microscopic organisms. It causes health problems and death in humans. Pollution upsets the natural cycles on which all life depends, causing a ripple effect that can harm organisms hundreds of miles away from the pollutant. For example, pollutants in a body of water can harm the sea life and poison the plants that depend on the water. In turn, surrounding animals that depend on the plants for food and shelter, such as birds, will need to either move to another location or die. Water and air pollution also destroy Earth's natural beauty.

What you can't see...

Air is essential for life on Earth. It provides oxygen for animals and carbon dioxide for plants. It encircles Earth to form its atmosphere, protecting the planet against harmful rays and causing its weather. Air pollution comes in the form of gases—such as nitrogen dioxide, sulfur dioxide, and carbon monoxide—as well as solid and liquid particles called **particulate matter.** Measuring about 0.0001 inch (0.0025 mil-

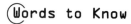

Words to Know

Control experiment:
A setup that is identical to the experiment, but is not affected by the variable that affects the experimental group.

Eutrophication:
The process by which high nutrient concentrations in a body of water eventually cause the natural wildlife to die.

Greenhouse effect:
The warming of Earth's atmosphere due to water vapor, carbon dioxide, and other gases in the atmosphere that trap heat radiated from Earth's surface.

Did You Know?

- The average adult is estimated to breathe about 460 cubic feet (13 cubic meters) of air per day. Children breathe more air per pound of body weight than adults.

- One of the largest oil spills occurred in 1989 when the Exxon Valdez tanker spilled about 11 million gallons (42 million liters); that's about equal to 125 Olympic-sized swimming pools. The oil impacted 1,300 miles (2,080 kilometers) of coastline and killed hundreds of thousands of marine animals.

- Each year, 120 million tons (110 million metric tons) of sulfur dioxide are released into the atmosphere. Sulfur dioxide is a major cause of acid rain, which can harm plants and animals.

- The United States generates 275 million tons (250 million metric tons) of waste each year.

Words to Know

Hypothesis:
An idea in the form of a statement that can be tested.

Particulate matter:
Solid matter in the form of tiny particles in the atmosphere. (Pronounced par-TIK-you-let.)

Pollution:
The contamination of the natural environment, usually through human activity.

Radon:
A radioactive gas located in the ground; invisible and odorless, radon is a health hazard when it accumulates to high levels inside homes and other structures where it is breathed.

Smog:
A form of air pollution produced when moisture in the air combines and reacts with the products of fossil fuel combustion. Smog is characterized by hazy skies and a tendency to cause respiratory problems among humans.

limeters, also called 2.5 microns) in diameter, particulate matter is small enough to be suspended, or float, in the air.

There are several major categories of air pollution produced by humans. Pollutants include the gases nitrogen dioxide, sulfur dioxide, and carbon monoxide, along with lead pollution and particulate matter.

Gases: In most industrial nations the majority of air pollution comes from the automobile. The exhaust in cars and trucks releases carbon monoxide, carbon dioxide, nitrogen oxides, and sulfur dioxide. Automobiles, especially diesel vehicles, also release smoke particles. The burning of fossil fuels—such as gas, oil, and coal—is also a major source of air pollution. Power plants that burn coal and oil release nitrogen oxides, sulfur oxides, carbon dioxide, and particles. Various industrial processes also produce large amounts of these pollutants.

Scientists generally agree that the **greenhouse effect,** also called global warming, comes from the buildup of carbon dioxide, methane, and other gases in the atmosphere. The increased levels of carbon dioxide and other greenhouse gases trap heat close to Earth, resulting in an overall increase in temperature. This warmer climate could produce extreme weather events, such as droughts and floods, raise the sea level, and alter the life populations.

Another planetwide effect of air pollution is the breakdown of the layer of air in Earth's upper atmosphere. The upper atmosphere protects people and animals from dangerous ultraviolet rays produced by the

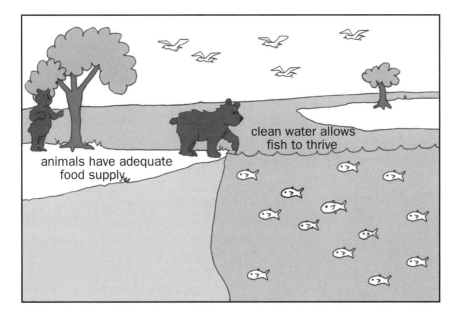

Clean air and water support a healthy life cycle for all organisms.

clean water allows fish to thrive

animals have adequate food supply

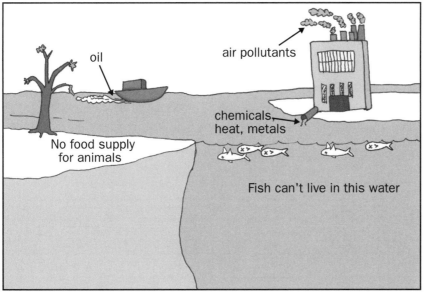

Air and water pollutants can affect a wide variety of surrounding life.

air pollutants

oil

chemicals, heat, metals

No food supply for animals

Fish can't live in this water

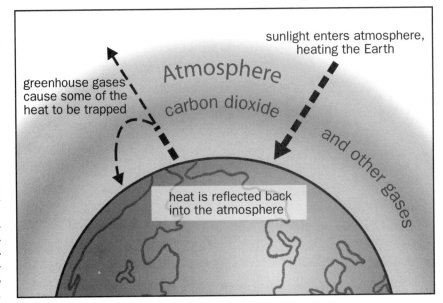

TOP:
Carbon dioxide and other gases trap heat close to Earth, causing a warming in Earth's climate.

greenhouse gases cause some of the heat to be trapped

Atmosphere
carbon dioxide
and other gases

sunlight enters atmosphere, heating the Earth

heat is reflected back into the atmosphere

BOTTOM:
In a thermal inversion, a layer of warm air traps the cool air close to Earth. When this happens the polluted air cannot rise and disperse into the atmosphere, causing pollution to build up to dangerous levels.

warm air

cooler polluted air

Sun. In humans, exposure to ultraviolet rays is linked to skin cancer and harm to the immune system. Chlorofluorocarbon (CFC) gases are one of the main pollutants that bore holes in Earth's upper atmosphere.

Lead: Lead is a toxic or lethal metal that was once a common component of gasoline, paints, and various industrial processes. Unleaded gasoline and paint, along with improvements in industrial processes, have brought about a decrease in the release of lead in the air. Especially harmful to young children, lead can slow down mental development, and can harm the kidneys, liver, nervous system, and other organs.

Particulates: Particulate matter varies in size. Larger particles settle near their source after a few minutes in the air; small particles can remain in the air for several days and spread over a wide area. Particles that are especially small can cause health problems in humans and animals. Particles enter the respiratory system and penetrate deeply into the lungs. Brief exposure can result in symptoms ranging from coughing to a sore throat. Long-term exposure can cause asthma and congestion.

Suspended particles in the atmosphere are seen as dust, smoke, soot, and haze. These particles can also cause **smog.** Smog is a type of large-scale outdoor pollution caused by reactions between strong sunlight and different pollutants, primarily automobile exhaust and industrial emissions. Smog appears as a haze over wide areas.

Smog often worsens in warm temperatures when a **thermal inversion** can occur. In a thermal inversion, a layer of warm air traps the cool air close to Earth. When this happens the polluted air cannot rise and disperse into the atmosphere. The pollution can build up to dangerous levels. In 1952, thermal inversion caused a London smog that killed over four thousand people. In the United States, Los Angeles, California, is the city most profoundly affected by smog, according to a 2003 American Lung Association report.

Pollutants from nature

Air inside homes can also become polluted. Trapped in an enclosed area, indoor pollution can cause people serious health problems because of the large amount of time people spend indoors. Cigarette smoke, cooking and heating appliances, paints, and some cleaning products are all possible sources of indoor pollution. **Radon**, an odorless natural gas released from the ground, is another possible pollutant. Radon can enter buildings through cracks and can seep into basements of homes. Lung cancer is one health effect of radon.

Words to Know

Thermal inversion:
A region in which the warmer air lies above the colder air; can cause smog to worsen.

Thermal pollution:
The discharge of heated water from industrial processes that can kill or injure water life.

Variable:
Something that can affect the results of an experiment.

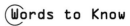

Smog appears as a haze over large areas. Here, the skyline of New York City is wrapped in a veil of smog. (Courtesy of National Archives and Records Administration.)

Radon is an example of a natural pollutant. Other types of naturally occurring pollutants include erupting volcanoes, which produce large amounts of sulfur oxides and particulate matter. Some microorganisms that break down plant material also release methane gas, a contributor to the greenhouse effect. Among the places these microorganisms live is in cows' stomachs to help with their digestion. When the cows belch, methane gas gets released.

Sickly water

About 70 percent of Earth is covered by the ocean, which makes up almost all the water on the planet. All life on Earth needs water to survive. Oceans, rivers, lakes, and other bodies of water hold a rich diversity of animal, plant, and microscopic life that organisms in both the water and on land depend upon to live. Oil, pesticides, fertilizers, litter, wastes, heat, and toxic chemicals are several major sources of water pollution. Polluted water kills sea life and causes disease in humans.

Oils: While oil spills from cargo ships make headline news, these accidents make up only a fraction of the oil released into the oceans. The majority of oil in North American waters comes from industry and road runoff, along with boating. Other sources of oil pollution include drilling, shipping, and improper disposal of oil waste. Oils are also released naturally from eroding rocks at the bottom of the ocean.

The impact of oil on marine life depends upon the amount of oil, where it is located, and the amount of toxic chemicals in the oil. Oils spills form a visible film on the water called an **oil slick.** Oil in a slick sticks to birds, fish, and plants, blocking their breathing and possibly causing death. The reduced food supply can have a long-term impact for

An oil-soaked bird washes up on a beach in northern Spain in November 2002, after a tanker leaked 3,000 tons of oil off the western coast of Spain before eventually sinking. (Reproduced by permission of AP/Wide World.)

whole ecosystems. Oils also wash up on beaches and other human recreational areas. Researchers are working to discover how the steady, relatively small release of oil affects ocean and human life.

Chemicals: Chemical water pollutants are substances not naturally occurring in the waters. Industrial compounds, such as sulfur and nitrogen oxides, along with herbicides and pesticides are common chemicals released into the waters. Rainwater can carry chemicals from the land into waterways. Heavy metals, such as copper, lead, and mercury, enter the water from industries, automobile exhaust, mines, and even natural soil.

Heat: When hot water is poured into a cooler body of water it is called **thermal pollution.** All life forms have a range of temperature in which they can live. If the water temperature is outside that range it will upset and kill organisms. Thermal pollution is common near factories and power plants, where water is heated to high temperatures. Although the water is cooled before it is added to natural bodies of water, it often remains hotter than the natural water. Thermal pollution is also caused by the removal of trees and vegetation that shade bodies of waters.

Natural substances: Upsetting the balance of nutrients can also pollute the waters in a process called **eutrophication**. Nitrates and phosphates are natural nutrients that plants such as algae use for growth. Fertilizers and untreated sewage can contain many of these nutrients. Rain washes the nutrients into bodies of water where they accumulate and stimulate algae growth. The algae grow more rapidly than fish can eat them, causing two major effects. When the algae die it causes decomposing organisms to thrive, depleting the water of oxygen. The lack of oxygen causes fish and surrounding plants to die. Also, the abundance of algae clog the waters and block sunlight for the plants underneath. These plants, which provide food and shelter for sea life, then die.

Solid Matter: Along with blemishing water's natural beauty, litter can significantly harm sea life. Litter is often made of plastic, which takes hundreds of years to break down. Birds and fishes can mistake such litter for food. When enough litter is consumed, the animal's intestines become blocked and it dies. Plastic bags can also suffocate small sea life. Plastic fishing lines and other debris can entangle seabirds and other life. Some estimates put the number of plastic-related deaths at 2 million seabirds and 100,000 marine mammals each year.

OPPOSITE PAGE:
The process of eutrophication depletes the water of oxygen and blocks needed sunlight, causing fish and plant life to die.

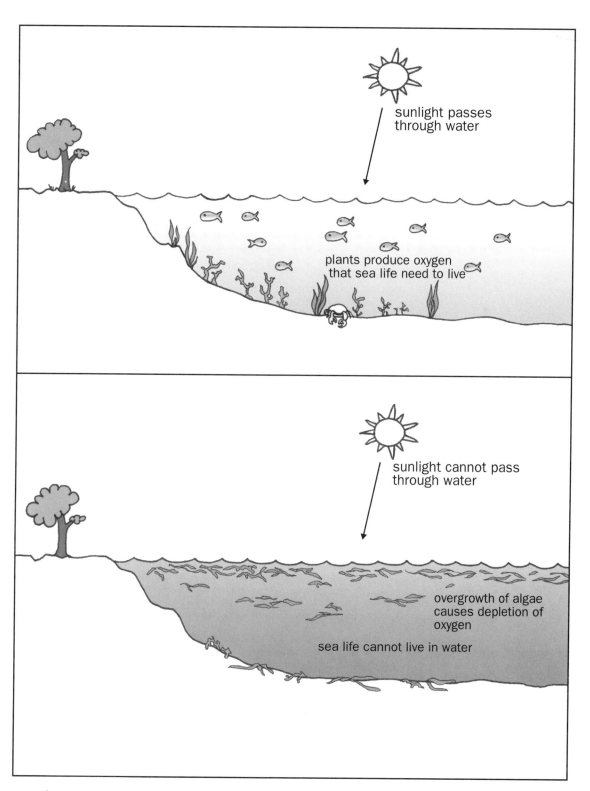

sunlight passes
through water

plants produce oxygen
that sea life need to live

sunlight cannot pass
through water

overgrowth of algae
causes depletion of
oxygen

sea life cannot live in water

Pollution prevention

In the mid-to-late 1900s, the U.S. government began to enact regulations on pollutants that have helped clear much of the waters and air. In 1970 the Clean Air Act established standards for air quality and emissions. The act required automobile manufacturers to produce cars that use unleaded fuel, which has reduced pollutants, and to install pollution-control devices on the exhaust. Factories, incinerators, and power plants were also required to install pollution-control mechanisms. In the 1970s the Safe Water Drinking Act and the Clean Water Act were enacted. These acts set water standards for public water systems and established regulations for the discharge of pollutants into waters.

Other governments also have enacted regulations against releasing pollutants. Companies have developed improved methods to clean up pollution, such as a genetically modified type of bacteria that eats oil from oil spills. As almost all pollutants are the result of human activity, there are multiple ways that individuals can help reduce pollutants. Producing less garbage by recycling, not littering, avoiding disposing of oil or oil-related products down the drain, and driving less and using a car that conserves fuel are a few ways that one person can reduce air and water pollutants.

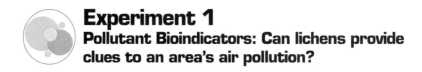

Experiment 1
Pollutant Bioindicators: Can lichens provide clues to an area's air pollution?

Purpose/Hypothesis

Lichens are organisms that are extremely sensitive to air pollution. These life forms are actually two types of organisms living in partnership: fungi and either a green algae or a blue-green bacterium. Lichens grow on rocks, buildings, and on trees. These organisms receive virtually all their water and nutrients from the air. Lichens are especially sensitive to certain air pollutants, such as sulfur dioxide. When lichens are exposed to these pollutants they will die. Automobile emissions and some industrial processes can produce these pollutants. Because of this, scientists use lichens as indicators of pollution, or bioindicators.

The quantity, diversity, and colors of the lichens all provide evidence of the area's pollutants. These organisms are colored red, orange, yellow, gray, black, brown, and green. When lichens are affected by pollutants, they turn from their usual color and can peel away from the surface they live on. There are three main types of lichens: Fruticose lichens look like miniature 1-inch (25-millimeter) tall shrubs or lettuce leaves and hang from branches; foliose lichens appear like flat leafs; and crustose lichens sit closely to their surface and appear crustlike. The crustose lichens are the most resistant to air pollution, and are often seen in cites. Fruticose lichens are the most sensitive to pollutants.

In this experiment you will measure an area's air pollution by using lichens as the bioindicator. You will choose three different areas and randomly select three trees of similar sizes in each area. You may need to look at pictures of the different types of lichens before you begin. By placing a transparent grid over the tree you can count the amount and type of lichens covering each tree.

Before you begin, make an educated guess about the outcome of this experiment based on your knowledge of air pollution and lichens. This educated guess, or prediction, is your **hypothesis.** A hypothesis should explain these things:

- the topic of the experiment
- the **variable** you will change
- the variable you will measure
- what you expect to happen

There are three main types of lichens.

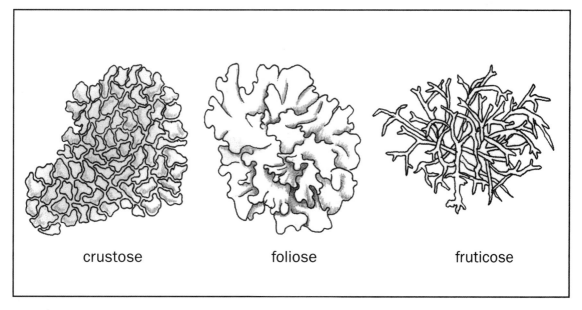

crustose   foliose   fruticose

What Are the Variables?

Variables are anything that might affect the results of an experiment. Here are the main variables in this experiment:

- the location
- types of trees
- the size of trees

In other words, the variables in this experiment are everything that might affect the growth of lichens. If you change more than one variable at the same time, you will not be able to tell which variable had the most effect on inhibiting lichen growth.

A hypothesis should be brief, specific, and measurable. It must be something you can test through further investigation. Your experiment will prove or disprove whether your hypothesis is correct. Here is one possible hypothesis for this experiment: "There will be fewer and less diversity in the lichens living near high traffic and/or industrial areas than the lichens in more remote areas."

In this case, the variable you will change is the location. The variable you will measure is the quantity and type of lichens.

Level of Difficulty

Moderate.

Materials Needed

- three locations (sites) of different environments; all should have trees (example: a city street, in a park, near a school parking lot)
- trees in each area, of the same or similar species (kinds)
- magnifying glass
- ball of string or twine
- tape measure
- transparent piece of grid paper (1x1 inch squares work well, or slightly larger squares)
- marking pen
- partner (optional but helpful)

How to Experiment Safely

If studying trees near the road, be careful of traffic. Try to conduct your experiment during a low-traffic time of the week and day; and ask an adult to accompany you to a high-traffic area.

Approximate Budget

$5.

Timetable

2.5 hours (including travel time).

Step-by-Step Instructions

1. Create a chart for each area, listing "Tree 1," "Tree 2," and "Tree 3" across the top columns. Label the rows: "Fruticose," "Foliose," "Crustose," "Bark," and "Other."
2. Choose a tree at random in the first area of study. The tree should have lichen growing on it. Circle the string around the trunk at a height that you can comfortably observe, such as 3 feet (.9 meters).
3. Tie a knot in the string and cut. Mark the string with a 1 or one mark.
4. Starting at the marked line, place the transparency directly below the string. Count and note the squares covered by each group of lichens, bare bark, and other life forms, such as moss. You may want to use the magnifying glass. Have your partner write down the results for each grid. Continue this along the tree until you have made a complete circle. Repeat the process above the string.
5. Add up the numbers of squares covered by each lichen, bark, and any other growth and then note those numbers on the chart.
6. Also note the color of the lichens on the chart.
7. Repeat this process with two more randomly chosen trees nearby at the same site. For each tree, tie a fresh piece of string at the same height. Mark the second string with a 2 or two marks and the third tree with a 3 or three marks.
8. At the second site, use the three pieces of string that are marked. Try to measure three trees that have roughly the same circumference as each of the trees at the first site. Again, note the types of lichens and the number of squares each fills.

Step 4: Count the squares that each type of lichen, plain bark, and other life form(s) takes up on the tree.

9. Repeat the process at the third site, choosing three trees randomly that are roughly the same diameter.

Summary of Results

Calculate the average numbers for each site. Use the averages of your data to create a graph of the three sites. How do the numbers of lichens compare between the sites? Is your hypothesis correct? For the same type of lichens, is there a difference in their colors? Determine if there was one dominant type of lichen in each area. How does that dominant type compare to the lichens in the other two areas? Examine the possible pollutants in each area. Write a brief summary of your findings and analysis.

Change the Variables

To change the variables in this experiment you can focus on one location and measure the lichens on different trees. You can focus on spe-

Troubleshooter's Guide

Below is a problem that may arise during this experiment, some possible causes, and some ways to remedy the problem.

Problem: All the lichen looked the same.

Possible cause: It is possible that much of the lichen was the same, especially if the sites were close to one another. To categorize lichens it is also helpful to refer to reference material. If possible, take a book out of the library with pictures of the different types of lichen and repeat the experiment, using the photographs as a guide.

cific parts of the trees also, such as a shady or sunny section. You can also concentrate your research on different pollutants, such as automobile exhaust and industrial processes. You can then find areas where you observe each pollutant occurring, and determine its effect on the lichen.

Experiment 2
Eutrophication: The effect of phosphates on water plants.

Purpose/Hypothesis

Phosphorus is a vital nutrient that both plants and people need. Plants use phosphorus for converting sunlight into energy, cell growth, and reproduction. Organisms usually take in phosphorous in the form of phosphate, a phosphorous compound. Because they promote plant growth, phosphates are one of the nutrients in many agricultural and garden fertilizers. Many dishwasher detergents add phosphates to reduce spotting on glasses and dishes. Laundry detergents can contain phosphates to soften the water.

In this experiment, you will explore how an excess of phosphates can affect life in lakes, streams, and oceans. When too many nutrients accumulate in a body of water, it can spark eutrophication. This process begins with the growth of algae. Algae are simple water plants that are found near the surface of waters. There are many types of algae, and sea life depends upon them for food. In waters, phosphorous is naturally present in low concentrations, as algae require only small amounts of it to live.

In this experiment you will add phosphates to healthy water plants that are living in water with a natural amount of algae. You will add two different concentrations of the phosphate and then observe their effect on the plant. By observing the water plants daily you will be able to determine the effect of the phosphate.

Before you begin, make an educated guess about the outcome of this experiment based on your knowledge of water pollution and eutrophication. This educated guess, or prediction, is your **hypothesis.** A hypothesis should explain these things:

- the topic of the experiment
- the **variable** you will change
- the variable you will measure
- what you expect to happen

A hypothesis should be brief, specific, and measurable. It must be something you can test through further investigation. Your experiment will prove or disprove whether your hypothesis is correct. Here is one possible hypothesis for this experiment: "Water with the highest concentrations of phosphates will cause the algae to clog the waters and cause the plants to die."

In this case, the variable you will change is the amount of phosphate added to the water. The variable you will measure is the plant's health. To measure the plant's health you can observe its height, color, root structure, and leaves.

Conducting a **control experiment** will help you isolate each variable and measure the changes in the dependent variable. Only one variable will change between the control and the experimental setup, and that is the amount of phosphate-soap added to the water. The control in this experiment will be to add no additive to the plant's water.

Note: When making a solid/liquid solution, it is standard to use weight/weight (grams/grams) or weight/volume (grams/milliliters). With water, one gram of water equals 1 milliliter. In this experiment, teaspoons and tablespoons are used to measure the solid.

What Are the Variables?

Variables are anything that might affect the results of an experiment. Here are the main variables in this experiment:

- the type of plant
- the soap
- the quantity of soap
- the environmental conditions (sunlight, air temperature, water temperature, etc.)

In other words, the variables in this experiment are everything that might affect the growth of the plants. If you change more than one variable at the same time, you will not be able to tell which variable had the most effect on how the algae affected the plants' health.

Level of Difficulty

Easy.

Materials Needed

- three small water plants of the same type with roots; elodea work well (available at pet shops)
- pond water (preferred) or water that plants were living in: collect enough to fill each of the jars about three-quarters full
- three glass jars, large enough to hold plants
- detergent with high phosphate content (preferably, a detergent with 7 percent or higher phosphate content)
- masking tape
- marking pen
- measuring spoons

Approximate Budget

$8.

Timetable

20 minutes to set up; 5 minutes daily for about 10 days.

Step-by-Step Instructions

1. Label the jars "High Phosphate," "Low Phosphate," and "Control." Fill each jar with the pond water.

How to Experiment Safely
There are no safety hazards in this experiment.

2. Create a chart with "Day 1," "Day 5," and "Day 10" written across the top and the jar labels written down the side.

3. Measure out 1 tablespoon of the detergent and mix into the High Phosphate water.

4. Measure out 1 teaspoon of the detergent and mix into the Low Phosphate water.

5. Place one of the plants in each of the three jars. Do not add detergent to the Control jar.

6. Fill in the physical description of the plant and water for Day 1 on the chart.

7. Place the three jars in the same sunny location.

8. Observe each plant's health and its water daily for about 10 days (time will vary depending on the amount of algae in the control water and the amount of sun).

9. On Day 5 and Day 10, note in a chart the color of the water for each jar and any physical properties of the plant.

Measure the water color and plant health at Day 1, Day 5, and Day 10.

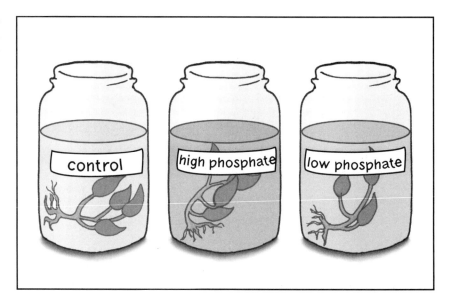

Troubleshooter's Guide

Below is a problem that may arise during this experiment, some possible causes, and some ways to remedy the problem.

Problem: The water in the experiment jars remained the same as the Control.

Possible cause: You may not have collected enough algae to foster growth. Try to find a pond in your area or use water from another shop. Repeat the experiment with this new water.

Possible cause: Algae grow best in a sunny environment. It also might look like nothing is growing when they will suddenly bloom. Make sure the jars are in a sunny window and continue your observations.

Summary of Results

Examine the results of your data chart. Hypothesize how phosphates would have different effects in shallow and slow-moving waters compared to that of deep and flowing waters. In which types of water would sea life be the most in danger? Many states now limit the use of phosphates in their detergents. You can research if your state has regulations on phosphate usage and calculate how those amounts compare to the amount used in your experiment.

Change the Variables

There are several ways that you can alter this experiment. Try using different brands of detergent, either dishwashing or laundry. You can use the same amount of detergent in the water and place the jars in varying environments, by placing them in a hot- or cold-water bath (you will have to change it daily). Will a cool, sunny environment stimulate algae growth more than a warm, sunny environment? You can also change the type of water plant that you use.

Design Your Own Experiment

How to Select a Topic Relating to this Concept

Air and water pollution is all around, no matter what your location. To think of a topic, you can first observe the pollution in the waters, cities, and roadways. Think about methods of measuring the air and water pollution. Check the For More Information section and talk with your science teacher to learn more about air pollution. You may also want to explore any companies in your area that measure pollutants.

Steps in the Scientific Method

To conduct an original experiment, you need to plan carefully and think things through. Otherwise, you might not be sure what question you are answering, what you are or should be measuring, or what your findings prove or disprove.

Here are the steps in designing an experiment:

- State the purpose of—and the underlying question behind—the experiment you propose to do.
- Recognize the variables involved and select one that will help you answer the question at hand.
- State your hypothesis, an educated guess about the answer to your question.
- Decide how to change the variable you selected.
- Decide how to measure your results.

Recording Data and Summarizing the Results

Your data should include charts and graphs such as the one you did for these experiments. They should be clearly labeled and easy to read. You may also want to include photographs and drawings of your experimental setup and results, which will help other people visualize the steps in the experiment.

If you are preparing an exhibit, you may want to display your results, such as any experimental setup you designed. If you have completed a nonexperimental project, explain clearly what your research question was and illustrate your findings.

Related Projects

Projects related to air and water pollution include examining its effects on organisms. You can visit a lake or stream in your area and collect water samples to determine its pollutants, then compare that to its plant and animal life. You can collect samples of particulate matter in the air by hanging papers smeared with petroleum jelly. After collecting the data, you can compare the test sites to the animal and plant life in the area. For a research project, you could examine how pollutants affect people's health and determine if those health problems are correlated to locations with high levels of pollution. Other projects include examining methods that scientists have developed to clean up pollutants. Taking a look at pollution around the world and its impact is another area of exploration.

For More Information

"Air." *U.S. Environmental Protection Agency Student Center.* http://www.epa.gov/students/air.htm (accessed on August 24, 2003) ❖ A comprehensive web site with links and information on a wide range of environmental issues including air pollution, air quality standards, and more.

Exxon Valdez Oil Spill Trustee Council. http://www.oilspill.state.ak.us (accessed on August 24, 2003) ❖ Information about the spill and the ongoing efforts to clean up the damage and restore the natural habitat in the affected area.

"Indoor and Outdoor Air Pollution." *Lawrence Berkeley National Laboratory.* http://www.lbl.gov/Education/ELSI/pollution-indoor.html (accessed on August 24, 2003) ❖ Information on sources of air pollution.

I Want Clean Air. http://www.iwantcleanair.com/ (accessed on August 24, 2003) ❖ Information and products relating to clean air.

"Loveable Lichens." *Earthlife.* http://www.earthlife.net/lichens/intro.html (accessed on August 24, 2003) ❖ Photos and information on all types of lichens.

Macmillian Encyclopedia of Science: The Environment. New York: Macmillan Publishing USA, 1997. ❖ Covers all aspects of our environment and how pollution affects it.

"Sources of Water Pollution." *The Global Development Research Center.* http://www.gdrc.org/uem/water/water-pollution.html (accessed on August 24, 2003) ❖ Lots of information on water pollution.

"State of the Air 2002." American Lung Association. http://www2.lungusa.org/press/envir/sota_rankingsa.html http://www2.lungusa.org/press/envir/sota_050103a.html (accessed on August 24, 2003) ❖ Report on air quality in the United States, 2002.

"Water Quality Standards Handbook." *U.S. Environmental Protection Agency.* http://www.epa.gov/waterscience/standards/handbook/ (accessed on August 24, 2003) ❖ Hundreds of pages of information on water quality, allowable levels of pollutants, and more.

Bacteria

You cannot see them with the naked eye, but the world is teeming with **bacteria**. They live around you, inside of you, and are found in environments that would kill most every other life form. Bacteria are microbes, organisms that are so small they can only been seen with a microscope. They are the simplest, most abundant, and oldest life form on Earth, having evolved roughly 3.5 billion years ago. That beats other life forms by a long shot including dinosaurs, which only arrived on the scene 250 million years ago, and humans, who appeared a mere 2 million years ago. Scoop up a teaspoon of soil and, if you could see them, you would count about a billion bacteria.

While bacteria often make headline news as the cause of disease, the vast majority are either harmless or helpful to humans. Many bacteria live in the soil and decompose dead plants and animals. This process returns needed nutrients back into the environment, which plants and animals then use to live and grow. Other bacteria change the nitrogen gas from the air into a form of nitrogen that plants needs to survive. For humans, they are used to produce foods, such as yogurt and cheese. Humans and some animals depend on bacteria in their digestive tract to break down the plants they eat so they can process the food. Bacteria are an integral part to all life on Earth.

Wretched beasties

The discovery that bacteria exist is one of the major breakthroughs in science. It began with the development of the microscope. In the late 1600s Dutch merchant and amateur scientist Antony van Leeuwenhoek (1632–1723) had built microscopes that magnified objects up

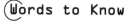
Words to Know

Antibiotic:
A substance derived from certain fungi, bacteria, and other organisms that can destroy or inhibit the growth of other microorganisms; widely used in the prevention and treatment of infectious diseases.

Antibiotic resistance:
The ability of microorganisms to change so that they are not killed by antibiotics.

Did You Know?

- There are more bacteria on a person's hand than there are people on the entire planet.

- Bacteria were unknown to people until the 1600s, when Antony van Leeuwenhoek first observed them in his newly made microscope.

- In 1999 researchers discovered the largest bacteria found to date. A single *Thiomargarita namibiensis*, can reach the size of 750 micrometers (that's about the size of the period at the end of this sentence).

- The holes in Swiss cheese are made by a type of bacteria that produces gas, which pushes the cheese out of the way and forms the holes.

- It is the excreted waste from sweat-eating bacteria that causes the stink of feet. In one day, feet can produce over a pint (2 cups) of sweat that is trapped inside shoes and socks, so bacteria that feed on sweat thrive in this dark environment and create quite an odor.

Words to Know

Bacteria:
Single-celled microorganisms found in soil, water, plants, and animals that play a key role in the decay of organic matter and the cycling of nutrients. Some are agents of disease. (Singular: bacterium.)

Colony:
A visible growth of microorganisms, containing millions of bacterial cells.

Control experiment:
A setup that is identical to the experiment, but is not affected by the variable that acts on the experimental group.

Cytoplasm:
The semifluid substance inside a cell that surrounds the nucleus and other membrane-enclosed organelles.

Deoxyribonucleic acid (DNA):
Large, complex molecules found in the nuclei of cells that carry genetic information for an organism's development.

Extremophiles:
Bacteria that thrive in environments too harsh to support most life forms.

to two hundred times their size. While he was examining water droplets and the white matter on teeth he noted the existence of these "wretched beasties" wriggling about. Although he did not know it, this was the first recorded sighting of bacteria.

Two hundred years later researchers connected these tiny microbes to some of the deadly diseases that were sweeping through the world and killing hundreds of millions of people. For thousands of years, people did not understand the cause of disease; they often blamed a disease on evil spirits or as a punishment to the victim.

Then in the 1860s scientists Louis Pasteur (1822–1895) and Robert Koch (1843–1910) conducted a series of experiments that showed microbes could cause disease. They called their evidence the **germ theory of disease.** Pasteur discovered bacteria could cause food to spoil and he developed a method to destroy these bacteria, now called pasteurization. Koch isolated the individual bacteria that caused the deadly diseases anthrax, tuberculosis, and cholera. Understanding

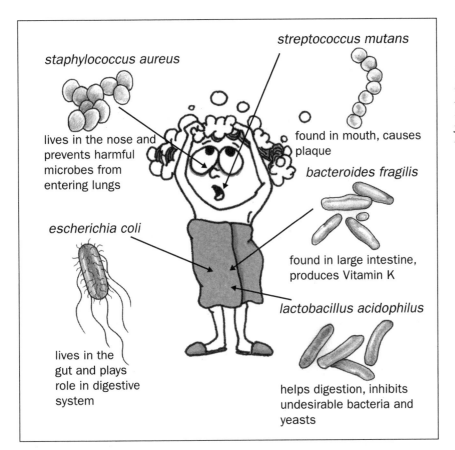

staphylococcus aureus

lives in the nose and prevents harmful microbes from entering lungs

streptococcus mutans

found in mouth, causes plaque

bacteroides fragilis

found in large intestine, produces Vitamin K

lactobacillus acidophilus

helps digestion, inhibits undesirable bacteria and yeasts

escherichia coli

lives in the gut and plays role in digestive system

The human body houses trillions of bacteria. Bacteria can cause disease if they get out of control, yet many help humans stay healthy.

that microbes acted upon other life forms opened the door to an entirely new field of research. Scientists learned how to destroy and protect against these microbes, saving millions of lives.

What they look like

There are thousands of species of bacteria, yet all share some basic features. Bacteria are single-celled organisms and fall into a category of life called **prokaryotes.** Prokaryotes do not have certain specialized structures in their cells and they do not have a cell nucleus, which humans have. A **nucleus** is a cellular compartment inside cells that surrounds DNA and other **organelles.** An organelle is an enclosed structure in a cell that performs a specific function, much like the role of an organ in the body.

What the typical bacteria does have is a fluid called **cytoplasm** inside its cell. Cytoplasm is a gooey, gel-like substance that holds everything and helps move materials around inside the cell. All the

Words to Know

Flagella:
Whiplike structures used by some organisms for movement. (Singular: flagellum.)

Germ theory of disease:
The theory that disease is caused by microorganisms or germs, and not by spontaneous generation.

Hypothesis:
An idea in the form of a statement that can be tested by observation and/or experiment.

Cell structure of the typical bacterium.

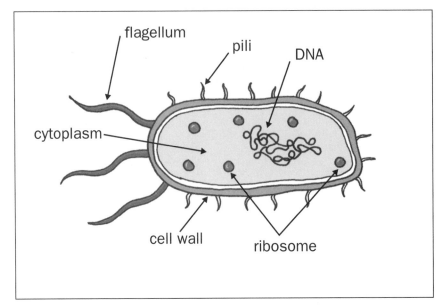

flagellum

pili

DNA

cytoplasm

cell wall

ribosome

Closeup of the Leptospira *bacteria. (Reproduced by permission of Custom Medical Stock Photo.)*

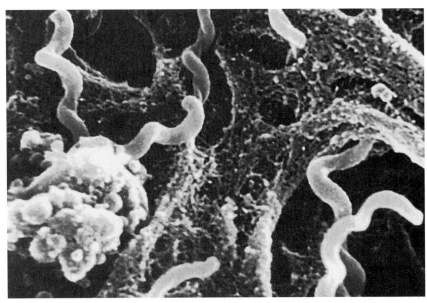

Words to Know

Nucleus, cell:
Membrane-enclosed structure within a cell that contains the cell's genetic material and controls its growth and reproduction. (Plural: nuclei.)

Organelle:
A membrane-enclosed structure that performs a specific function within a cell.

Pili:
Short projections that assist bacteria in attaching to tissues.

Prokaryote:
A cell without a true nucleus, such as a bacterium.

genetic information is contained in the **deoxyribose nucleic acid (DNA)** molecule. The DNA in bacteria sits loosely in the **cytoplasm.** Also located in the cytoplasm are the **ribosomes.** Ribosomes play a key role in translating the information from DNA into proteins.

The cytoplasm is surrounded by a simple cell membrane, which has a variety of functions, including bringing nutrients and chemicals into the cells. The cell membrane is enclosed by a rigid cell wall that provides

experiment
CENTRAL

the overall shape. Bacteria come in three basic shapes. There are bacteria shaped like rods, those that are spherical or round, and those that are helical or spiral.

Some bacteria have whiplike structures called **flagella** that they use to move forward. Some also have small hairlike projections from the cell surface called **pili.** Pili help the cell stick to surfaces or to each other.

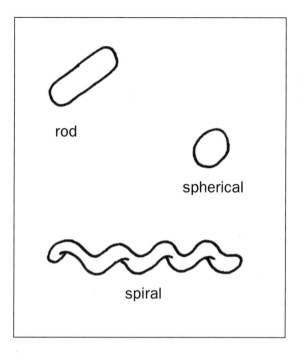

rod

spherical

spiral

Bacteria come in three basic shapes: rod, spherical or round, and spiral.

The typical bacteria range in size from 1 to 5 micrometers (μm). One micrometer equals one millionth of a meter. Scientists use micrometers as the unit of measurement because bacteria are too small to be measured in inches or millimeters. A large clump of bacteria growing together is called a **colony.** A colony can have millions of individual bacteria and is visible to the naked eye.

Living and eating

Bacteria have survived on Earth for billions of years because they are able to adapt relatively quickly to changing environments. One of the ways they adapt is by having a speedy reproduction rate. Bacteria usually reproduce by simply dividing into two cells. All the genetic information, the DNA, is passed along to each of the cells. Sometimes bacteria reproduce sexually: one bacterium transferring part of its DNA to another bacterium. This allows bacteria to quickly create or pass along new traits that help them adapt to different environments.

Given ideal conditions, bacteria can reproduce about every twenty minutes. That means one bacterium could multiply to more than five billion in about ten hours. If all bacteria really were to reproduce this quickly, the world would soon be overtaken with these microorgan-

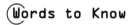

Words to Know

Ribosome:
A protein composed of two subunits that functions in protein synthesis (creation).

Variable:
Something that can affect the results of an experiment.

Bacteria that live in extreme habitats, such as the boiling hot geysers at Yellowstone National Park, are called extremophiles. (© Pat O'Hara/CORBIS. Reproduced by permission.)

isms. Luckily, in the real world, conditions are never ideal. Once there are too many bacteria in one place their food runs out, they crowd each other, and eventually they start dying.

Bacteria have a wide range of diets and living conditions. Some bacteria eat other organisms. Many of these feed off dead organisms, the waste of other organisms, or get their food from living in or on other organisms. Many of these bacteria depend on such foods as sugars, proteins, and vitamins. The bacteria in the human gut, for example, get their food from digested food. Other bacteria make their own food either from sunlight, like plants, or from different chemicals in their environment. The chemicals these bacteria use for foods are often unusual, such as iron and sulfur.

Scientists have found bacteria in practically every known locale and environment. Until the late 1960s, it was thought that no organism could survive in certain extreme environments, meaning environments that would kill other creatures such as humans. Then a researcher discovered there were bacteria living in the hot springs of Yellowstone National Park, which reached temperatures over 158°F (70°C). The bacteria that live in these extreme habitats are called **extremophiles.** Since that time scientists have discovered an increasing number of extremophiles. There are extremophiles that live in sub-freezing temperatures under sheets of ice; thrive in highly acidic environments; and withstand blasts of radiation thousands of times greater than the level that would kill a human.

Extremophiles are of great interest to both industry and basic research. Researchers are interested in how these organisms survive. NASA is conducting experiments on extremophiles to investigate survival in outer space. The biotechnology industry uses extremophiles to manufacture items, such as detergents, diagnostics, and food products.

Building up resistance

While most bacteria are harmless or helpful to humans, there are a number of bacteria that do cause disease. Lyme disease, anthrax, tuberculosis, and salmonellosis are examples of diseases caused by bacteria. Many bacterial diseases are deadly without treatment and can cause widespread infections.

Antibiotics are substances that harm or kill bacteria. Erythromycin and penicillin are examples of commonly used antibiotics. Discovered in the 1920s, these substances are produced naturally by a variety of organisms, such as bacteria themselves and fungi. (See Fungi chapter.) The production and use of antibiotics has dramatically reduced the number of deaths and illnesses from bacterial disease.

In modern day, people are facing the growing public-health problem of **antibiotic resistance.** This is when disease-causing bacteria have become resistant to an antibiotic, thereby lessening the effectiveness of the drug. Resistance can occur when a single bacterium acquires the genetic ability to resist, or block, the antibiotic. This one bacterium will rapidly reproduce and produce an antibiotic-resistant population. An over-exposure to an antibiotic is one way bacteria can acquire resistance. The antibiotic will kill the weak bacteria and allow the stronger, resistant ones to survive. Patients who are prescribed antibiotics but do not take the full dosage can also contribute to resistance. If all the bacteria are not killed, the strong, resistant bacteria that live can pass on resistance to the next generation.

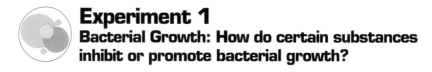

Experiment 1
Bacterial Growth: How do certain substances inhibit or promote bacterial growth?

Purpose/Hypothesis
There are many kinds of bacteria, but a great many of the bacteria that you encounter daily share similar growth requirements.

In this experiment you will investigate substances that affect the growth of common household bacteria. You will collect a sample of bacteria from one of numerous possible sources. You can use your imagination on where to collect the bacteria. Because bacteria need moisture to live, possible sources include the base of a faucet, on someone's hands, inside someone's cheek, or on a bathroom doorknob. You will then streak the bacteria on a growth substance. Bacteria grow well on a substance called agar. Nutrient agar is a jellylike substance that contains food for the bacteria. You can order prepared nutrient agar in a petri dish.

You will use paper disks to place the substances on a section of the bacteria. You can use the suggested liquids or select different ones. Saturate each paper disk with the item to be tested, and place the disk on the bacteria. After giving the bacteria time to grow, you will measure the diameter of the clear area around the paper disk where the bacteria did not grow. This area is called the zone of inhibition. If there is a large zone of inhibition, the substance inhibits bacteria growth. If there is no clear zone of inhibition, the substance does not inhibit bacterial growth. If there is a larger amount of bacteria around and under the disk than when you started, the substance promotes growth.

In this experiment, you will be using more than one type of bacteria. Different types of bacteria often live together. When you collect your sample, you will probably gather more than one type. The experiment will still be valid because bacteria that grow together naturally usually do so because they respond the same way to their environment—something

What Are the Variables?

Variables are anything that might affect the results of an experiment. Here are the main variables in this experiment:

- the size of the paper disks
- the growth substance
- the temperature of the bacteria's environment
- the substance placed on the bacteria
- the type of bacteria

In other words, the variables in this experiment are everything that might affect the zone of inhibition. If you change more than one variable at a time, you will not be able to tell which variable impacted bacterial growth.

that promotes growth for one of them will be good for all of them, and something that inhibits growth for one will be bad for all.

Before you begin, make an educated guess about the outcome of this experiment based on your knowledge of bacteria. This educated guess, or prediction, is your **hypothesis.** A hypothesis should explain these things:

- the topic of the experiment
- the **variable** you will change
- the variable you will measure
- what you expect to happen

A hypothesis should be brief, specific, and measurable. It must be something you can test through further investigation. Your experiment will prove or disprove whether your hypothesis is correct. Here is one possible hypothesis for this experiment: "The acidic and cleaning substances will inhibit bacterial growth; the protein and sugary substances will promote bacterial growth."

In this case, the variable you will change is the substance you place on the bacteria. The variable you will measure is the distance from the disk to the bacterial growth.

Conducting a control experiment will help you isolate each variable and measure the changes in the dependent variable. Only one variable will change between the control and the experimental bacterial growth. The control experiment will have no substance on the paper disk. At the end of the experiment, you will compare the growth of the control bacteria with the experimental bacteria.

Level of Difficulty
Medium to Difficult.

Materials Needed
- rubbing alcohol
- small cup
- tweezers
- paper hole puncher
- white nonglossy paper
- cotton swab
- nutrient agar plates* (available from a biological supply company)
- bacteria source
- test substances: chicken broth (can be made from bouillon), coffee, lemon juice, syrup, vinegar, liquid soap
- distilled water
- five small cups or plates
- marking pen
- filter paper
- ruler, with millimeters
- magnifying glass (optional)
- microscope (optional)

*Depending on how many bacteria experiments you plan to conduct, you may consider less expensive options than that of purchasing ready-made nutrient agar plates. You can order the nutrient agar and plates separately and pour the agar into the plates yourself. You can also order nutrient agar that needs to be made. This process may take some practice so allow yourself extra time. There are also recipes for agar using common household items. Gelatin is also an alternative for nutrient agar. Look on the Internet for these recipes or ask your science teacher. Allow extra time for this process, as you may have to experiment with what recipe best promotes bacterial growth.

Approximate Budget
$25.

How to Experiment Safely

When working with bacteria, you should consider the bacteria capable of causing disease and follow the appropriate safety procedures. Handle the cultures carefully. If there is a spill, wipe up the material using a disinfectant-soaked paper towel, then throw the towel away immediately. Throw away or sterilize all items that touch the bacteria.

Always wash your hands after using live materials. Thoroughly wipe your working area with a disinfectant cleansing agent after you have finished with the setup. Keep your plate closed and store it in a safe area that will not be disturbed. Keep younger children away from the experiment area.

Be careful when working with the hot water.

Timetable

1 hour setup and followup; 2 days waiting.

Step-by-Step Instructions

1. Turn the covered petri dish upside down. Use the marker to divide the dish into six even sections, like a pie. On each section write the name of one of the five substances. Write "Control" on the sixth section.
2. Write the date on the side of the dish.
3. Dip a cotton swab in distilled water.
4. Run the swab over the source of bacteria.
5. Spread the bacteria over the entire plate. Hold the swab flat or at a slight angle so as not to puncture the agar. (See illustration on page 50.)
6. Cover the plate and throw the swab away.
7. Use a hole puncher to make at least 5 paper disks.
8. Sterilize the tweezers: Pour rubbing alcohol into a small cup to cover the bottom. Hold or place the end of the tweezers into the alcohol and wait at least one minute. Rinse in water and shake any excess off the tweezers.
9. Pour several drops of each of the substances you are to test into its own cup or small plate.

experiment
CENTRAL

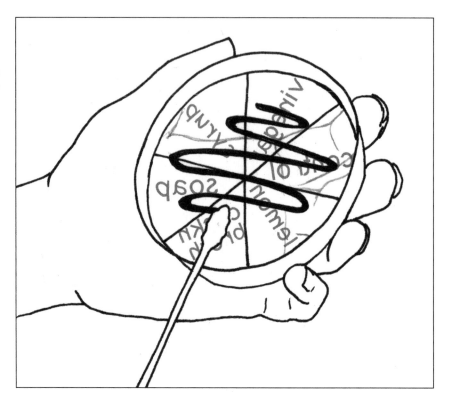

Step 5: Spread the bacteria over the entire plate.

10. Pick up a paper disk with the tweezers and dip it into one of the liquids. The disk should be wet but not dripping.

11. Lift the petri lid just high enough to place the paper disk into the middle of its marked section.

12. Hold the tweezers under running water for at least 5 seconds to clean.

13. Continue wetting each paper disk in the liquid, and placing the disk in its allotted section. Rinse the tweezers in hot water between each paper disk.

14. With clean tweezers, put a plain paper disk in the Control section.

15. Invert or turn the plate upside down. (Condensation may collect on the top lid. Turning the plates upside down prevents the condensation from falling on the bacteria and allows a clear view of growth.)

16. Store the plate in a warm, nonbright area for 24 hours.

17. Check the plate for growth. If there is little to no growth, wait another 24 hours.

18. Observe each section for zones of inhibition, the clear area around the disk in which bacteria have not grown.

19. Measure the diameter of the zone of inhibition, in millimeters, from the left edge of the clear area to the right edge. Repeat this

experiment
CENTRAL

Step 11: Lift the petri lid just high enough to place the paper disk into its marked section.

step for all 6 substances.

20. Record the measurements in a data chart. Note also if there is no zone of inhibition, or if there is increased growth compared to that of the Control.

21. When you have completed the summary, throw away the agar plate.

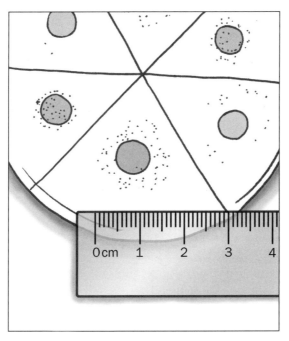

Step 19: Measure the diameter of the zone of inhibition, in millimeters, from the left edge of the clear area to the right edge.

experiment
CENTRAL

Troubleshooter's Guide

Below are some problems that may arise during this experiment, some possible causes, and some ways to remedy the problems.

Problem: Bacteria grew in some areas of the plate but not in others.

Possible cause: You may not have streaked the entire plate with the bacteria. Repeat the experiment, spreading the bacteria around so that the entire plate is covered with the microorganism.

Problem: There was no growth.

Possible cause: You may have stored the plate in an environment that harmed the bacteria or caused it not to grow, such as if it was too cold. Repeat the experiment, storing the plate in a warm environment.

Possible cause: You may not have picked up enough bacteria on the swab. Make sure the cotton swab is wet and repeat the experiment, using the same or a different source for the bacteria.

Problem: My results were not as expected.

Possible cause: You may not have rinsed off the tweezers thoroughly after touching each paper disk, mixing together some of the substances on a disk. Repeat the experiment, making sure to rinse the tweezers in the hot water after each disk is complete.

Summary of Results

Create a graph illustrating the data chart. Make sure you label the graph carefully. Can you tell if the bacteria grew more in certain substances than in others? What substances inhibited bacterial growth the greatest amount? Were there any substances that promoted bacterial growth?

Compare each substance to the control experiment. Examine the differences between the growth in the Control section and growth in any substances that were not inhibited by the substance. Analyze the main ingredient in each of your substances that may have inhibited or promoted growth,

Change the Variables

You can vary this experiment in several ways.

- Change the substance on the paper disks
- Use one substance and change the concentration of that substance
- Alter the growing temperature of the bacteria
- Isolate one type of bacteria before you begin the experiment (the easiest way is to purchase a single type of bacteria from a biological supply company; you could also streak a bacteria mix onto an agar plate to thin out the population until a bacteria of one color and shape grow; see For More Information).
- Grow the bacteria under different lighting conditions

Experiment 2
Bacterial Resistance: Can bacteria gain resistance to a substance after exposure?

Purpose/Hypothesis

Antibiotic resistance is a growing health problem around the world. In this experiment, you will explore bacterial resistance by experimenting with bacteria and antibacterial soap.

Ever since the mid 1990s, soap manufacturers have put antibacterial agents in their products, such as body washes, toothpaste, and hand soaps. The number of antibacterial soaps has increased over the years. In modern day, the majority of soaps carry some antibacterial agent. Researchers have theorized that bacteria may develop a resistance to antibacterial agents over time. If the bacteria develop a resistance to the agent, the agent will no longer be effective in slowing down their growth or killing them.

In this experiment, you will collect a sample of bacteria and spread it on a growth substance. Bacteria grow well on a substance called agar. Nutrient agar is a jellylike substance that contains food for the bacteria. You can order prepared nutrient agar in a petri dish. On top of the nutrient agar you will spread a low concentration of antibacterial soap. The bacteria that survive this concentration of soap will be introduced to a higher concentration of soap. You will continue this process for five growth cycles. After the last plate of bacteria has grown, you can compare the surviving bacteria with the bacteria that have had no exposure to antibacterial soap. You will measure the bacterial growth by counting the number of colonies.

The concentrations of soap provided in this experiments are guidelines. The type of soap you use and the bacteria you collect will influence how bacteria respond to the different concentrations. If you want to determine the concentration that would best suit your materials, read the Troubleshooter's Guide before you begin.

In this experiment, you will be using more than one type of bacteria. Different types of bacteria live together. When you gather a swab of bacteria you have gathered a number of different populations. To draw conclusions about a single type of bacteria, you can order one from a biological supply house.

Before you begin, make an educated guess about the outcome of this experiment based on your knowledge of bacteria and resistance. This educated guess, or prediction, is your **hypothesis.** A hypothesis should explain these things:

- the topic of the experiment
- the **variable** you will change
- the variable you will measure
- what you expect to happen

A hypothesis should be brief, specific, and measurable. It must be something you can test through further investigation. Your experiment will prove or disprove whether your hypothesis is correct. Here is one possible hypothesis for this experiment: "Bacteria that are exposed to an increasingly greater concentration of soap will survive a concentration that will kill unexposed bacteria."

In this case, the variable you will change is the concentration of the soap. The variable you will measure is the number of bacteria colonies that grow.

Conducting a control experiment will help you isolate each variable and measure the changes in the dependent variable. Only one variable will change between the control and the experimental bacterial growth. Each phase of this experiment will have a control. The control bacteria will grow on nutrient agar with no soap. At each phase of the experiment, you should compare the growth of the control bacteria with the experimental bacteria.

What Are the Variables?

Variables are anything that might affect the results of an experiment. Here are the main variables in this experiment:

- the concentration of soap
- the type of bacteria
- the type of soap
- the environmental conditions of each plate

In other words, the variables in this experiment are everything that might affect the zone of inhibition. If you change more than one variable at a time, you will not be able to tell which variable impacted bacterial growth.

Level of Difficulty

Difficult.

Materials Needed

- cotton swabs
- six (at least) nutrient agar plates* (available from a biological supply company)
- antibacterial liquid soap
- measuring cups
- measuring spoons
- five containers with covers
- stirring spoons
- marking pen
- magnifying glass (optional)
- microscope (optional)

*Depending on how many bacteria experiments you plan on conducting, you may consider less expensive options than that of purchasing ready-made nutrient agar plates. You can order the nutrient agar and plates separately and pour the agar into the plates yourself. You can also order nutrient agar that needs to be made. This process may take some practice so allow yourself extra time. There are also recipes for agar using common household items. Gelatin is also an

How to Experiment Safely

When working with bacteria, you should consider the bacteria capable of causing disease and follow the appropriate safety procedures. Handle the cultures carefully. If there is a spill, wipe up the material using a disinfectant-soaked paper towel, then throw the towel away immediately. Throw away or sterilize all items that touch the bacteria.

Always wash your hands after using live materials. Thoroughly wipe your working area with a disinfectant cleansing agent after you have finished with the setup. Keep your plate closed and store it in a safe area that will not be disturbed. Keep younger children away from the experiment area.

alternative for nutrient agar. Look on the Internet for these recipes or ask your science teacher. Allow extra time for this process, as you may have to experiment with what recipe best promotes bacterial growth.

Approximate Budget
$20.

Timetable
1 hour and 30 minutes working time; 6 days' waiting time.

Step-by-Step Instructions

1. Turn the covered petri dish upside down and use a pen to divide the plate in half. Mark the left half ".0001 percent" and the right half "Control." Write the date on the side of the dish.

2. Make up the concentrations by first mixing a 1 percent concentration of soap water. Stir 1 teaspoon (5 milliliters) of liquid soap with 2 cups and 4 teaspoons (500 milliliters) of water. Mix thoroughly, cover, and label "1 percent."

OPPOSITE PAGE:
Experiment 2 setup. Plate progression: Bacteria exposed to soap move to increasingly higher concentrations; the control bacteria are never exposed to soap.

3. To make a .1 percent concentration: Measure 1 teaspoon of the 1 percent solution and add to a clean container. Mix in 9 teaspoons of water. Mix thoroughly, cover, and label ".1 percent."

4. To make a .01 percent concentration: Measure 1 teaspoon of the .1 percent solution and add to another clean container. Mix in 9 teaspoons of water. Mix thoroughly, cover, and label ".01 percent."

experiment
CENTRAL

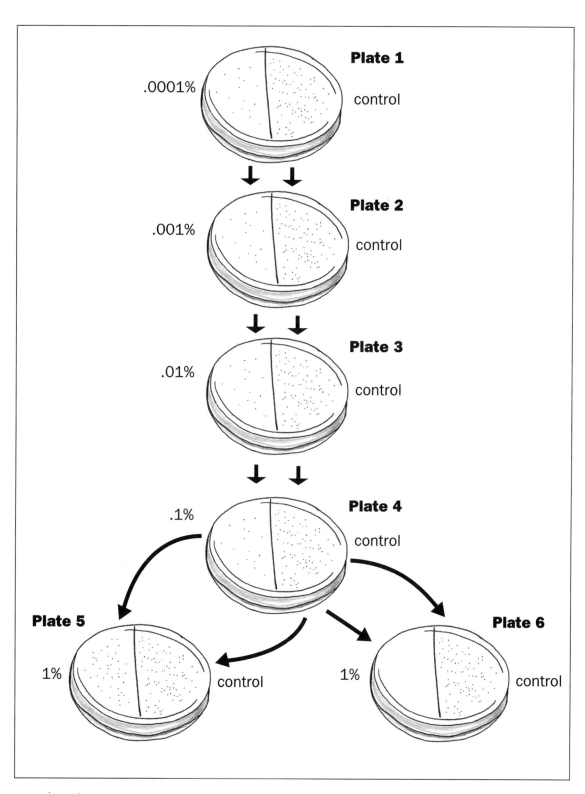

Plate 1

.0001%   control

Plate 2

.001%   control

Plate 3

.01%   control

Plate 4

.1%   control

Plate 5

1%   control

Plate 6

1%   control

5. To make a .001 percent concentration: Measure 1 teaspoon of the .01 percent solution and add to another clean container. Mix in 9 teaspoons of water. Mix thoroughly, cover, and label ".001 percent."

6. To make a .0001 percent concentration: Measure 1 teaspoon of the .001 percent solution and add to another clean container. Mix in 9 teaspoons of water. Mix thoroughly, cover, and label ".0001 percent."

7. Use a fresh cotton swab to spread the .0001 percent solution over the agar that is marked ".0001 percent." Keep the swab flat or at a slight angle so as not to puncture the agar.

8. Dip a cotton swab in distilled water.

9. Run the swab over a source of bacteria and spread the bacteria over the agar in the soap half of the dish.

10. Get a new cotton swab. Use the same source of bacteria and spread the bacteria over the Control half of the dish.

11. Place the lid on Plate 1 and turn it upside down. Store it in a warm temperature for 24 hours. (If there is little to no growth on both the Control and soap sides, let sit another 24 hours.)

Repeat Step 1 with Plate 2, marking the left half ".001 percent."

12. With a fresh cotton swab, collect bacteria from the soap water side of Plate 1 and spread it on the half of the agar marked ".001 percent" in Plate 2.

13. Use a fresh cotton swab to collect bacteria from the Control side of Plate 1 and spread it on the half of the agar marked Control in Plate 2. Throw Plate 1 away. Place the lid on Plate 2 and turn it upside down. Store in a warm temperature for 24 hours.

14. Repeat this process for the .01 percent (Plate 3) and .1 percent (Plate 4), waiting 24 hours or longer between new plates.

15. Have ready Plate 5 and Plate 6. After dividing the plates, mark the left-hand side of both plates "1 percent."

16. Use a cotton swab to collect bacteria from the .1 percent side of Plate 4 and spread it on the 1 percent half of Plate 5.

17. With a new swab, collect some of the Control bacteria from Plate 4 and spread it on the Control on Plate 5, the Control for Plate 6, and the 1 percent on Plate 6. This bacteria has had no exposure to any soap.

18. Place lids on Plates 5 and 6 and turn them upside down. Store in a warm temperature for 24 hours.

19. Count the colonies on the 1 percent solution on both Plate 5 and Plate 6.

Troubleshooter's Guide

Below are some problems that may arise during this experiment, some possible causes, and some ways to remedy the problems.

Problem: There was no difference in the amount of growth between the bacteria on Plates 5 and 6.

Possible cause: The soap that you used may need a higher concentration than 1 percent to inhibit bacterial growth. Spread varying concentrations of the soap on nutrient agar plates and grow bacteria on each concentration. When you have determined the concentration that kills most of the bacteria, use that figure as the end concentration that will go on Plates 5 and 6. Dilute that concentration one thousand fold and repeat the experiment, increasing the concentration by tenfold each growth period.

Problem: At one point there was no growth on a plate.

Possible cause: You may have stored the plate in an environment that harmed the bacteria or caused it not to grow, such as if it was too cold. Continue the experiment at the last plate with growth, storing the plate in a warm environment.

Summary of Results

Examine your data. How do the bacterial growths on Plates 5 and 6 compare with each other? Was your hypothesis correct? Write a description of the bacteria on both plates. If you have a magnifying glass or microscope you could take a closeup look at the bacteria. What was the main difference between the bacteria spread on both plates? Write a summary of the experiment that explains each step in the process and the reason for it.

Change the Variables

There are several variables you can change in this experiment to provide new data:

- Change the brand or type of soap, to a nonantibacterial soap, for instance, or to an antibacterial soap that has a different main ingredient
- Use a cleansing agent instead of soap
- Alter the growing temperature of the bacteria
- Use one type of bacteria by isolating one type before you begin the experiment (the easiest way is to purchase a single type of bacteria from a biological supply company; you could also streak a bacteria mix onto an agar plate to thin out the population until a bacteria of one color and shape grow; see For More Information)
- Use a mixture of different bacteria by collecting it from another source

 Design Your Own Experiment

How to Select a Topic Relating to this Concept

There are thousands of species of bacteria living and growing around you, in you, and on you. For a project, you could examine the differences among different types of bacteria. You could also examine bacteria's growth requirements, or how bacteria have impacted life on Earth.

Check the For More Information section and talk with your biology teacher to learn more about bacteria. You could also try to get access to a microscope so that you can look at the bacteria in more detail.

Steps in the Scientific Method

To conduct an original experiment, you need to plan carefully and think things through. Otherwise, you might not be sure what question you are answering, what you are or should be measuring, or what your findings prove or disprove.

Here are the steps in designing an experiment:

- State the purpose of—and the underlying question behind—the experiment you propose to do.
- Recognize the variables involved and select one that will help you answer the question at hand.
- State your hypothesis, an educated guess about the answer to your question.

- Decide how to change the variable you selected.
- Decide how to measure your results.

A decomposing house plant is a common example of bacteria at work. Many bacteria live in soil and decompose dead plants, returning needed nutrients back into the environment. (Copyright © Kelly A. Quin. Reproduced by permission of Kelly A. Quin.)

Recording Data and Summarizing the Results

In any experiment you conduct, you should look for ways to clearly convey your data. You can do this by including charts and graphs for the experiments. They should be clearly labeled and easy to read. You may also want to include photographs and drawings of your experimental setup and results, which will help others visualize the steps in the experiment. You might decide to conduct an experiment that lasts several months. In this case, include pictures or drawings of the results taken at regular intervals.

If you are preparing an exhibit, you may want to display your results, such as any experimental setup you designed. If you have completed a nonexperimental project, explain clearly what your research question was and illustrate your findings.

Related Projects

Bacteria are in and around people every day, opening the door to many projects that are interesting and inexpensive. You could experiment with different growth mediums, making your own or adding variables to one medium. You could explore bacteria's role in the life cycle, conducting a project with plants and bacteria. You could look at how different plants use bacteria. Other bacteria roles you could look at are in the soil and natural water sources. People and animals also house thousands of different bacteria. You could try to isolate some types of bacteria and determine their role and growing requirements.

You can also examine people's use of bacteria. Foods make use of these microorganisms' natural role. You could also examine how bacteria cause foods to spoil (see Spoilage chapter). Bacteria are the key to making cheeses. Yogurt and buttermilk are made from the bacteria in milk. You could experiment with using bacteria to grow yogurt. In biotechnology, people use bacteria to produce medicines, improve cleaning products, and make proteins. You could conduct a research project on how extremophiles and other more common types of bacteria are used.

For More Information

"Bacteria." *Stalking the Mysterious Microbe.* http://www.microbe.org/microbes/bacterium1.asp (accessed on August 24, 2003). ❖ Clear, concise information on bacteria and other microorganisms.

"Bacteria Divide and Multiply." *Cells alive!* http://www.cellsalive.com/ecoli.htm (accessed on August 24, 2003). ❖ Pictures and information on bacterial cells.

"The Bad Bug Book: Foodborne Pathogenic Microorganisms and Natural Toxins Handbook." *Center for Food Safety & Applied Nutrition.* http://vm.cfsan.fda.gov/~mow/intro.html (accessed on August 24, 2003). ❖ Detailed information on microbes that can contaminate food and cause diseases.

"Extremophiles." *University of New South Wales.* http://www.micro.unsw.edu.au/rick/extremophiles.html (accessed on August 24, 2003). ❖ Basic introduction to extremophiles.

Facklam, Howard, and Margery Facklam. *Bacteria.* New York: Twenty-First Century Books, 1994. ❖ Clear, detailed text with graphics.

Harder, Ben. "Germs That Do a Body Good: Bacteria might someday keep the doctor away." *Science News.* February 2, 2002. http://www.sciencenews.org/20020202/bob9.asp (accessed on August 24, 2003). ❖ How bacteria can help humans stay healthy.

"How big is a ...?" *Cells Alive!* http://www.cellsalive.com/howbig.htm (accessed on August 24, 2003). ❖ Interactive look at the size of different organisms relative to each other.

Madigan, Michael T., and Barry L. Marrs. "Extremophiles." *Scientific American.* April, 1997. ❖ Article on microbes that that survive under extreme conditions.

MicrobeWorld. http://www.microbeworld.org/ (accessed on August 24, 2003). ❖ News and information on microbes.

"Streaking for Isolation." *Hendrix College.* http://www.hendrix.edu/homes/fac/ sutherlandM/CellWeb/Techniques/micoiso.html (accessed on August 24, 2003). ❖ One technique on streaking plates.

Travis, J. "Pearl-like bacteria are largest ever found." *Science News.* April 17, 1999. http://www.sciencenews.org/sn_arc99/4_17_99/fob5.htm (accessed on August 24, 2003). ❖ The discovery of the largest bacteria in the world.

"Unsung Heroes." *Timeline Science.* http://www.timelinescience.org/resource/ students/pencilin/unsuhero.htm (accessed on August 24, 2003). ❖ A brief history of the many people who helped develop the antibiotic penicillin.

chapter 4

Bones and Muscles

Whenever you run, sit, walk, or even stand, your bones and muscles are working together in the activity. Bones are similar to the framework of a building; they provide the shape and protection. Our bones also produce our much-needed supply of daily blood cells—about 200 billion a day! They are the holding places for minerals and other key substances the body needs.

Many muscles are attached to bones and they pull the bones for movement. Other muscles provide much-needed functions for daily life. Even when you are just sitting still, your muscles are at work. They are allowing you to breath, swallow, smile, and even move your eyes. And it is a muscle that powers your entire body—the heart muscle. Working nonstop through a person's life, this vital muscle beats an average of seventy times per minute.

Bones, bones, bones

An adult body has about 206 bones. The number varies from person to person because of differences in the number of small bones. Some bones are responsible for movement, including bones in the hands, feet, and limbs. Other bones primarily give protection to the internal structures, such as the skull protecting the brain and the ribs shielding the heart, lungs, and liver.

When looking at animal bones or at a skeleton, bones may appear to be static and dead, but in the body they are actually full of activity. Bones grow and change along with the person. They are made of living and nonliving materials: About 70 percent of an adult's bones are composed of minerals. The remaining part is **bone tissue,** a group of

(W)ords to Know

Bone joint:
A place in the body where two or more bones are connected.

Bone marrow:
The spongy center of many bones in which blood cells are manufactured.

Bone tissue:
A group of similar cells in the bone with a common function.

Cancellous bone:
Also called spongy bone, the inner layer of a bone that has cells with large spaces in between them filled with marrow.

experiment
CENTRAL

Did You Know?

- The thighbone is the largest bone in your body, and the tiniest bones are the three deep inside your ear.

- Each of your feet and hands has twenty-six bones.

- When a person is said to be double jointed, they can have extra-long ligaments in their joints, allowing them to bend or twist farther than the average person.

- It takes fourteen muscles to smile and forty-three muscles to frown.

- The strongest muscle in your body is the gluteus maximus (the buttocks), and the second strongest is your tongue.

Words to Know

Cartilage:
The connective tissue that covers and protects the bones.

Collagen:
A protein in bone that gives the bone elasticity.

Compact bone:
The outer, hard layer of the bone.

Contract:
To shorten, pull together.

Control experiment:
A setup that is identical to the experiment, but is not affected by the variable that acts on the experimental group.

Hypothesis:
An idea in the form of a statement that can be tested by observation and/or experiment.

Ligaments:
Tough, fibrous tissue connecting bones.

similar cells with a common function. Bone tissue is constantly building new bone. In fact, about every seven years your bone tissue makes essentially a whole new skeleton.

Wherever two bones meet there is a **joint.** In some places, such as the bones in the skull, the joints are locked together and do not move. Most joints are movable, though, and are coated with a fluid that acts as a lubricant. **Ligaments** are a tough connective tissue that links bones together at the joints. Ligaments prevent the bones at the joints from becoming dislocated. **Cartilage** is another connective tissue found at the end of the bones and in the joints. This is a smooth and flexible tissue that lets one bone slide smoothly over another.

Hard and spongy

Almost every bone in the body is made of the same materials: The outside of the bone is the hard layer that is strong. It is made of living cells and is called **compact** or hard bone. Holes and channels run through the compact bone, carrying blood vessels and nerves to its inner parts. Inside this layer is **cancellous bone** or spongy bone. Cancellous bone has cells with large spaces in between them like a honeycomb. The spaces in this network are filled with a jellylike red-and-yellow **bone marrow.** Red bone marrow, found mainly at the

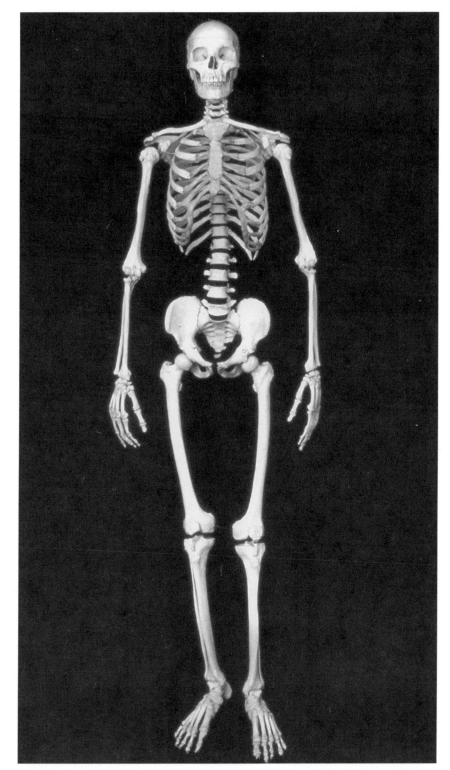

Full frontal view of a
human skeleton.
(Reproduced by permission
of Photo Researchers Inc.)

(W)ords to Know

Muscle fibers:
Stacks of long, thin cells
that make up muscle;
there are three types of
muscle fiber: skeletal,
cardiac, and smooth.

Nucleus, cell:
Enclosed structure
within a cell that
contains the cell's
genetic material and
controls its growth and
reproduction. (Plural:
nuclei.)

Tendon:
Tough, fibrous
connective tissue that
attaches muscle to
bone.

Variable:
Something that can
affect the results of an
experiment.

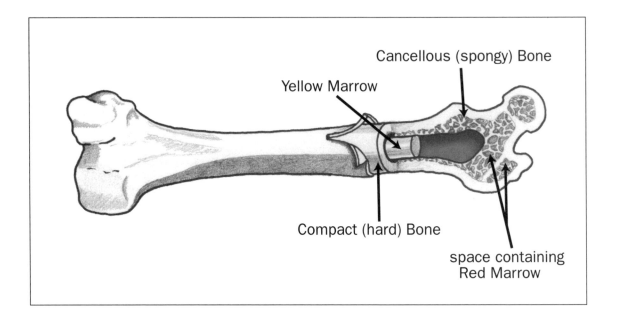

Parts of the human bone.

ends of bones, makes most of our body's blood cells. Red bone marrow also produces white blood cells, which help fight infection, and platelets, which help blood clot. Yellow bone marrow stores fat and releases it when it is needed somewhere in the body.

Bones contain large amounts of a protein called **collagen** as well as minerals, including calcium and phosphorous. Collagen gives bones their elasticity. Calcium is what gives bones their strength. Extra minerals are stored in the bone, and the bones release them when they are needed by other parts of the body. The amount of minerals that a person eats affects how many minerals the bones contain and store.

As a person gets older, the amount of new bone created slows down and bones break down at a faster rate than they are being made. Women especially may lose the stored calcium in their bodies that helps keep their bones strong and healthy. This causes the bones to become weak, which can lead to breaks. The disease **osteoporosis** occurs most often among older people. In osteoporosis bone tissue becomes brittle and thin. Bones break easily, and the spine can begin to collapse. Building up adequate stores of calcium in the bones as a young adult is one important way people can prevent or delay the development of this disease.

Muscular strength

Bones are moved by muscles attached to them. These muscles are fas-

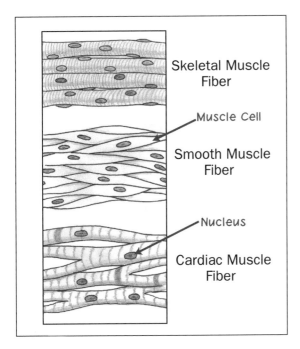

Skeletal Muscle Fiber

Muscle Cell

Smooth Muscle Fiber

Nucleus

Cardiac Muscle Fiber

tened to bones by a thin, tough tissue called **tendons,** which also link muscles to other muscles.

Muscles come in all shapes and sizes. The human body has about 650 muscles, which make up about 40 percent of a person's body weight. Muscles are classified as voluntary or involuntary. Voluntary muscles are those you can control at will, such as moving your arm. Involuntary muscles act automatically, such as your stomach muscles digesting food. Some muscles fit into both categories, such as the muscle used in blinking your eyes.

Muscles are made of stacks of long, thin cells called **muscle fibers.** Each muscle fiber is a single cell and contains at least one **nucleus.** The nucleus (plural: nuclei) is an enclosed structure that contains the cell's genetic material and controls its growth and reproduction. There are three types of muscle fibers: skeletal, smooth, and cardiac. Skeletal muscle fibers are attached to bone and are voluntary muscles. They are the most abundant and largest of the three, with some fibers running more than a foot long. Each skeletal muscle fiber has several nuclei. Smooth muscle fibers are involuntary, as in the stomach and intestines. They are smaller than the skeletal muscles and are narrow at the ends, with one nucleus in each cell. Cardiac muscles are found

LEFT:
The three types of muscle fibers.

RIGHT:
A humped back is a sign of osteoporosis. Elderly women especially are prone to developing this disease. (© Lester V. Bergman/CORBIS. Reproduced by permission.)

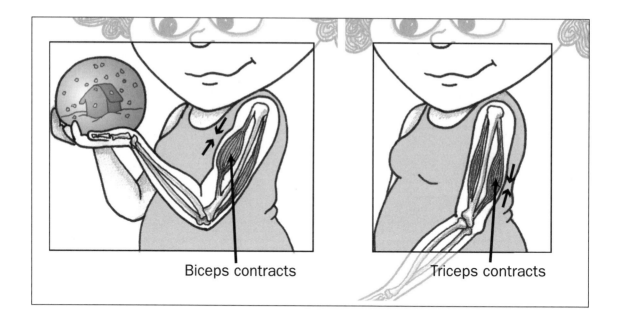

Biceps contracts

Triceps contracts

only in the heart. These muscles have fibers that are tightly packed together and have branches. A cardiac muscle cell usually has a single nucleus.

When muscles go into action they work in terms of contractions and relaxations. Muscles can only pull bones because they can only **contract,** or get shorter. They cannot push bones back into their original position. Because of this, muscles work in pairs. When one muscle contracts it can bend a limb; then when that muscle is finished contracting, its partner muscle contracts to extend or straighten the limb. Whenever you bend your arm, for example, the bicep muscle in the front of the upper arm contracts. When the arm straightens, the bicep relaxes and the tricep muscle at the back of the upper arm contracts.

All the energy that muscles use is created when muscle cells process the carbohydrates, fats, and proteins in foods. Healthy muscles burn nutrients efficiently. The amount a person exercises and his or her general health will make muscles work better and become less fatigued. Muscle fatigue occurs when the muscle stops contracting. When muscle cells run out of oxygen, they reach a point where the muscles have a reduced ability to contract. When a person builds his or her muscles, the muscle fibers grow. This increases the blood flow in the fibers, increasing their ability to contract.

experiment
CENTRAL

Regular exercise allows muscles to burn nutrients more efficiently and increases their ability to contract. (© Karl Weatherly/CORBIS. Reproduced by permission.)

Experiment 1
Bone Loss: How does the loss of calcium affect bone strength?

Purpose/Hypothesis

Your bones are lightweight and incredibly strong. Bones get their strength from a hard outer shell that contains the mineral calcium carbonate. The calcium keeps the bone stiff and rigid. A strong acid can chemically react with the bones and remove much of the calcium carbonate.

In this experiment you will determine how the loss of calcium carbonate affects the strength of bones. You will use vinegar as the acid. The vinegar will react with three bones for varying lengths of time. The longer the vinegar reacts with the bone, the more calcium the vinegar will remove from the bone. How much you can bend the bone will allow you determine the bone's strength.

Before you begin, make an educated guess about the outcome of this experiment based on your knowledge of bones and the mineral calcium. This educated guess, or prediction, is your **hypothesis.** A hypothesis should explain these things:

- the topic of the experiment
- the **variable** you will change

What Are the Variables?

Variables are anything that might affect the results of an experiment. Here are the main variables in this experiment:

- the type of bone you use
- the thickness of the bone
- the cleanliness of the bone
- the solution the bone is soaked in
- residue in the jars
- the environment of the bones when they are not soaking

In other words, the variables in this experiment are everything that might affect the vinegar reacting with the bone. If you change more than one variable at the same time, you will not be able to tell which variable had the most effect on bone strength.

- the variable you will measure
- what you expect to happen

A hypothesis should be brief, specific, and measurable. It must be something you can test through further investigation. Your experiment will prove or disprove whether your hypothesis is correct. Here is one possible hypothesis for this experiment: "The more calcium a bone loses, the weaker the bone will be and the more it will bend."

In this case, the variable you will change is the amount of time the bones react with the vinegar or acid. The variable you will measure is the bone's strength or how much the bone bends.

Conducting a **control experiment** will help you isolate each variable and measure the changes in the dependent variable. Only one variable will change between the control and the experimental bones, and that is the solution that immerses the bones. For the control, you will soak a bone in plain water, which does not react with the bone. At the end of the experiment you will compare the water-soaked bone with each of the vinegar-soaked bones.

For your experiment you will select four bones of the same type that are of equal thickness and general appearance. You will soak three of the bones in vinegar and one of the bones in water. Every four days you will remove each of the vinegar-soaked bones and test its strength. To compare the bones again at the end of the experiment, you will wrap each of the bones after the allotted period of time. If you leave them in the open air, the bone will react with the carbon dioxide in the air and harden again.

Level of Difficulty

Easy/Moderate.

Materials Needed

- four similar chicken bones (drumsticks from chicken wings work well)
- vinegar, white
- four glass jars with lids, large enough to hold a bone
- marking pen
- masking tape
- plastic wrap

Approximate Budget

$5.

Timetable

20 minutes initial setup time; another 30 minutes spread out over the next 12 days.

Step-by-Step Instructions

1. Clean the four bones thoroughly, scrubbing them with water.

Steps 2 and 3: Label each jar. Cover the bone in the control jar with water; cover the bones in the other jars with vinegar.

2. Place a piece of masking tape on each jar and label the first jar "Control," the second jar "4 Days," the third "8 Days," and the last "12 Days."

3. In the control jar, cover the bone with water. In the other three jars, cover the bones with vinegar. Set the jars aside.

4. After four days, open the "4 Day" jar and rinse off the bone with water. Test the strength of the bone by trying to bend it. While the bone is still wet, wrap it in plastic wrap thoroughly. Rinse the jar clean and place the wrapped bone back in the jar, screw on the lid and set it aside.

5. Repeat Step 4 after another four days for the bone in the "8 Day" jar. Repeat again four days later for the "12 Day" jar, except do not place the bone in plastic wrap.

6. Unwrap the other bones and examine how far each bone bends. Rinse the control bone with water and compare the strength of the three bones to the control.

7. Create a graph of the results, using an estimate of the degree the bones bend for the y-axis, and the number of days of calcium loss on the x-axis.

Summary of Results

Examine your graph of the data. How did the control bone compare to the bone with the greatest calcium loss? What do the bones feel

like? Do they feel different from each other? Think about how the loss of calcium in bones would affect a person. What can this experiment teach you about osteoporosis in older people?

Change the Variables

You can vary this experiment by changing the thickness or type of bone you use. Do you get the same results with a turkey bone as a chicken bone? You could also try leaving the bones out in the air for several days after they have finished soaking in vinegar and compare the results. You could also try comparing the same type bone from a young animal and an old animal. You may have to talk with your local butcher for help in selecting the bones.

Experiment 2
Muscles: How does the strength of muscles affect fatigue over time?

Purpose/Hypothesis

Skeleton muscles are the muscles attached to bones that are at work during physical activity. A muscle contracts when it is flexed or at work. The number of contractions a muscle can make is affected by fatigue.

In this experiment you will examine if a muscle can increase the number of contractions with muscle use, thereby reducing muscle fatigue. You will measure your muscle contractions through squats. The quadriceps muscles in the front of the upper legs are one of the main muscles used in a squat. A squat also uses the gluteus, hamstrings, and calf muscles.

A friend or family member will time the length of time you conduct the activity before you are fatigued. This partner will also count the number of squats you carry out and note them in a chart that you should not look at until you have completed the entire experiment. Not allowing you to know the number of muscle contractions you have completed will make the experiment more objective by not giving you a number to "beat." Try to think of something else during the experiment so you do not count the squats for yourself.

You will repeat the experiment every other day, until you have completed ten trials.

Before you begin, make an educated guess about the outcome of this experiment based on your knowledge of muscle strength and fatigue. This educated guess, or prediction, is your **hypothesis.** A hypothesis should explain these things:

- the topic of the experiment
- the **variable** you will change
- the variable you will measure
- what you expect to happen

What Are the Variables?

Variables are anything that might affect the results of an experiment. Here are the main variables in this experiment:

- The time of day

- Your nutritional level before you conduct the trial

In other words, the variables in this experiment are everything that might affect how many times you can complete a squat. If you change more than one variable at the same time, you will not be able to tell which variable had the most effect on fatigue.

How to Experiment Safely

Working a muscle too hard can cause soreness and damage to your muscle. Stop the activity if you feel dizzy or experience physical discomfort. Keep your feet firmly on the floor at all times and breathe regularly. If you have knee problems, do not do this experiment. Check with a parent or physical education teacher for a replacement activity.

A hypothesis should be brief, specific, and measurable. It must be something you can test through further investigation. Your experiment will prove or disprove whether your hypothesis is correct. Here is one possible hypothesis for this experiment: "The stronger muscles will become less fatigued and will gain strength over time."

In this case, the variable you will change is the strength of the muscles. The variable you will measure is the number of times your muscles can contract. To equate all the other variables, conduct the experiment at roughly the same time of day. At the end of the experiment you will examine how your muscles have changed over time.

Level of Difficulty
Easy

Materials Needed
* partner
* watch with second hand

Approximate Budget
$0

Timetable
Approximately 5 minutes per trial for a period of ten trials.

Step-by-Step Instructions
1. Have your partner begin timing when you start your first squat. Your partner will count the number of squats you do at each trial. Try to think of something else during the experiment so you do not count the squats for yourself.

Step 3: Squat until your knees are above your toes; stop when you get fatigued.

2. To conduct the squat, get into a comfortable upright stance, with your feet shoulder-width apart and your toes pointed straight ahead. Don't point your toes inward, because this will put a lot of strain on your knees.

3. Extend your arms. Squat down until your knees are over your toes. Pretend you are sitting in a chair.

4. Make sure to keep your heels planted firmly on the floor.

5. Return in an upright position and repeat at a regular pace.

6. When your muscles become fatigued then stop. Have your partner note the number of squats and the amount of time. Do not look at the chart.

7. Repeat this process every other day for a period of ten trials.

Summary of Results

Graph the results of your data from your first trial to the last trial, making the x-axis the number of squats and the y-axis the trial number. Does the number of muscles' contractions change over time?

Troubleshooter's Guide

Below is a problem that may arise during this experiment, a possible cause, and a way to remedy the problem.

Problem:: There is no change in muscle fatigue over the trials.

Possible cause: You may be squatting further down over the trials, which uses more muscle. Repeat the experiment making sure to stop your squat each time when your knees are over your toes.

Construct a second graph that marks the length of time of each trial on the x-axis with the trial number on the y-axis. How does the length of time you were able to contract your muscles change over time? Write a brief summary of the experiment that relates your results to muscle strength and movement.

 # Design Your Own Experiment

How to Select a Topic Relating to this Concept

To select a related project, you can explore the different ways that you use your bones and muscles throughout the day. An experiment with bones could include comparing bones from different species. An experiment with muscles could work to identify the characteristics of each of the three muscle fibers. Check the For More Information section and talk with your science, health, or physical education teacher to learn more about bones and muscles.

Steps in the Scientific Method

To do an original experiment, you need to plan carefully and think things through. Otherwise, you might not be sure what question you are answering, what you are or should be measuring, or what your findings prove or disprove.

Here are the steps in designing an experiment:

- State the purpose of—and the underlying question behind—the experiment you propose to do.
- Recognize the variables involved and select one that will help you answer the question at hand.
- State your hypothesis, an educated guess about the answer to your question.
- Decide how to change the variable you selected.
- Decide how to measure your results.

Recording Data and Summarizing the Results

Your data should include charts and graphs such as the one you did for these experiments. They should be clearly labeled and easy to read. You may also want to include photographs and drawings of your experimental setup and results, which will help others visualize the steps in the experiment.

If you are preparing an exhibit, you may want to display your results, such as any experimental setup you designed. If you have completed a nonexperimental project, explain clearly what your research question was and illustrate your findings.

Related Projects

You can design your own experiments on bones and muscles. Think of some other reasons why people might experience bone decalcification. Investigate a method for testing the impact of other minerals in a bone. You could explore how the bones in different species compare to each other. Do species that are physically similar have similar bone structures?

For a muscle experiment, you could examine the characteristics of each of the three types of muscle fibers by purchasing the three different muscles from a butcher. Examine muscle fatigue further by investigating if fatigue is greater at certain times of the day. You could investigate if there are particular activities that women find fatiguing and men do not. Are there different muscles in the bones of women and men?

For More Information

Ávila, Victoria. *How Our Muscles Work.* New York: Chelsea House, 1995. ❖ Includes introduction to muscles with full illustrations.

"Bones, Muscles, and Joints." *KidsHealth.* http://kidshealth.org/teen/your_body/ body_basics/bones_muscles_joints_p8.html (accessed August 24, 2003). ❖ Collection of articles for teenagers that explains how the bones, muscles, and joints work.

Human Anatomy Online. http://www.innerbody.com/htm/body.html (accessed August 24, 2003). ❖ An interactive look at the skeleton and muscular systems, with descriptions and animations.

Jacoby, Mitch. "Tough Bones," *Chemical & Engineering News.* December 17, 2001. http://pubs.acs.org/cen/topstory/7951/7951notw4.html (accessed August 24, 2003). ❖ Looks at findings on the bonds that make bones so tough.

Simon, Seymour. *Bones: Your Skeleton System.* New York: Morrow Junior Books, 1998. ❖ Clear introduction to the skeleton system using photographs.

Simon, Seymour. *Muscles: Your Muscular System.* New York: Morrow Junior Books, 1998. ❖ Clear introduction to the muscular system using photographs.

White, Katherine. *The Muscular System.* New York: Rosen Publishing, 2001. ❖ Basic information about the muscular system.

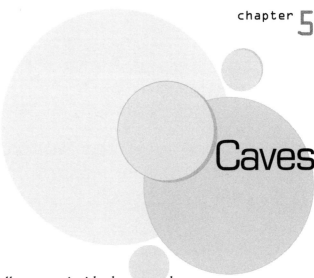

chapter 5

Caves

Caves, also called **caverns,** are natural hollow areas inside the ground that are large enough for a person to fit inside. There are millions of caves on Earth. Some caves, are only a few yards (meters) deep. Others stretch hundreds of miles underground, splitting into numerous rooms and passageways. There are caves underwater, on the sides of mountains, and beneath flat land. Interiors of caves often contain unique landscapes and life forms that are spectacular sights.

Along with their awesome beauty, caves have provided people with important clues to ancient life and geology. The scientific study of caves is called **speleology** (pronounced spee-lee-AH-lu-gy), from the Greek words for cave, *spelaion,* and knowledge, *logos.* Scientists who study these caves are known as **speleologists** and they are only beginning to unearth the treasure of information that caves contain. Speleologists have found unique animals, new plant life, and clues to Earth's history.

Forming the holes

Caves take hundreds of thousands of years to form. There are caves in the process of forming right now, and already-formed caves that are undergoing continuous change. The majority of caves are made out of the rock limestone. Limestone is a rock formed millions of years ago out of the hardened remains of layers of sea animals.

The formation of a limestone cave begins with water. When rain falls it collects a small amount of the gas carbon dioxide from the air. As the water trickles into the soil, it passes through tiny pockets of air in the soil. The soil is where it picks up most of the carbon dioxide.

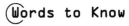

Words to Know

Carbonic acid:
A weak acid that forms from the mixture of water and carbon dioxide.

Cave:
Also called cavern, a hollow or natural passage under or into the ground large enough for a person to enter.

Control experiment:
A setup that is identical to the experiment, but is not affected by the variable that acts on the experimental group.

Words to Know

Hypothesis:
An idea in the form of a statement that can be tested by observation and/or experiment.

Lava cave:
A cave formed from the flow of lava streaming over solid matter.

Sea cave:
A cave in sea cliffs, formed most commonly by waves eroding the rock.

Speleologist:
One who studies caves.

Speleology:
Scientific study of caves and their plant and animal life.

Spelunkers:
Also called cavers, people who explore caves for a hobby.

Stalactite:
Cylindrical or icicle-shaped mineral deposit projecting downward from the roof of a cave. (Pronounced sta-LACK-tite.)

Carbon dioxide that mixes with water causes the water to change into an acid, called **carbonic acid**. Carbonic acid water slowly eats away at the soft limestone. It seeps into small cracks, causing the cracks to widen and allowing more water to flow through. Gradually, the water causes the rock to dissolve. The dissolved area grows into a hole, then a larger hole, and still larger. Eventually, over a few million years, the water carves an underground room where there was once only rock. In time, that room increases in size and can become many rooms with passageways between them.

A newly formed cave is filled with water. This water can stay in the cave for hundreds or thousands of years. Water drains out of the cave only when some type of geological shift occurs. The cave may be lifted above the water by a gradual uplifting of the ground. Or a nearby stream of water can flow through the cave, slicing a deep swath through the cave and causing the water level to drop. Caves often contain remnants of the water in streams or ponds. When the cave is lifted above the water, water flows out of the hole and the cave fills with air.

There are several other types of caves also. **Sea caves** form along rocky shores from the constant pounding of ocean waves. The waves

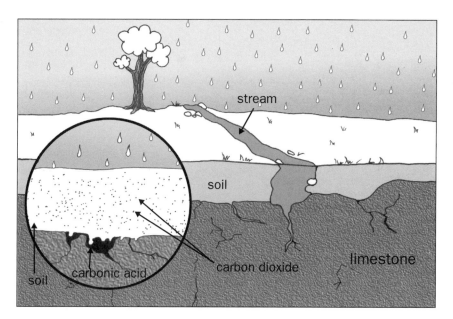

Cave formation begins: Water mixes with carbon dioxide to form carbonic acid, which seeps into small cracks in the limestone.

stream

soil

soil

carbonic acid

carbon dioxide

limestone

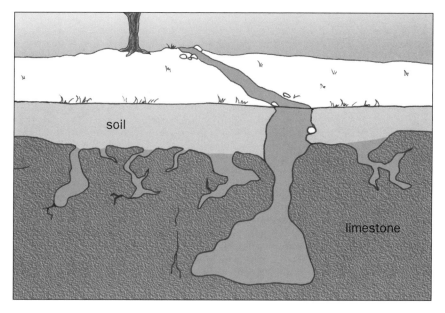

Cave formation continues: The dissolved rock grows in an increasingly larger hole, eventually forming a cave.

soil

limestone

(W)ords to Know

Stalagmite:
Cylindrical or icicle-shaped mineral deposit projecting upward from the floor of a cave. (Pronounced sta-LAG-mite.)

Troglobite:
An animal that lives in a cave and is unable to live outside of one.

Troglophile:
An animal that lives the majority of its life cycle in a cave but is also able to live outside of the cave.

wear away the base of the rocky cliff where the rock is soft or has cracks in it. Seawater carries the rock away and, over time, a cave forms. **Lava caves** are made after a volcano erupts and the molten, hot lava flows down the side of the volcano. The outer layer of the lava cools and hardens; hot lava continues to flow underneath. When this hot lava drains away it can leave a cave behind.

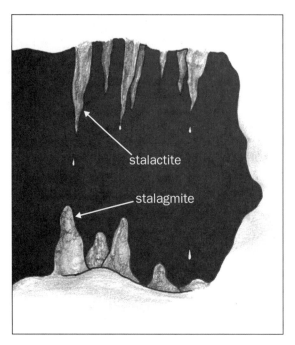

Stalactites and stalagmites, common in limestone caves, form gradually over time from the buildup of calcite.

More recently, scientists have discovered that caves can also form from a type of bacteria that live deep beneath Earth. These bacteria use oil for food and release the gas hydrogen sulfide. Hydrogen sulfide reacts with oxygen to produce sulfuric acid, which can dissolve limestone. The Carlsbad Caverns in New Mexico is an example of a limestone cave carved out of sulfuric acid. These caverns contain eighty-three caves and include the nation's deepest limestone cave at 1,567 feet (478 meters), and one of the world's largest chambers.

Natural extensions

The slow drainage of carbonic acid water can cause the formation of dramatic cave features created after the underground chamber is formed. These features come in many shapes and several different colors. Two types of attributes common in limestone caves are icicle-like extensions that sprout up from the floor or hang down from its ceiling. **Stalactites** are cave features that hang from the ceiling; **stalagmites** grow upward from the floor.

The formation of these two types of features begins with water droplets. After most of the water has drained from a cave, water continues to flow through layers of the limestone rocks. All the water droplets contain a small amount of dissolved limestone, which carries the mineral calcite. A stalactite begins when a drop of this water hangs from the ceiling. The water evaporates or drips to the ground and the calcite in the water remains. One droplet builds upon another, the calcite deposits increase and a stalactite grows. Stalactites can reach down hundreds of meters, but watching one grow is a lengthy process. On average, a stalactite grows only about half an inch every hundred years.

OPPOSITE PAGE:
Sea caves form along rocky shores from the constant pounding of ocean waves. (Reproduced by permission of Field Mark Publications.)

experiment
CENTRAL

The upward-growing stalagmites form when water droplets drip from the ceiling or a stalactite above. When the water droplet hits the floor it spatters the calcite deposits outward, but close together. The calcite builds up over time to create finger-like shapes with rounded tops. Stalagmites can grow to both amazing widths and heights, some growing more than 45 feet (13 meters) wide and 30 feet (9 meters) tall.

Stalactites and stalagmites are often white or nearly white because the most common form of calcite is white. Iron and other minerals or materials mixing with the calcite create rich-colored stalactites and stalagmites, including red, yellow, orange, and black.

Life in the dark lane

A cave's darkness may deter many life forms from making a home inside, but caves are crawling with organisms that like what a cave offers. Scientists have separated cave animals into three distinct types.

Animals that can only survive in the deep interior of caves' pitch-blackness are called **troglobites,** from the Greek word meaning cave life. Types of troglobites include species of shrimp, insects, and spiders. Many of these animals feature small eyes or blindness, no pigment, and a well-developed sense of touch and smell. Other animals are part-time cave dwellers. Called **trogloxenes,** meaning cave guest, these animals stay in the cave for sleep, warmth, protection, and to raise their young. Bats are an example of this type of animal. The nocturnal bats doze away the sunny hours in the darkness of a cave. Bats live in colonies and feed at night, catching insects such as moths, beetles, and mosquitoes. Bat colonies are among the largest grouping of mammals in the world. The Bracken Cave in Texas houses twenty million Mexican free-tail bats that eat more than 250,000 pounds of insects every night. Bears, crickets, and pack rats are other examples of trogloxenes.

The last type, **troglophiles,** meaning cave lovers, are animals that live most of their lives in caves but also have the ability to live outside. They like the dampness of the cave and may venture outside to forage for food. Troglophiles include species of salamanders, frogs, beetles, millipedes, snails, and mites.

Because green plants need light to live, plants only grow near the entrance where light penetrates. Mosses and ferns are the plants commonly found near the cave opening; algae grows on the rocks. Caves

(Words to Know

Trogloxene:
An animal that spends only part of its life cycle in a cave and returns periodically to the cave.

Variable:
Something that can affect the results of an experiment.

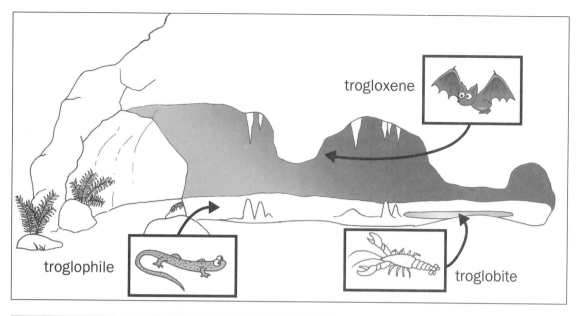

are also teeming with fungi and bacteria that keep the chain of cave life flowing. Droppings from animals, such as bats, can provide the major food source for other cave life, yet few animals can feed on these. Bacteria and fungi decompose these materials into simple foods and nutrients. Small animals, such as insects, also munch on fungi and bacteria for their food supply. These insects then become food, in turn, for larger predators.

TOP:
Cave life includes three general categories of animals that live in different areas of the cave.

BOTTOM:
Fruit bats hang from the walls of a cave in Bali, Indonesia. (© Robert Gill/CORBIS. Reproduced by permission.)

experiment
CENTRAL

Some like it dark

Speleologists are not the only people who like to study caves. People who explore caves for a hobby are called cavers or **spelunkers.** Spelunking can be a somewhat dangerous hobby. There are narrow passages, steep cliffs, and long distances–all in the dark. With caves that stretch steeply downward, spelunkers need to have many of the skills and equipment of mountain climbers. The darkness of a cave and its vastness also take some skill to navigate.

Experiment 1
Cave Formation: How does the acidity of a substance affect the formation of a cave?

Purpose/Hypothesis

The majority of caves are formed when limestone is dissolved by carbonic acid. In this experiment you will determine why acidic substances form caves by comparing how acidic and nonacidic solutions react with different geologic materials. You will use chalk, seashells, and rocks as the geologic materials. Chalk and seashells are both types of limestone.

Carbonic acid, a mixture of carbon dioxide and water, is the same compound found in soda. Carbonic acid is a weak acid. It is carbonic acid that makes soda fizz. A liquid can also be a base or it can be neutral. Pure water is an example of a neutral. A mixture of baking soda in water is an example of a base.

After determining the acidity of the liquids, you will place drops of the liquids on each material and note the results.

Before you begin, make an educated guess about the outcome of this experiment based on your knowledge of limestone and carbonic acid. This educated guess, or prediction, is your **hypothesis.** A hypothesis should explain these things:

- the topic of the experiment
- the **variable** you will change
- the variable you will measure
- what you expect to happen

A hypothesis should be brief, specific, and measurable. It must be something you can test through further investigation. Your experi-

What Are the Variables?

Variables are anything that might affect the results of an experiment. Here are the main variables in this experiment:

- the solid material
- the liquid
- the liquid's acidity
- the amount of liquid poured

In other words, the variables in this experiment are everything that might affect limestone's reaction with the liquid. If you change more than one variable at the same time, you will not be able to tell which variable had the most effect on dissolving the limestone.

ment will prove or disprove whether your hypothesis is correct. Here is one possible hypothesis for this experiment: "Only the limestone materials will have a reaction with the acidic liquids."

In this case, the variable you will change is the acidity of the solution. The variable you will measure is the reaction of the liquid on the geologic substance.

Conducting a **control experiment** will help you isolate each variable and measure the changes in the dependent variable. Only one variable will change between the control and the experimental setup, and that is the solution you drop on the solid material. For the control in this experiment you will use plain water.

Level of Difficulty
Easy to Moderate.

Materials Needed
- acid/base indicator strips
- baking soda
- clear soda pop
- distilled water
- dropper or spoon
- six clear or plastic cups

Some of the materials needed for Experiment 1.

- spoon
- measuring spoon
- dropper
- 3 pieces pure white chalk
- 3 small rocks/pebbles
- 3 seashells or seashell pieces

Approximate Budget
$5.

Timetable
30 minutes.

Step-by-Step Instructions
1. Create a data chart, listing the liquids across the top columns and the different substances in the rows.

How to Experiment Safely
There are no safety hazards in this experiment.

2. Prepare a basic solution: Mix 1 teaspoon (5 milliliters) of baking soda with one cup of water. Stir thoroughly and label the cup "Baking soda."

3. Pour water in another cup and label as "Water"; pour soda in yet another cup and label as "Soda."

4. With an acid/base indicator strip, first test the water, then the baking-soda solution, and, finally, the soda for acidity. Use a new strip for each test and dip the strip briefly in each liquid. An acid will turn the paper red, a base will turn the paper blue, and a neutral substance will not change the color of the strip. Note on your chart whether each liquid is an acid, base, or neutral.

5. Take three new, empty cups: Place one piece of chalk in one; one pebble in a second; and one seashell piece in the third.

6. Use a dropper to drip 3 to 4 drops of the soda on the limestone chalk. Note in your chart a description of the sound and appearance. Does the limestone absorb the soda? Does the soda give any indication that it is dissolving the chalk?

7. Drip the same amount of soda over a piece of the seashell and the pebble. Describe the reaction of each on the seashell and the pebble.

8. Repeat Steps 6 and 7, replacing the soda with the baking-soda solution, and then with the water. (You may use the same cups to test all three liquids.) Note the reactions in the chart.

Summary of Results

Examine the reactions of each liquid on the solid material. How did the acidity level of the liquid affect the reaction? Was your hypothesis

Troubleshooter's Guide

Below is a problem that may arise during this experiment, a possible cause, and a way to remedy the problem.

Problem: There was no reaction with any of the substances.

Possible cause: You may have used soda that was flat, meaning that all the carbon dioxide has escaped and there is no carbonic acid. Repeat the experiment, making sure to use a fresh, fizzy can of soda.

correct? Hypothesize what would occur to each material if you soaked it in the liquids for several weeks. What would happen to each substance if you dropped a stronger acid on it? Write a brief summary of the experiment and your analysis.

Change the Variables

There are several ways you can modify the experiment by changing the variables. You can change the type of geologic substance, using different types of rocks or granite, for example. You can vary the acidity level of the liquid, such as by using vinegar (an acid) or soap (a base). There are charts available where you can look up the strengths of the acids and bases. Many cleaning products also contain strong acidic substances: Use these carefully and with adult supervision. You can also alter the experiment by lengthening the amount of time the liquid sits on the substance.

Experiment 2
Cave Icicles: How does the mineral content of water affect the formation of stalactites and stalagmites?

Purpose/Hypothesis

The formation of stalactites and stalagmites in a cave is a slow process that depends on the mineral content of the water and the evaporation rate. In this experiment, you will form your own mini-cave icicles using two different types of minerals.

Most caves are formed in limestone. Limestone is a form of the mineral calcite, which is made up largely of calcium carbonate. In this experiment, you will use two compounds made from similar minerals: baking soda and Epsom salt. Baking soda is sodium bicarbonate, a mineral that is a form of carbonate; Epsom salt is magnesium sulfate, another type of mineral, but not a carbonate.

In order for the minerals to join together to make a stalactite or stalagmite, you have to make a water solution brimming with the minerals. Hot water can dissolve more minerals than cold water. When as much of a substance as possible is dissolved in hot water and the water is allowed to cool, that solution is called supersaturated. The molecules in a supersaturated solution are so crammed together that they readily

What Are the Variables?

Variables are anything that might affect the results of an experiment. Here are the main variables in this experiment:

- the saturation level of solution

- the environment allowed to grow

- the string

- the mineral

In other words, variables in this experiment are everything that might affect the formation of the stalactites. If you change more than one variable, you will not be able to tell which variable impacted their formation.

stick to each other. When you dip a length of yarn in this solution, the solution will creep up the yarn. As the air evaporates some of the water, the solid material will remain on the string. Just as stalactites and stalagmites form in a cave, the minerals will build up over time.

Before you begin, make an educated guess about the outcome of this experiment based on your knowledge of the formation of stalactites and stalagmites. This educated guess, or prediction, is your **hypothesis.** A hypothesis should explain these things:

- the topic of the experiment
- the **variable** you will change
- the variable you will measure
- what you expect to happen

A hypothesis should be brief, specific, and measurable. It must be something you can test through further investigation. Your experiment will prove or disprove whether your hypothesis is correct. Here is one possible hypothesis for this experiment: "The cave formations will accumulate better when they are made out of baking soda, the same carbonate mineral that is in a cave."

In this case, the variable you will change is the type of mineral in each solution. The variable you will measure is the formation of the stalactites and (perhaps) stalagmites.

Level of Difficulty

Moderate.

Materials Needed

- four clear glasses or small glass jars (same size)
- hot water
- baking soda
- Epsom salt
- two spoons
- dark construction paper, 8.5 x 11 inches (22 x 28 centimeters)
- four small washers (or paper clips)
- scissors
- bowl
- thick woolen yarn, about 2 feet (0.6 meters)
- masking tape
- marking pen

Approximate Budget

$5.

Timetable

45 minutes for setup and followup; 5 to 10 minutes per day for about 8 to 12 days to observe and record the results.

Step-by-Step Instructions

1. Pour 2 cups of very hot water into a bowl and dissolve as much baking soda as you can to make a saturated solution. Stir after every addition. When the solution is saturated, small bits of baking soda will fall to the bottom and will not dissolve no matter how hard you stir.
2. Pour half the water in one cup and half in another cup.
3. Cut the construction paper in half. Place the two glasses close to either end of the dark paper.

How to Experiment Safely

Have an adult present when handling hot water. Be careful when handling the scissors.

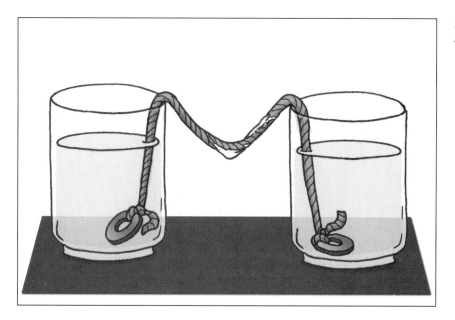

Step 6: The yarn should sag slightly in the center.

4. Stretch the yarn between the glasses and cut a piece that is about double that length. The yarn should be long enough to go inside each glass and hang loosely.
5. Tie a washer or paper clip to each end of the yarn.
6. Carefully lower the weighted ends of the yarn into the two glasses. The yarn should sag slightly in the center.
7. Label the two glasses "sodium bicarbonate."
8. Repeat Steps 1 through 7, replacing the baking soda with Epsom salt. Label the second set of glasses "magnesium sulfate."
9. Allow the glasses to sit undisturbed for at least 8 to 12 days. (A warm, sunny area works well.)
10. Illustrate what happens each day.

Summary of Results

Look at your progression of pictures over the time of the experiment. What has formed on the string? Has anything begun to form on the construction paper? Compare the pictures of the two types of minerals? Write up a summary of the experiment, explaining the process of the mineral formations.

Change the Variables

There are several ways you can vary this experiment. You can use a different type of mineral to form the solution, such as sodium carbon-

Troubleshooter's Guide

Below is a problem that may arise during this experiment, some possible causes, and some ways to remedy the problem.

Problem: No crystals grew in one or more of the solutions.

Possible cause: The solution may not have been saturated when the water was hot. You may not have stirred enough to dissolve the solids. Pour the solution back in the saucepan. Reheat the solution, adding more of the substance and stirring well after each addition until you see bits of the substance fall to the bottom.

Possible cause: The water may not have been hot enough. It does not need to be at the boiling point, but it does need to be hot. Pour the solution back in the saucepan. Reheat the solution, adding more of the substance and stirring well after each addition until it is saturated.

ate (washing soda) or sodium chloride (salt). You can also alter the environment that the minerals form in, such as a humid or a dry environment.

 Design Your Own Experiment

How to Select a Topic Relating to this Concept

Cave formations are often intriguing to view and study. These structures are continuing to provide new information to spelunkers, speleologists, and other explorers. For a related project, you could investigate the history, geology, life, and formation of caves. You could also find out if there are any caves in your area that are open to visitors.

Check the For More Information section and talk with your science teacher to learn more about caves. If you decide to visit a cave, make sure you are accompanied by an adult knowledgeable about caving.

Steps in the Scientific Method

To conduct an original experiment, you need to plan carefully and think things through. Otherwise, you might not be sure what question you are answering, what you are or should be measuring, or what your findings prove or disprove.

A Native American cave dwelling at Canyonlands National Park, Utah. (© PBNJ Productions/CORBIS. Reproduced by permission.)

Here are the steps in designing an experiment:

- State the purpose of—and the underlying question behind—the experiment you propose to do
- Recognize the variables involved and select one that will help you answer the question at hand
- State your hypothesis, an educated guess about the answer to your question
- Decide how to change the variable you selected
- Decide how to measure your results

Recording Data and Summarizing the Results

Your data should include charts and graphs such as the one you did for these experiments. They should be clearly labeled and easy to read. You may also want to include photographs and drawings of your experimental setup and results, which will help other people visualize the steps in the experiment.

If you are preparing an exhibit, you may want to display your results, such as any experimental setup you designed. If you have completed a nonexperimental project, explain clearly what your research question was and illustrate your findings.

Related Projects

There are multiple projects related to caves that you can undertake. You can study the animal and plant life in a cave through research and visits to museums or other facilities that may house some cave creatures. If there is a cave in your area that is open to the public, you could visit the cave and use a magnifying glass to examine the plant and animal life. Make sure you do not collect or touch any of the plant or animal life so as not to disturb their habitat. This project could also include an examination of how each type of animal and plant has adapted to the cave environment. If you decide to conduct a cave exploration, make sure an adult who is knowledgeable in caving accompanies you.

You can also investigate the formation of different types of caves, such as caves that form from volcanoes or out of ice. You could conduct a research project on the information that caves have provided in many fields of study. Another research project could be to examine how cultures throughout history have used caves in their daily life and rituals.

For More Information

"Biology of Caves." *National Park Service.* http://www.nps.gov/ozar/cavelife.html (accessed on August 24, 2003). ❖ Information on caves and cave life.

Groleau, Rick "How Caves Form." *NOVA.* http://www.pbs.org/wgbh/nova/caves/form.html# (accessed on August 24, 2003). ❖ Animated depiction of the formation of caves with clear explanations.

Hadingham, Evan. "Subterranean Surprises." *Smithsonian Magazine.* October 2002: pp. 68–74. ❖ Detailed article on new information scientists are learning about caves.

The National Speleological Society. http://www.caves.org/ (accessed on August 24, 2003). ❖ Homepage for the National Speleological Society describing its purpose and activities.

experiment
CENTRAL

chapter 6

Chemosenses

People depend on taste and smell to recognize a delicious meal, but these senses also play a key part in survival helping keep us alive. Both senses can warn us of trouble and both are linked to what we eat. Pleasant tastes and smells ensure that a person or animal continues to eat and acquire energy from foods. Unpleasant tastes and smells are one way to ensure a person does not ingest poisons or other materials that can harm him or her.

People get information about the world around them through their senses of hearing, touch, sight, taste, and smell. Each of these five senses is tuned to a specific sensation. You are always using at least one of your senses. The senses send messages to the brain, which processes the information. Taste and smell belong to the chemical-sensing system group, known as **chemosenses,** which means that the sense is stimulated by specific chemicals. These chemicals trigger a nerve signal to the brain that then "reads" the signal.

How taste works

When people say something tastes good, they are usually referring to the flavor of the food or drink. Flavor is a combination of taste, smell, texture, and other characteristics of the food itself, such as temperature. The sense of taste is complex because it is so intricately linked with flavor and weaves in many of the other senses, especially the sense of smell. There are five basic tastes: sweet, sour, salty, bitter, and umami (pronounced oo-MAM-ee). Umami was described in the early 1900s, but only in the late 1990s did food researchers officially recognize it as a distinct taste. Umami is the taste that occurs when foods with the

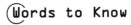

Words to Know

Chemosense:
A sense stimulated by specific chemicals that cause the sensory cell to transmit a signal to the brain.

Cilia:
Hairlike structures on olfactory receptor cells that sense odor molecules.

Control experiment:
A setup that is identical to the experiment, but is not affected by the variable that acts on the experimental group.

Did You Know?

- The numbers of taste buds and olfactory receptors differ widely across species. Cows have about 25,000 taste buds, and insects only about 4. For olfactory receptors, humans have an estimated 40 million, but there are some dogs that have about 2 billion.

- Catfish have taste buds on their whiskers, and butterflies taste with their feet!

protein glutamate are eaten. Glutamate is found in meat, fish, and the flavor-enhancing chemical monosodium glutamate, or MSG.

Humans get the sensation of taste through their taste cells, which lie within the taste bud. The average person has about 10,000 **taste buds.** People regenerate new taste buds every three to ten days. As people grow older their taste buds regenerate at a slower rate, causing their sense of taste to lessen. An elderly person may have only 5,000 taste buds.

Taste buds are onion-shaped structures located primarily on a person's tongue. The majority of buds on the tongue are scattered on the **papillae** (pronounced pah-PILL-ee), the small projections that give

Taste buds are onion-shaped structures located primarily on a person's tongue.

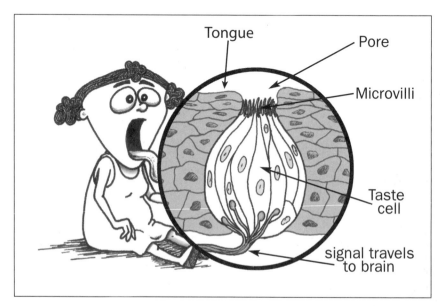

your tongue its rough appearance. Taste buds are also located on the throat, roof of the mouth, and pharynx, but the buds on your tongue provide most of your taste experience. Each taste bud is made up of about 50 to 150 taste cells. Every cell has a fingerlike extension called a **microvilli** that connects with an opening at the top of the taste bud, called the **taste pore.**

For food to have taste, its chemicals need to reach your taste cells. The instant you take a bite of food, saliva or spit in the mouth starts breaking down the food's chemical components. These components, or molecules, travel through the pores in the papillae to bind to specific taste cells. The chemicals cause a change in the taste cell, sending a signal via nerves to the brain, which processes the signals.

The chemical reaction in the taste cells varies depending on the taste group involved. For example, salty foods trigger a change in taste cells when enough sodium (the main component of salt) molecules enter the cells through the microvilli. Each taste cell has the ability to recognize different taste groups, yet taste cells specialize in processing

In order for food to have taste, its chemical components need to reach the taste cells in your mouth. (Copyright © Kelly A. Quin. Reproduced by permission of Kelly A. Quin.)

one particular group. Researchers have found that taste buds with common taste perceptions may be bunched together on the papillae. Many of the taste buds more sensitive to bitterness, for example, are located on the back of the tongue. This can cause an automatic gag-reflex to help prevent poisoning if something too bitter is ingested.

Smells at work: Lime or lemon?

It is the **olfactory** sense, or sense of smell, that plays a key role in determining your perception of how tasty something is, or its flavor. Flavor is so strongly linked to the olfactory sense that researchers estimate 70 to 75 percent of what humans perceive as taste actually comes from the sense of smell.

Special olfactory cells, located inside the uppermost part of the nose, recognize specific odors. These odors, or chemical molecules, enter the nose and rise upward until they reach the **olfactory epithelium**, a postage-stamp-size area that contains **olfactory receptor cells.** Olfactory receptor cells are nerve cells, and each cell lasts about four to five weeks before it is replaced with a new one. These cells have hairlike projections called **cilia** that are sensitive to odor molecules. A specific odor molecule dissolves in the mucus of the nose. Mucus is a slippery substance that protects and moistens. The odor molecule binds to specific receptors on the cilia, which trigger a chemical signal in the receptor cell. The cell then sends its signal to the **olfactory bulb** of the brain, and then on to other areas of the brain that recognize it as a specific odor. There can be hundreds of receptors that take part in recognizing one smell.

Olfactory cells can recognize thousands of different odors. The chemical molecules reach the cells through the air you breathe and the food you eat. When you put food in your mouth, chemicals are released while you are chewing. Molecules from the food travel through the passage between your nose and mouth to the olfactory epithelium.

If a person's nose is congested, mucus in the nasal passages can block the odor molecules from reaching the olfactory cells. This will block surrounding smells, and food will lose much of its flavor.

All senses are not created equal

Because the chemosenses are complex mechanisms, there are several reasons why people have varying preferences for smells and tastes. A person's genetics (physiological makeup), upbringing, and familiarity with specific smells and foods can influence his or her likes and dislikes.

Words to Know

Hypothesis:
An idea in the form of a statement that can be tested by observation and/or experiment.

Microvilli:
The extension of each taste cell that pokes through the taste pore and first senses the chemicals.

Mucus:
A thick, slippery substance that serves as a protective lubricant coating in passages of the body that communicate with the air.

Olfactory:
Relating to the sense of smell.

Olfactory bulb:
The part of the brain that processes olfactory (smell) information.

Olfactory epithelium:
The patch of mucous membrane at the top of the nasal cavity that contains the olfactory (smell) nerve cells.

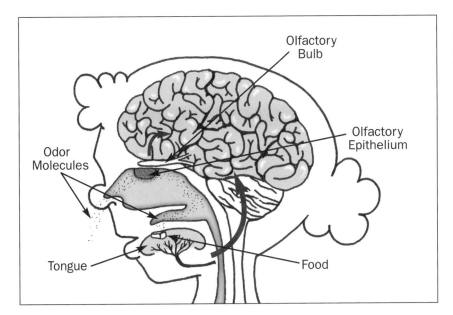

How tastes and smells are recognized. Food and odor molecules attach to olfactory cells that send signals to the brain.

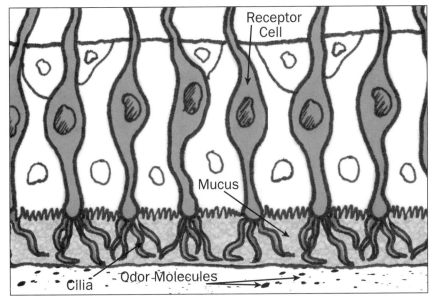

The olfactory epithelium. Odor molecules bind to specific receptors on the cilia, which triggers a chemical signal in the receptor cell. The cell then sends its signal to the olfactory bulb of the brain, and then on to other areas of the brain that recognize it as a specific odor.

Odor molecules transmit their signals to areas of the brain that are involved with emotional behavior and memory. When a person smells something, it often brings back memories associated with the object, and those memories can help shape a person's perception of that smell.

Genetics is also a factor in tasting ability. In the early 1930s researchers discovered an inherited trait that determined people's sensitivity to a bitter taste. They classified people as "tasters" or "nontasters" based on whether they were able to detect a specific chemical, which tastes bitter to some people and tasteless to others. Later research found that some people are especially sensitive to this bitter taste. These people are born with more than the average number of taste buds and, as a result, perceive tastes more intensely than the average person. For these supertasters bitter tastes more bitter, sweet tastes sweeter, and salt tastes saltier. Researchers theorize that about 25 percent of the people in the United States are supertasters, 25 percent are nontasters, and the remaining 50 percent are regular tasters.

In the two experiments that follow, you will use the scientific method to examine if genetics affects the sense of taste and how closely linked these two senses are.

Experiment 1
Supertasters: Is there a correlation between the number of taste buds and taste perception?

Purpose/Hypothesis
In this experiment, you will test varying concentrations of three tastes on people to predict whether they fall into the category of nontaster, taster, or supertaster. Then you will test your hypothesis by counting the number of papillae of each person to estimate the number of taste buds each person has. If a person has more than twenty-five in a punch-hole-size area, then he/she is classified as a supertaster, five or less is considered a nontaster, and anywhere in between is an average taster.

Before you begin, make an educated guess about the outcome of this experiment based on your knowledge of the sense of taste. This educated guess, or prediction, is your **hypothesis.** A hypothesis should explain these things:

- the topic of the experiment
- the **variable** you will change
- the variable you will measure
- what you expect to happen

A hypothesis should be brief, specific, and measurable. It must be something you can test through further investigation. Your experiment will prove or disprove your hypothesis. Here is one possible hypothesis for this experiment: "People who are more sensitive to tastes will have a greater number of taste buds."

Variables are anything you can change in an experiment. In this case, the variable you will change will be the concentration of the solutions. The variable you will measure will be the number of taste buds.

Setting up a **control experiment** will help you isolate each variable and measure the changes in the dependent variable. Only one variable will change between the control and the experimental setup, and that is the concentration of the solution. For the control in this experiment you will use a cup of plain water (tasteless). For your experiment, you will determine sensitivity to three tastes: bitter, salty, and sweet.

You will first make a 10 percent solution for each substance, then dilute the solutions. Sugar and salt are solids and you will make a 10 percent weight/weight (gram/gram) solution. For liquids you will make a 10 percent volume/volume (milliliter/milliliter) solution. One gram of water equals 1 ml of water.

You will rate people's sensitivity to varying concentrations of grapefruit juice (bitter), sugary water, and salty water. Then you will use blue dye to color each person's tongue's papillae. Because you are

If a person's nose is congested, mucus in the nasal passages can block the odor molecules from reaching the olfactory cells; thus, the brain receives no signal telling it what the object smells like. (Copyright © Kelly A. Quin. Reproduced by permission of Kelly A. Quin.)

What Are the Variables?

Variables are anything that might affect the results of an experiment. Here are the main variables in this experiment:

- The participants in the experiment
- The cleanliness of the person's palette before the experiment
- The size of the paper hole
- The concentration of the taste
- The substance people are tasting

In other words, the variables in this experiment are everything that might affect the relationship between a person's sensitivity to taste and the number of his or her taste buds. If you change more than one variable at the same time, you will not be able to tell which variable had the most effect on taste.

relying on human subjectivity, the more people you test, the more accurate your results.

Level of Difficulty

Easy to Moderate.

Materials Needed

- grapefruit juice
- sugar
- salt
- water
- measuring spoons
- gram scale
- three to four helpers
- sixteen small disposable paper cups
- light-colored pen
- blue food coloring
- cotton swabs
- piece of paper

 How to Experiment Safely
Check with an adult before you or your helpers taste
any of the foods to make sure none of you has any
allergies to the foods, or other dietary restrictions.

Use each cotton swab only once, one per person. Tasters should also use a fresh cup for their
water. You might want to wear an old shirt in case
any dye should spill.

- hole punch (standard 1/4-inch size)
- mirror
- magnifying glass

Approximate Budget
$5.

Timetable
1 hour.

Step-by-Step Instructions
1. Measure out 10 Tablespoons (150 milliliters of water) and pour into
   a cup. Add 4 teaspoons (15 grams) of sugar for a total volume of 150
   ml and stir until all the sugar is dissolved. Write on the cup: "10%
   sugar." Repeat this process for the salt, labeling the cup: "10% salt."
2. Measure out 9 Tablespoons (135 ml) water and pour into a cup.
   Add 1 Tablespoon (15 ml) grapefruit juice for a total volume of
   150 ml and stir thoroughly. Label the cup: "10% grapefruit."
3. Dilute each solution by 10 percent. From the sugar solution measure out 1 Tablespoon (15 ml) and pour into a clean cup. Add 9
   Tablespoons (135 ml) of water and stir until all sugar is dissolved.
   Label the cup: "1% sugar."
4. To make a 0.1% solution: From the 1% sugar solution measure
   out 1 Tablespoon (15 ml) and pour into a clean cup. Add 9 Tablespoons (135 ml) of water and stir until all sugar is dissolved. Label
   the cup: "0.1% sugar."
5. To make a 0.01% solution: From the 0.1% sugar solution measure out 1 Tablespoon (15 ml) and pour into a clean cup. Add 9

Tablespoons (135 ml) of water and stir until all sugar is dissolved. Label the cup: "0.01% sugar."

6. To make a 0.001% solution: From the 0.01% sugar solution measure out 1 Tablespoon (15 ml) and pour into a clean cup. Add 9 Tablespoons (135 ml) of water and stir until all sugar is dissolved. Label the cup: "0.001% sugar."

7. Repeat this process for the salt solution and the grapefruit juice.

8. Place plain water in a cup for the control solution.

9. Create a chart that lists the concentrations and the control on the left, and the three tastes across the top.

10. Have the taster rinse out his/her mouth with water and make sure the mouth is relatively dry before beginning.

11. Start with one taste. Switch the five cups around, including the cup of water, not allowing the taster to see the labels. Have the taster dip a clean cotton swab into the solution, smear it over his/her tongue, and wait a few moments. Ask the taster if he/she can identify a taste. If the taster can identify a taste, make a "✓" sign in the box; if not, make a "x" in the box.

12. Have the taster rinse out his/her mouth with water and repeat the process for all the dilutions, including the control. Once the taster has completed one taste, repeat the process with another taste.

13. When one taster has finished sampling the three sets of tastes, repeat the process with another helper. Have a helper mix the samples so that you can also sample the dilutions yourself.

14. Punch a hole in a piece of paper for each taster.

15. Dip a cotton swab in the blue food coloring and have the tasters wipe the blue swab on the tip of their tongues.

16. Place the paper hole on the blue area of each tongue.

17. Using a magnifying glass, look at each tongue and count the round structures, the papillae, that are visible in the paper hole. Look in the mirror to count your own papillae. Write down the results for each taster.

Summary of Results

Compare the results of each person's data chart with the number of his or her taste buds. Did your results support your hypothesis? Did the people who were more sensitive to tastes have a greater number of taste buds? Could the people in the nontaster category only taste the higher concentrations, and the supertasters taste the lower concentrations? Share your results and discuss if the tasters with the greater number of taste buds have a higher sensitivity to tastes in general. If there are any

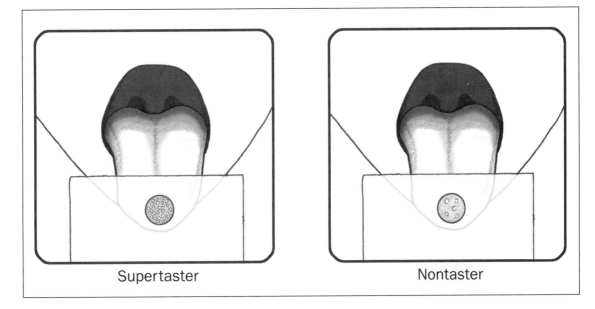

	Sweet	Bitter	Salty	# of Papillae
10%				
1%				
.1%				
.01%				
.001%				
water				

Supertaster

Nontaster

supertasters, do they have a strong dislike for broccoli, cabbage, and cauliflower (bitter tastes) and for strong sweet tastes such as frosting?

Change the Variables

Try repeating the experiment (with new helpers) using different concentrations of the solutions, both higher and lower, to get an increased number of data points. You can also change the type of bit-

TOP:
Step 9: Data chart for Experiment 1.

BOTTOM:
Step 17: Look at each tongue and count the round structures, the papillae, that are visible in the paper hole.

Troubleshooter's Guide

Below are some problems that may occur during this experiment, some possible causes, and some ways to remedy the problems.

Problem: A person's responses were inconsistent, sometimes saying he or she could taste the higher concentration and lower concentrated solution, but not the in-between solutions.

Possible causes: The person may have been mixing up tastes. Try repeating the test with that person, making sure the taster cleans his/her mouth with water carefully every time.

Problem: There was no correlation between number of taste buds and perceived taste.

Possible causes: Human error. Examine the taster's reaction to the control solution to ensure that he/she is not mistakenly identifying tastes where there is none. If the taste of water has a "✓," then try repeating the experiment with that person, or with someone else. The more people you test, the less chance human error will have a statistical impact on your results.

ter solution you use (for example, a beverage with caffeine in it or tonic water). Another variable you can change is to replace one of the tastes with the sour taste (lemon juice). Always check with an adult before you or anyone else tastes any of the solutions to make sure there are no dietary restrictions.

Experiment 2
Smell and Taste: How does smell affect the sense of taste?

Purpose/Hypothesis

Humans can perceive only five tastes, but can recognize thousands of smells. In this experiment you will test how closely the two

What Are the Variables?

Variables are anything that might affect the results of an experiment. Here are the main variables in this experiment:

- The participants in the experiment
- The cleanliness of the person's palate before the experiment
- The substance people are tasting

In other words, the variables in this experiment are everything that might affect the relationship between a person's ability to recognize foods by their smell and taste. If you change more than one variable at the same time, you will not be able to tell which variable had the most effect on identifying the foods.

chemosenses, the sense of smell and taste, are related. Blocking each sense independently, you will test and identify foods to determine which of the two senses sends the clearer message to the brain on what you are eating. You will use foods that have similar textures so that the feel of the food in your mouth is not a factor.

Before you begin, make an educated guess about the outcome of this experiment based on your knowledge of the sense of taste. This educated guess, or prediction, is your **hypothesis.**. A hypothesis should explain these things:

- the topic of the experiment
- the **variable** you will change
- the variable you will measure
- what you expect to happen

A hypothesis should be brief, specific, and measurable. It must be something you can test through further investigation. Your experiment will prove or disprove your hypothesis. Here is one possible hypothesis for this experiment: "Humans need both the sense of smell and taste working together to identify foods."

Variables are anything you can change in an experiment. In this case, the variable you will change will be which sense or senses you use. The variable you will measure will be the identification of the food. You will test each sense separately, then together.

Level of Difficulty
Easy.

Materials Needed
- onion
- raw potato
- roll of flavored candy
- chocolate ice cream
- strawberry ice cream
- knife
- four spoons
- helper

Approximate Budget
$5.

Timetable
About 20 minutes.

Step-by-Step Instructions
1. Carefully cut off a small piece of the onion and potato and then cut each into even smaller pieces. Place each on a separate spoon.
2. Ready spoonfuls of the chocolate ice cream and strawberry ice cream.
3. Set out two different-flavored hard candies; (e.g., one green and one red).
4. Make a chart listing the foods across the top and writing "Smell," "Taste," and "Both" down the page on the left.

How to Experiment Safely
Check with an adult before you or your helpers taste any of the foods to make sure none of you has any allergies to the foods, or other dietary restrictions. Use fresh utensils if more than one person conducts this experiment. Always use caution when working with any sharp objects, such as the knife.

Step 5: Block your sense of smell while tasting the food.

5. Close your eyes and hold your nose tightly. Have your helper hand you the spoons one by one, in groups of two: onion and potato, chocolate and strawberry ice creams, and red and green hard candies. Taste each one and say what you think it is—don't peek.
6. Have your helper write down what you guessed.
7. Keeping your eyes closed, have your partner refill the spoons and again hand you the spoons in the same groups of two as before. This time, only smell what is on the spoon and say what it is.
8. Have your helper write down what you guessed.
9. Repeat the procedure, keeping your eyes closed, this time using both your sense of taste and smell. Have your helper write down what you guessed.

Summary of Results

Examine your results and determine whether your original hypothesis was correct. Which sense identified the correct flavor more often? Did one sense tell your brain the specific food you were eating? Did you need both senses working together to identify the flavors? Summarize the results of your experiment.

Change the Variables

You can vary this experiment several ways. For example, why is it that you are keeping your eyes covered during this experiment? The sense of

Troubleshooter's Guide
Below is a problem that may occur during this experiment, some possible causes, and some ways to remedy the problem.

Problem: Results were not as hypothesized.

Possible causes: Make sure you do not have a cold or are congested during this experiment. Always make sure the utensils are clean. Make sure you dice the potato and onion into small enough pieces so that they have the same feel on the tongue.

vision plays a significant role in identifying foods. People have expectations that certain colors will relate to specific flavors, such as a green jellybean tasting like lime, even when the flavor is different than expected. Try putting different-flavored fruit juices in dark cups and testing how much of an impact your sense of vision has on your taste perception.

You can also try holding only half your nose, to see how much of an impact half of your olfactory receptors have on your taste perception.

Design Your Own Experiment

How to Select a Topic Relating to this Concept
If you are interested in the senses of taste and smell, there are many other possible experiments and projects. Because taste has a genetic component, you can try repeating Experiment 1 for groups of families. Compare family members' reactions to different tastes and their number of taste buds to each other. Then compare that data to a different family. Are members of one family more likely to all be either tasters, nontasters, or supertasters?

If you are interested in the sense of smell, you can examine the sensitivity of the olfactory sense by collecting and testing different concentrations of scents. Is there a genetic component to the sense of smell? How is the sense of smell different in other species from that of humans? What are some possible explanations for this?

experiment
CENTRAL

Check the For More Information section and talk with your science teacher or librarian to start gathering information on any questions that interest you.

Steps in the Scientific Method

To do an original experiment, you need to plan carefully and think things through. Otherwise, you might not be sure what question you are answering, what you are or should be measuring, or what your findings prove or disprove.

Here are the steps in designing an experiment:

- State the purpose of—and the underlying question behind—the experiment you propose to do.
- Recognize the variables involved and select one that will help you answer the question at hand.
- State your hypothesis, an educated guess about the answer to your question.
- Decide how to change the variable you selected.
- Decide how to measure your results.

Recording Data and Summarizing the Results

Your data should include charts, such as the ones you did for these experiments. They should be clearly labeled and easy to read. You may also want to include photos, graphs, or drawings of your experimental setup and results. If you have done a nonexperimental project, explain clearly what your research question was and illustrate your findings.

Related Projects

Besides completing your experiments, you could prepare a model that demonstrates a point that you are interested in with regard to the chemosenses. For example, you could construct a model of the brain and illustrate the pathway of the taste and olfactory cells sending signals as they travel to certain parts of the brain. You could also try a similar dilution experiment with smell, observing the effect of varying dilutions of an odor, such as a perfume or a beverage. The effect of temperature also has an effect on smell, and you could chart people's perception of an odor that is cold, room temperature, and warm.

For More Information

Hesman, T. "Researchers enjoy bitter taste of success." *Science News.* March 25, 2000. http://www.sciencenews.org/20000325/fob2.asp (accessed August 24, 2003). ❖ Article looks at research revealing how taste buds handle the chemical information they receive.

Neuroscience for Kids. http://faculty.washington.edu/chudler/chsense.html (accessed August 24, 2003). ❖ Clear explanations and activities of the chemosenses.

Rouhi, Maureen I. "Unlocking the Secrets of Taste." *Chemical and Engineering News.* September 10, 2001. http://pubs.acs.org/cen/coverstory/7937/7937 taste.html (accessed August 24, 2003). ❖ Article on recently identified taste receptors and the molecules that stimulate them.

Smith, David V., and Robert F. Margolskee. "Making Sense of Taste." *Scientific American.* March 18, 2001. http://www.sciam.com/article.cfm?articleID=000641 D5-F855-1C70-84A9809EC588EF21 (accessed August 24, 2003). ❖ A look at how taste cells work, with detailed graphics.

"The Vivid World of Odors." *Howard Hughes Medical Institute.* http://hhmi.org/senses/d110.html (accessed August 24, 2003). ❖ Report from the Howard Hughes Medical Institute on odor and taste receptors.

"Your Sense of Smell." *Your Gross and Cool Body.* http://yucky.kids.discovery.com/noflash/body/pg000150.html (accessed August 24, 2003) ❖ Introductory information on smells and how the sense works.

chapter 7

Comets and Meteors

Earth is part of a solar system that is filled with celestial objects moving about. Scientists theorize that many of these objects are materials left over from when the solar system formed—about 4.6 billion years ago. **Comets** and **meteors** are two such chunks of materials in the solar system. Every so often these objects are visible to the naked eye as brilliant streaks of light across the sky. Meteors appear regularly and are sometimes called "shooting stars"; comets show themselves with far less frequency. Astronomers look to these objects to learn more about the universe around Earth and the early history of the solar system.

Hot snowballs

Comets are often referred to as dirty snowballs because of their make-up: a mixture of ice and dust. They typically move through the solar system in orbits or revolutions around the Sun ranging from a few years to several hundred thousand years.

Astronomers theorize there may be more than one trillion comets zipping about the solar system, yet spotting a comet is rare. Most comets are located on the outskirts of the solar system in a giant sphere called the **Oort cloud,** which surrounds the solar system. The comets in the Oort cloud can take over a million years to make a single revolution around the Sun. Occasionally one of these comets is pulled by a nearby star and gets pushed closer to the Sun. When it approaches the Sun it becomes visible to astronomers. About a dozen of these new comets are discovered every year.

A few comets have a relatively short orbit. For example Halley's Comet orbits the Sun about every seventy-six years. This comet is

Words to Know

Coma:
Glowing cloud of gas surrounding the nucleus of a comet.

Comet:
An icy body orbiting in the solar system, which partially vaporizes when it nears the Sun and develops a diffuse envelope of dust and gas as well as one or more tails.

Comet head:
The nucleus and the coma of a comet.

Comet nucleus:
The core or center of a comet. (Plural: Comet nuclei.)

Did You Know?

- In 1947 one of the largest fireballs in recorded history exploded over Siberia and caused at least 122 craters; the largest was 85 feet (26 meters) wide and almost 20 feet (6 meters) deep.

- The largest meteorite ever found on Earth is the Hoba in South Africa. This metal meteorite weighs an estimated 66 tons (60 metric tons) and is unusual in that it did not make a crater.

- Scientists estimate that between 1,000 tons (907 metric tons) to more than 10,000 tons (9,070 metric tons) of meteoritic material falls on Earth every day. Most of this material is incredibly tiny.

- Before people knew the cause of meteors, there were many myths associated with shooting stars. Some of these myths included beliefs that they were an omen for disaster or the weapons of angels, and that each meteor was actually a fire dragon.

- If you discover a comet, you can name it after yourself—and there are many comets discovered by amateurs.

Words to Know

Comet tail:
The most distinctive feature of comets; comets can display two basic types of tails: one gaseous and the other largely composed of dust.

Control experiment:
A setup that is identical to the experiment, but is not affected by the variable that acts on the experimental group.

Crater:
An indentation caused by an object hitting the surface of a planet or moon.

Dust tail:
One of two types of tails a comet may have, it is composed mainly of dust and it points away from the Sun.

Fireball:
Meteors that create an intense, bright light and, sometimes, an explosion.

named after English astronomer Edmond Halley (1656–1742), who was the first person to work out the elliptical orbits of comets. After Halley spotted a comet in 1682, he started reading through historical records. He found that two previous comets, in 1531 and 1607, had orbital paths similar to the one he had witnessed. These three comet sightings, he concluded, were actually the same object making three appearances. Halley predicted this comet would pass through again in 1758 and, although he did not live to see it, the comet appeared as predicted.

A tail's story

For a short time during each orbit around the Sun, comets can become visible from Earth. When a comet approaches the Sun, it develops three basic parts: a **nucleus,** a **coma,** and a **tail.**

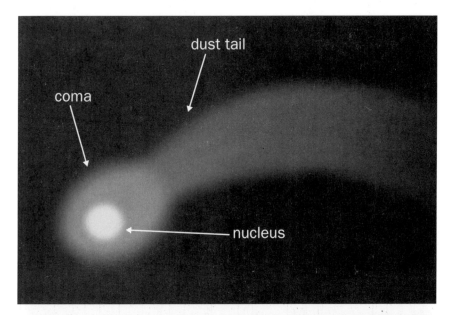

Components of a comet.

dust tail

coma

nucleus

Halley's Comet orbits the Sun about every seventy-six years. (Reproduced by permission of AP/Wide World Photos.)

The nucleus is the dirty snowball part of the comet, made of ice and a small amount of dust and other solids. It ranges from about 1 to 10 miles across and is at the center of the comet. The nucleus and the coma make up the **comet head** of the comet. The coma is the blob of gas that roughly encircles the nucleus. It is the brightest part of the comet. This region is formed as the comet approaches the Sun and becomes warmer. The coma is made up of water vapor, carbon dioxide, and other gases that have **sublimed** from the solid nucleus. Subliming is when a material goes directly from being a solid to being a gas without becoming a liquid.

One of the most impressive sights of a comet is its **tail,** a long extension from the head that always points away from the Sun. Even though it does not have much mass, a comet's tail can stretch into space several million miles.

Comets often have two tails. One type of tail is a **dust tail.** This is made of dust leaving the nucleus. Gas and heat from the Sun push the tail backward into its long streak. The dust tail is often curved or spread out, and yellowish in appearance. Another type of tail is an **ion tail.** An ion tail forms when the gas particles become ionized or charged by the Sun. The molecules are pushed away from the nucleus by charged particles streaming out of the Sun. An ion tail is usually very straight and bluish.

A meteor's story

As a comet hurls close to the Sun and its ice melts, pieces of rock sometimes loosen. These tiny solid remnants traveling through space are called **meteoroids.** While the majority of meteoroids come from comets, some are fragments of planets or other celestial bodies. They are chunks of stone, metal, or a combination of the two. Wherever they originate, all meteoroids are small. Most range in size from a grain of sand to a pebble. They are the smallest known particle to orbit the Sun. They are also fast. Meteoroids are usually traveling at speeds ranging from 25,000 miles per hour (40,000 kilometers per hour) to 160,000 miles per hour (256,000 kilometers per hour).

When a speedy meteoroid tears into Earth's atmosphere, the layer of air encircling our planet, it produces a streak of light known as a shooting star, or meteor. The blaze occurs as the meteor's intense speed heats up the air around it to more than 3,000°F (1,650°C). This in turn heats up the meteor and creates a flash of light visible from the ground below. Some large meteors can produce a brilliant flash. These meteors are called **fireballs** and they can create an explosion that can be heard up to 30 miles (48 kilometers) away.

While the intense heat burns up the vast majority of meteors, a small percentage make it through the Earth's atmosphere. These are called **meteorites.** Because of their high speeds, meteorites can some-

Words to Know

Hypothesis:
An idea in the form of a statement that can be tested by observation and/or experiment.

Ion tail:
One of two types of tails a comet may have, it is composed mainly of charged particles and it points away from the Sun..

Meteor:
An object from space that becomes glowing hot when it passes into Earth's atmosphere; also called shooting star.

Meteor shower:
A group of meteors that occurs when Earth's orbit intersects the orbit of a meteor stream.

Meteorites:
A meteor that is large enough to survive its passage through the atmosphere and hit the ground.

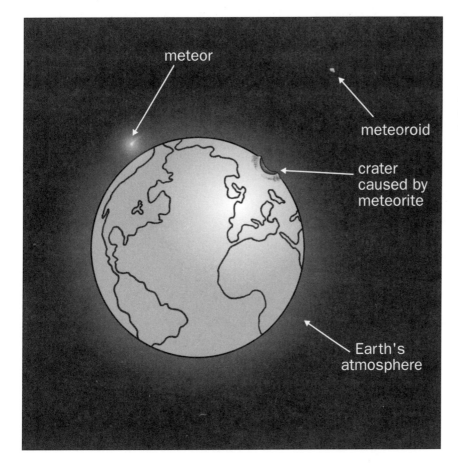

meteor

meteoroid

crater caused by meteorite

Earth's atmosphere

The progression of particles that break away from a comet: They first become meteoroids, then meteors, and, finally, meteorites.

times make huge **craters** when they hit the ground. A crater is a circular pit created when a celestial object crashes into a planet or other orbiting mass.

These craters are found almost everywhere in the solar system and they pocket the surface of the Moon. As of 2003, scientists have found about 150 craters on Earth. One of the largest and best preserved craters on Earth is the Barringer Meteor Crater in Arizona, which formed about 50,000 years ago. It stretches nearly 1 mile (1.6 kilometers) wide and is 570 feet (174 meters) deep.

The size, speed, and angle of impact of the meteor all determine whether the crater will be simple or complex. Simple craters have a smooth, bowl shape and a raised outer rim. Complex craters have a central peak, or peaks, and a relatively shallower depth. These large craters form this shape when their initial steep wall collapses downward and inward. The explosion of the impact causes the fallen crater

Words to Know

Meteoroid:
A piece of debris that is traveling in space.

Oort cloud:
Region of space beyond our solar system that theoretically contains about one trillion inactive comets.

Sublime:
The process of changing a solid into a vapor without passing through the liquid phase.

Variable:
Something that can affect the results of an experiment.

A fragment of a meteorite found in 1891 in Arizona, on display at the Monnig Meteor Gallery in Fort Worth, Texas. (Reproduced by permission of AP/Wide World.)

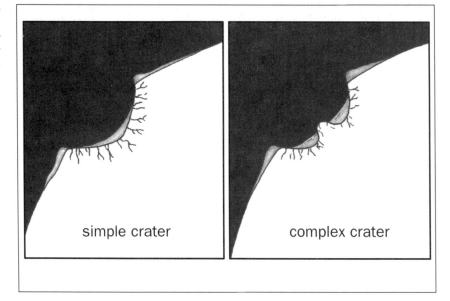

Because of their high rates of speed, meteorites can sometimes make huge craters when they hit the ground.

simple crater

complex crater

floor to rebound. Rock fragments blast outward, creating the central peak or peaks.

Showering shooting stars

On any clear night, a person can probably spot some meteors. Several times every year, though, storms of meteors will fill the night sky in what is called a **meteor shower.**

experiment
CENTRAL

A meteor streaks through the sky over Joshua Tree National Park in California, November 17, 1998. Stars moving through the sky are seen as a series of short lines across this 30-minute time exposure frame. (Reproduced by permission of AP/Wide World.)

Meteor showers occur when Earth moves through a stream of particles produced by comet leftovers. Since the orbits of comets are known, it is possible to predict many meteor showers. These showers can create a brilliant light show as they enter the atmosphere.

Project 1
Comet Nucleus: Linking a Comet's Composition to its Properties.

Purpose/Hypothesis

In this project, you will construct a comet* using either the same or similar ingredients that make up a real comet. Comets are composed of bits of dirt or dust, held in place by ice. The ice is a combination of water and carbon dioxide ice. Comets contain carbon-based or organic molecules and ammonia. Sodium or salt was found to be in the comet Hale-Bopp. Trapped gas and an uneven surface are other features of a comet.

It is these materials in the nucleus that form the brilliant head and tail when they come close to the Sun. Once you have constructed the comet, you can then observe its behavior.

*Adapted from "Making A Comet in the Classroom" by Dennis Schatz, Pacific Science Center, 1985.

Level of Difficulty
Moderate (because of the number of trials and careful measurements needed).

Approximate Budget
$15.

Timetable
45 minutes for initial setup; several hours observation time.

Materials Needed
- 2 cups (500 milliliters) of water
- 2 cups (500 milliliters) of dry ice, broken into pieces if possible (dry ice is available at ice companies and some butcher shops)
- 2 to 3 spoonfuls of dirt (a small dinner spoon is fine; the exact size is not important)
- 1 spoonful of ammonia
- 1 spoonful of organic material (dark or light corn syrup works, or Worcester sauce works well)
- thick gloves
- large plastic bowl

How to Work Safely
Dry ice is carbon dioxide frozen at −110°F (−79°C). If you touch a piece of dry ice too long, it will freeze your skin and feel like a burn. Wear gloves when working with dry ice and do not place dry ice in your mouth. Also be careful when you pour the ammonia into the spoon to prevent it from splashing into your eyes.

- 2 heavy-duty garbage bags
- self-sealing plastic bag
- hammer or mallet
- mixing spoon
- salt
- paper towels

Step-by-Step Instructions

1. Cut open one garbage bag and use it to line your mixing bowl.
2. Add the water and dirt in the mixing bowl. Stir well.
3. Add a dash of ammonia
4. Add a sprinkle of salt and a spoonful of the organic material. Stir well.
5. Put on gloves and place the dry ice in the self-sealing plastic bag. Zip the bag closed and place the bag inside the second garbage bag. Pound the dry ice with a hammer until it is crushed.
6. Add the dry ice to the ingredients in the mixing bowl and stir rapidly. Continue stirring until the mixture is slushy and almost totally frozen.
7. Lift the garbage bag with the comet out of the bowl and shape it like a snowball. Shape the plastic bag and not the snowball. Wear gloves.
8. Unwrap the comet and place it on the bag.
9. After you have observed the comet for several hours, break it apart and look at the inside.

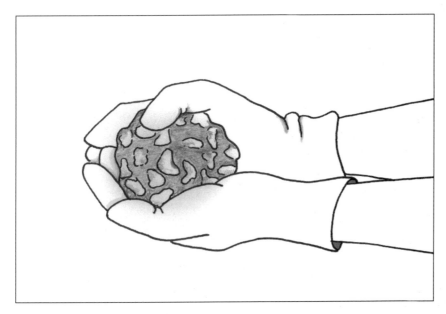

Step 7: Wearing gloves, pat the meteor into a snowball shape. Keep the comet in the plastic bag when shaping.

Troubleshooter's Guide

Below is a problem that may arise during this project, a possible cause, and a way to remedy the problem.

Problem: The comet fell apart during the snowball formation.

Possible cause: You may not have broken up the dry ice into small enough bits. Try the experiment again, pounding the dry ice thoroughly.

Summary of Results

Draw a picture of the comet and note how it appears. Gently blow on the comet and note your observation. After two hours have passed, note your observations of the comet and compare it to your first description. What has happened to the carbon molecules in the organic substance? Write a brief explanation of how this miniature comet relates to what occurs during a comet's orbit.

Experiment 2

Meteor Impact: How do the characteristics of a meteorite and its impact affect the shape of the crater?

Purpose/Hypothesis

It was in the early 1900s that scientists first concluded a meteorite caused the formation of a crater. (Most astronomers before that time had assumed that craters were formed by volcanoes.) The first crater that scientists proved had come from a meteorite was the Barringer Meteor Crater in the Arizona desert. This gigantic depression is nearly 1 mile (1.6 kilometers) wide and 570 feet (174 meters) deep. Since that time, scientists have studied both the many craters on the Moon and the ones on Earth to study meteorite impact.

In this experiment you will investigate the factors that affect the formation of simple meteor craters. You will examine how a meteor's size, angle of impact, and speed of impact affect the crater shape. Speed in this experiment is determined by the drop height. The higher the drop height, the faster the simulated meteor hits the surface.

Before you begin, make an educated guess about the outcome of this experiment based on your knowledge of meteors and craters. This educated guess, or prediction, is your **hypothesis.** A hypothesis should explain these things:

- the topic of the experiment
- the **variable** you will change
- the variable you will measure
- what you expect to happen

A hypothesis should be brief, specific, and measurable. It must be something you can test through further investigation. Your experiment will prove or disprove whether your hypothesis is correct. Here is one possible hypothesis for this experiment: "The faster and heavier the simulated meteor, the deeper and wider the crater; a meteor coming in at an angle will form an elongated crater."

In this case, the variables you will change, one at a time, are the weight of the meteor, the speed of the meteor, and the angle of impact. The variable you will measure is the depth and diameter of the crater.

Conducting a standard experiment will help you isolate each variable and measure the changes in the dependent variable. Only one

What Are the Variables?

Variables are anything that might affect the results of an experiment. Here are the main variables in this experiment:

- the shape of the object
- the weight of the object
- the angle of impact
- the speed of the object
- the substance the object impacts

In other words, the variables in this experiment are everything that might affect the shape of the crater. If you change more than one variable at a time, you will not be able to tell which variable changed the crater formation.

variable will change between the standard experiment and each of your trials. To change only one variable at a time, it is important to always use a simulated meteor of standard weight and use a standard drop height. Then you will change one variable at a time. Your control will be a medium-weight meteor, at a vertical, 180-degree drop, and a drop height of 39 inches (1 meter)

You will complete three tests in this experiment. You will measure how the weight of a simulated meteor, the speed of the simulated meteor, and the angle of impact of the simulated meteor affect the crater's physical characteristics. For each variable you will measure the crater's depth and diameter. The diameter is the measurement across a circle. In this case, it is a point on the peak of the rim to a point on the rim on the opposite side. In actuality there are many factors affecting a meteor's crater.

For increased accuracy, you will conduct three trials of each test, then average the measurements.

Level of Difficulty
Moderate (because of the number of trials and careful measurements needed).

Materials Needed
- shallow rectangle pan or plastic container, about 12 to 18 inches (30 to 46 centimeters) long and 2 inches (5 centimeters) deep
- fine, dry sand (available at hardware stores or greenhouses)
- powder of contrasting color to sand, such as cinnamon, cocoa, or paprika
- empty shaker, such as a saltshaker
- nine small round objects of similar shape to simulate meteors: three of the same light weight, three of the same medium weight, and three of the same heavy weight (marbles, candies, or pebbles work well)
- ruler
- protractor
- string, about 4 feet (30 centimeters)
- tape
- newspapers (optional)
- cardstock, cut into thin strips about 0.125 (⅛) inches (3 millimeters) wide

How to Experiment Safely
There are no safety hazards in this experiment.

Approximate Budget
$10.

Timetable
1 hour.

Step-by-Step Instructions
1. Weigh each of the simulated meteors and note on a chart. Create a separate chart for mass, speed, and angle of impact. Each chart should have separate rows for the diameter and depth measurements. Make a note of the standard meteor on the chart.
2. Place newspapers under the pan or conduct the experiment outside to avoid a sandy cleanup.
3. Fill the pan about three-quarters full with sand. Shake until the sand is level.
4. With the shaker, sprinkle a light layer of the contrasting colored powder over the sand. This will help you measure the crater's shape.

Step 1: Example of the "Mass" data chart; one of the three charts to be created for Experiment 2.

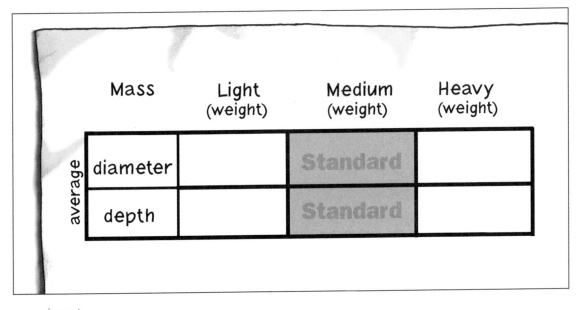

Mass		Light (weight)	Medium (weight)	Heavy (weight)
average	diameter		Standard	
	depth		Standard	

Step 6: One at a time, drop the three lightest-weight simulated meteors vertically from a height of 39 inches (1 meter) onto the surface.

5. Make sure the sand is level and the outer layer is even before you continue.

6. To test for the effect of size: One at a time, drop the three lightest-weight simulated meteors vertically from a height of 39 inches (1 meter) onto the surface (you may have to stand on a chair). Do not throw the object. Drop the objects so that the craters are several inches apart.

7. Measure the diameter of the resulting craters. Average the three measurements and record on a chart.

8. Measure the depth of the craters by carefully placing one of the narrow strips of paper at the bottom of the crater and marking on the paper where the paper meets the rim of the crater. Average the three measurements and record on chart.

9. Level out the sand and the contrasting-color layer.

10. To test for speed: Increase the drop heights to 79 inches (2 meters) and drop the three medium-weight simulated meteors. Again, drop them so the craters are several inches apart. Record the results. Level the sand and contrasting-color layer.

11. Using the same three medium-weight simulated meteors, decrease the drop height to 20 inches (0.5 meters). Average the measurement results and note in a chart. Level the sand and contrasting-color layer as before.

Troubleshooter's Guide

Below is a problem that may arise during this experiment, a possible cause, and a way to remedy the problem.

Problem: The crater depth was too shallow to measure in some craters.

Possible cause: You may have chosen projectiles that were too light. Set aside the small and medium projectiles, and select two new sets that are heavier than whatever was the heaviest object used before. Repeat the experiment.

12. To test for angle impact: Tie the piece of string to the midpoint of the protractor and tape the protractor to the bottom of the container. Use the string as a guide for the angle of impact.

13. Hold the string at a 75-degree angle and drop the three medium-weight meteors into the box at that angle, at the height of 39 inches (1 meter). Measure the diameter and depth of the resulting craters and record the averages on a chart. Level again.

14. Drop the three medium-weight meteors into the box at a 45-degree angle. Record the results.

Summary of Results

Create a graph illustrating the data in each chart. Make sure you use different colors or symbols for each of the variables in the chart and label each chart carefully.

Compare each of the variables to the standard projectile. How did the weight of the projectile affect the size of the crater? How did the angle of impact affect crater formation? For years astronomers hypothesized that objects that landed at an angle would produce an elongated-shape crater. Through experimentation scientists discovered that projectiles create round craters, independent of the angle of impact. Do your results match these findings?

Change the Variables

You can vary this experiment several ways:

• Try different angles of impact

- Alter the shape of the projectiles
- Change the surface the projectile impacts
- Change the consistency of the surface

Design Your Own Experiment

How to Select a Topic Relating to this Concept

Meteors and comets are amazing sights that can provide useful information about the universe. As both celestial bodies are visible to the naked eye, although comet sightings are quite rare, it may be possible to gather data on these objects through observation. Find an amateur astronomer who has observation equipment, and discuss a possible project with him or her. You may also want to investigate whether any science centers in your area have meteorite fragments that you can study.

Check the For More Information section for predicted comet and meteor sightings, along with information gathered from previous sightings. Talk with your science teacher, along with any professional or amateur astronomers, to learn more about comets and meteors. If you do choose to observe meteors or comets during the daylight, remember to never look directly at the Sun, as it can damage your eyes.

Steps in the Scientific Method

To conduct an original experiment, you need to plan carefully and think things through. Otherwise, you might not be sure what question you are answering, what you are or should be measuring, or what your findings prove or disprove.

Here are the steps in designing an experiment:

- State the purpose of—and the underlying question behind—the experiment you propose to do.
- Recognize the variables involved and select one that will help you answer the question at hand.
- State your hypothesis, an educated guess about the answer to your question.
- Decide how to change the variable you selected.
- Decide how to measure your results.

Recording Data and Summarizing the Results

In any experiment you conduct, you should look for ways to clearly convey your data. You can do this by including charts and graphs for the experiments. They should be clearly labeled and easy to read. You may also want to include photographs and drawings of your experimental setup and results, which will help others visualize the steps in the experiment. You might decide to conduct an experiment that lasts several months. In this case, include pictures or drawings of the results taken at regular intervals.

If you are preparing an exhibit, you may want to display your results, such as any experimental setup you designed. If you have completed a nonexperimental project, explain clearly what your research question was and illustrate your findings.

Related Projects

There are many related projects you can undertake to learn more about comets and meteors. Meteor showers occur throughout the year. Gathering data from observing meteors is one possible project. Because comet sightings are far more rare, you can create a model of an active comet orbiting the Sun, using household items to represent the objects in the solar system. Research the spatial relationships of celestial bodies in the solar system as you work on your project to ensure you have the model to scale.

You could also investigate if any craters are located in your surrounding area and, if so, set out on a field trip to examine the formation. If there are no craters in your area or you cannot visit one, you can use reference materials. You can compare how the sizes and shapes of craters relate to the meteor's composition. Why would one meteorite form a crater and another simply land on Earth? You can also conduct a research project to examine the data and theoretical information that astronomers have learned about the universe from their studies of comets and meteors.

For More Information

The Barringer Meteorite Crater. http://www.barringercrater.com (accessed on August 24, 2003). ❖ Story of the famous crater and the persistent scientist who proved a crater was caused by a meteorite, not a volcano.

Bonar, Samantha. *Comets.* New York: Franklin Watts, 1998. ❖ The makeup, orbits, and other information on comets, with illustrations.

Freudenrich, Craig C. "How Comets Work." *How Stuff Works.* http://science. howstuffworks.com/comet3.htm (accessed on August 24, 2003). ❖ Clear explanation of how comets work.

Koeberl, Christian, and Virgil L. Sharpton. *Terrestrial Impact Craters.* http://cass. jsc.nasa.gov/pub/publications/slidesets/impacts.html (accessed on August 24, 2003). ❖ Report on different types of craters, with photographs of craters around the world.

Kronk, Gary W. *Comets & Meteor Showers.* http://comets.amsmeteors.org/ (accessed on August 24, 2003). ❖ Site on comets and meteors includes clear explanations and a calendar of times for future sightings.

"Meteors and Meteor Showers: How They Work." *Space.com.* http://www.space. com/scienceastronomy/solarsystem/meteors-ez.html (accessed on August 24, 2003). ❖ Information on meteors and meteor showers, includes animation and meteor composition.

Milan, Wil. "Comet Photos." *Wil Milan's Astrophoto Gallery.* http://www.astrophoto grapher.com/cometphotos.html (accessed on August 24, 2003) ❖ Photographs and computer-generated pictures of comets with information.

National Optical Astronomy Observatory. http://www.noao.edu/education (accessed on August 24, 2003) ❖ Provides links to helps student researchers understand the field of astronomy.

"Orbits." *NEO Program.* http://neo.jpl.nasa.gov/orbits (accessed on August 24, 2003). ❖ Enter any asteroid or comet and see its orbit.

World Book's Young Scientist: Volume 1. Chicago: World Book, Inc., 1995. ❖ Well-illustrated reference with basics of space and space study.

chapter 8

Crystals

Crystals affect your life in countless ways, from what you eat to how your computer works. Any solid matter whose particles are arranged in a regular and repeated pattern is called a **crystal.** The type of particle and its geometric pattern determine the properties of the crystal. Salt, sugar, and rubies are all crystals, along with many metallic elements, such as iron. Both natural rock and artificial materials are often crystalline. Our bones even contain tiny crystals of a mineral called apatite.

All crystals have flat, smooth surfaces, called **faces.** Some crystals, such as diamonds, are formed over millions of years, while others, such as snowflakes, are formed in a matter of hours. Crystals of the same substance have the same geometric pattern between its particles. This pattern is called a **crystal lattice.** In crystals the smallest possible repeating structural unit is called a **unit cell.** The unit cell is repeated in exactly the same neat arrangement over and over throughout the entire material.

Symbols and surgery

Crystals have been a part of cultures throughout history, from ancient Egyptians to modern days. Topaz, emeralds, rubies, sapphires, and diamonds are examples of crystals long prized as gems. Their brilliance, durability, and rarity have caused people to attach superstitions and symbolism to them. Emeralds were once thought to blind snakes; amethysts to cure drunkenness; diamonds to make a soldier undefeatable; and rubies were a symbol of power.

In the 1900s, researchers began to use crystals to improve many areas of people's lives, from technology to medicine. The properties of

Words to Know

Atom:
A unit of matter, the smallest unit of an element, having all the characteristics of that element.

Control experiment:
A setup that is identical to the experiment, but is not affected by the variable that acts on the experimental group.

Crystal:
Naturally occurring solid composed of atoms or molecules arranged in an orderly pattern that repeats at regular intervals.

crystals, such as hardness, conductivity, insulation, and durability, make them valuable. In modern day crystals are used in electric fuses, control circuits, industrial tools, and communication equipment. Diamonds are used in drill bits, surgery scalpels, and saw blades. The television, radio, and camera all work because of crystals. Some laser beams used in surgery and welding are made using crystals. Crystals are also found in watches, flat panels for computer displays, and solar-powered calculators.

Shapes and structures

Crystals are made of either atoms or molecules. An **atom** is the smallest piece of an element that keeps the element's chemical properties. A **molecule** is composed of two or more atoms. It is the smallest particle of a substance that still has the properties of that substance. Inside the core of an atom are positive and negative charges.

The majority of crystals are made of **ions,** a charged atom or molecule. Inside the core of an atom are both positive and negative electrical charges. Atoms can either lose or gain negative charges. The charge of an atom is neutral when it has equal positive and negative charges. When an atom loses an electron it is called a positive ion and

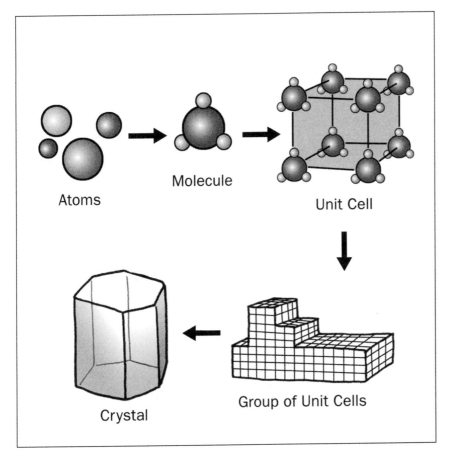

From an atom to a crystal: The smallest repeating unit in a crystal is the unit cell.

Atoms

Molecule

Unit Cell

Group of Unit Cells

Crystal

From televisions to wristwatches, crystals are a part of everyday life. (Copyright © Kelly A. Quin. Reproduced by permission of Kelly A. Quin.)

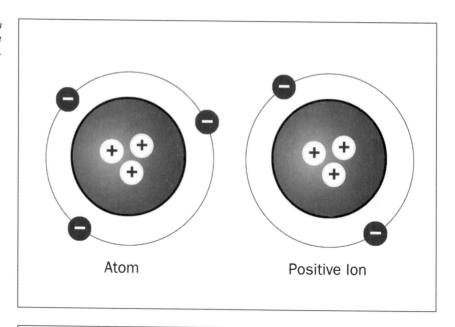

The majority of crystals are made of ions, a charged atom or molecule.

Atom   Positive Ion

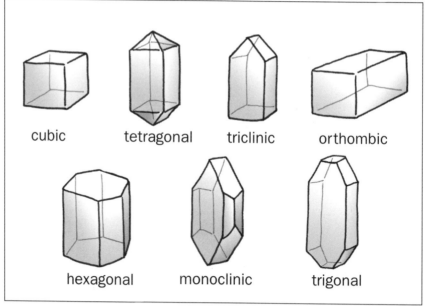

There are seven basic crystal systems, categorized by their geometric shapes.

cubic   tetragonal   triclinic   orthombic

hexagonal   monoclinic   trigonal

when it gains a negative charge it is called a negative ion. Most minerals and rocks are formed from ions.

The inner arrangement of the atoms or molecules, the unit cell, determines the outward shape of the crystal. Because of a crystal's geometric nature, many have strange and interesting shapes. There are seven basic crystal systems, categorized by their geometric shapes.

It is the internal structure of the crystal that determines its properties. Each atom has specific properties, yet crystals made of the same atoms can have unique properties. In graphite, the material in a pencil, carbon atoms are spaced far apart in layers. The layers are held together by weak bonds and can shift over one another. This makes graphite one of the softest minerals. On the other hand, the carbon atoms in diamond are bonded tightly to one another in closer layers. This makes a diamond a rigid and hard substance.

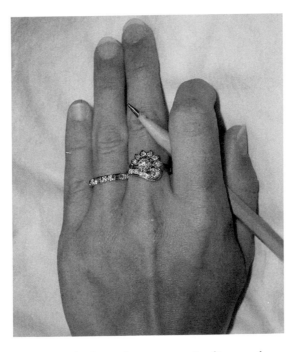

Though diamonds and graphite are comprised of carbon atoms, diamonds are rigid and hard, while the graphite used in lead pencils is soft. (Copyright © Kelly A. Quin. Reproduced by permission of Kelly A. Quin.)

How a crystal reacts to electrical forces and light, its shape, hardness, color, and the rate at which it conducts heat all depend on a crystal's internal structure. Some crystals will split light, for example, causing a double image. Other crystals will bend a beam of light.

Crystal formation

The size and shape of a crystal depends on how it is formed. Impurities, temperature, pressure, and the amount of space will affect what a crystal looks like. In snowflakes, for example, colder temperatures produce crystal snowflakes with sharper tips on the sides. Snowflakes that grow under warmer conditions grow more slowly, resulting in smoother shapes.

Crystals only grow large and perfect under specific conditions. Most crystals grow irregularly and sometimes it is difficult to distinguish their faces. It is rare to find a flawless crystal, which is why such perfect crystals are worth great amounts of money. While one crystal is growing it may enclose crystals of other minerals. These enclosures will appear as a visible mark in the crystal. A crystal pushed upon by some outside force can develop a twisted or bent shape.

Words to Know

Saturated:
In referring to solutions, a solution that contains the maximum amount of solute for a given amount of solvent at a given temperature.

Seed crystal:
Small form of a crystalline structure that has all the facets of a complete new crystal contained in it.

Solute molecules:
The substance that is dissolved to make a solution and exists in the least amount in a solution; for example, sugar in sugar water.

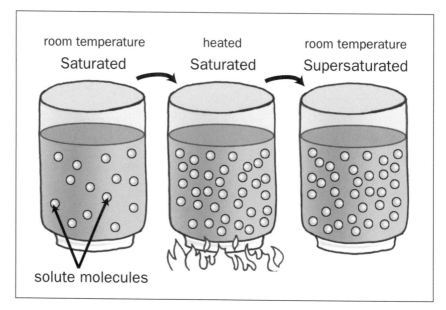

room temperature
Saturated

heated
Saturated

room temperature
Supersaturated

solute molecules

While natural crystals can often contain flaws, artificial or **synthetic crystals** can be made flawless. One reason why crystals are widely used in industry and technology is that scientists learned how to synthesize artificial crystals in the laboratory, making them flawless and relatively inexpensive.

Crystals start growing by a process called **nucleation.** Nucleation can start through the molecules themselves or through the help of solid matter already present. The nucleation process begins when the molecules in a solution, the **solute molecules,** have an attractive force to one another that pulls the molecules together. The more solute molecules in a solution, the greater the chance the molecules will come into contact with each other and form bonds.

When a solution contains as much dissolved solute molecules as it can hold at that temperature, it is **saturated.** The temperature of a solution will affect its saturation. A solution at higher temperatures will be able to dissolve more molecules than a solution at lower temperatures. If a solution is saturated at a high temperature and then cooled, it has a concentration above the saturation point. This solution is called a **supersaturated** solution. The molecules in a supersaturated solution are so crammed together they readily move together and can form a crystal.

The more molecules that are joined together, the stronger their attractive force. They continue to pull other molecules towards them.

Supersaturated:
Solution that is more highly concentrated than is normally possible under given conditions of temperature and pressure.

Synthetic crystals:
Artificial or manmade crystals.

Unit cell:
The basic unit of the crystalline structure.

Variable:
Something that can affect the results of an experiment.

A small crystal that provides the attractive force to begin forming larger crystals is called a **seed crystal.**

Experiment 1
Crystal Structure: Will varying shape crystals form from varying substances?

Purpose/Hypothesis

Crystals come in many shapes and sizes. The substance used to make a crystal and how this substance bonds together dictates the crystal's unit cell and, thus, its shape.

In this experiment you will compare the unique crystal formations that grow from four different substances. The four crystal substances you will use are alum, Epsom salt, sugar, and salt. You will create supersaturated solutions out of the four substances and examine the crystals that form.

To begin this experiment, make an educated guess about the outcome of the experiment based on your knowledge of crystals. This educated guess, or prediction, is your **hypothesis.** A hypothesis should explain these things:

Sugar and salt are examples of crystals that vary in size and shape. (Copyright © Kelly A. Quin. Reproduced by permission of Kelly A. Quin.)

What Are the Variables?

Variables are anything that might affect the results of an experiment. Here are the main variables in this experiment:

- the substances that make up the crystal
- the temperature of the beginning solution
- the temperature of the water
- the environment the crystal is grown in

In other words, the variables in this experiment are everything that might affect the growth of the crystals. If you change more than one variable at the same time, you will not be able to tell which variable had the most effect on the crystal's structure.

- the topic of the experiment
- the **variable** you will change
- the variable you will measure
- what you expect to happen

A hypothesis should be brief, specific, and measurable. It must be something you can test through further investigation. Your experiment will prove or disprove whether your hypothesis is correct. Here is one possible hypothesis for this experiment: "Crystals formed from different substances will develop unique shapes."

In this experiment the variable you will change will be the substance that will make up the crystal, and the variable you will measure will be the appearance of the crystal.

Level of Difficulty

Moderate.

Materials Needed

- alum (small jar, found in the spice section of the grocery store)
- Epsom salt
- sugar
- salt

- water
- black saucers (or any color saucers, black construction paper, and scissors)
- hot plate or stove
- saucepan
- four stirring spoons
- measuring cup
- measuring spoons
- glass cup or jars
- magnifying glass (optional)
- masking tape
- marking pen

Approximate Budget
$5 (most materials are common household items).

Timetable
45 minutes initial time; 30 minutes over the next week.

Step-by-Step Instructions
1. If you do not have black saucers, cut the black construction paper to fit tightly in the bottom of each saucer and place inside.
2. Make a supersaturated solution with the Epsom salt by bringing half a cup of water to the almost-boiling point, then transferring the hot water to a glass. Add 5 tablespoons Epsom salt and stir. Keep adding Epsom salt until no more salt can be absorbed by the water. You will know this when the salt begins to fall to the bottom no matter how hard you stir.
3. Pour the solution into a saucer and label the saucer accordingly on masking tape.

How to Experiment Safely
This experiment requires using very hot water to make a supersaturated solution. Ask an adult to help you when using the stove or hot plate. Do not put anything in your mouth, such as a sugar crystal, before checking with an adult.

Step 5: Set the four bowls aside in a quiet place until the liquid evaporates.

4. Repeat this process with each of the other substances. Make sure to rinse the pot and use a clean spoon. For the alum, begin with 3 tablespoons; for the salt begin with 1 tablespoon, and for the sugar begin with 4 tablespoons. The sugar solution should be thick.

5. Set the saucers in a quiet place and observe them over the next week until all the liquid evaporates. When all the liquid is gone you should see crystals coating the sides and bottoms of the saucers.

6. Examine the crystals with the magnifying glass.

Summary of Results

Draw the results of each of the crystals and write a written description. Was your hypothesis correct? How does the Epsom salt differ from the salt? How does the salt differ from the sugar? Compare the crystal formations with the physical shape of the substance they were made from. Can you identify to which of the seven basic crystal structures the four crystals belong?

Change the Variables

You can produce a variety of crystal colors and shapes by altering the substance used to form the crystal. Some substances you may have to order from a lab supply house or ask your science teacher where to get them: Potassium ferricyanide (red crystals); borax; copper acetate

experiment
CENTRAL

Troubleshooter's Guide

Below is a problem that may arise during this experiment, some possible causes, and some ways to remedy the problem.

Problem: No crystals grew in one or more of the solutions.

Possible Cause: The solution may not have been saturated when the water was hot. You may not have stirred enough to dissolve the solids. Pour the solution back in the saucepan. Reheat the solution, adding more of the substance and stirring well after each addition until you see bits of the substance fall to the bottom.

Possible Cause: The water may not have been hot enough. It should not be at the boiling point but it does need to be very hot. Pour the solution back in the saucepan. Reheat the solution, adding more of the substance and stirring well after each addition until it is saturated.

monohydrate (blue-green crystals); and calcium copper acetate hexahydrate (blue crystals). You can also vary the temperature of the water when making the saturated solutions and compare crystal growth.

Experiment 2
Cool Crystals: How does the effect of cooling impact crystal growth?

Purpose/Hypothesis

Temperature is one of the key environmental factors that affect crystal growth. This experiment examines the outcome of the same crystal-growing solution cooling at three different temperatures. You will place one jar in a cold environment while the crystals grow, the other jar will cool under room temperature conditions, and you will enclose the third jar and store it in a warm area so that it cools the slowest of the three. If the cooling is faster, the particles do not have time to

What Are the Variables?

Variables are anything that might affect the results of an experiment. Here are the main variables in this experiment:

- The solution's rate of cooling
- The crystal-growing substance
- The surrounding air temperature
- The container the crystals are grown in
- The string the crystals are grown on.

In other words, the variables in this experiment are everything that might affect the growth of the crystals. If you change more than one variable, you will not be able to tell which variable impacted crystal growth.

form a large-scale orderly arrangement and a mass of little crystals will form instead. The size of each crystal will demonstrate how temperature impacts the growth of a crystal.

To begin this experiment, make an educated guess about the outcome of the experiment based on your knowledge of crystals, temperature, and solutions. This educated guess, or prediction, is your **hypothesis.** A hypothesis should explain these things:

- the topic of the experiment
- the **variable** you will change
- the variable you will measure
- what you expect to happen

A hypothesis should be brief, specific, and measurable. It must be something you can test through further investigation. Your experiment will prove or disprove whether your hypothesis is correct. Here is one possible hypothesis for this experiment: "The slower a supersaturated solution cools, the larger the size of the crystal."

In this experiment the variable you will change will be the cooling rate of the solution, and the variable you will measure will be the size of the crystal. If the solution that cools the quickest forms the largest crystal, you will know the above hypothesis is incorrect and you will have to reevaluate your hypothesis.

Having a control or standard crystal will help you measure the changes in the dependent variable. Only one variable will change between the control and the experimental crystals, and that is the size of the crystal. For the standard crystal, you will soak a seed crystal in plain water, which will not react with the seed crystal. At the end of the experiment you will compare the size and shape of the seed crystal with each of the other crystals.

Level of Difficulty
Moderate.

Materials Needed
- Epsom salt
- dental floss
- glass saucepan
- hot plate or stove
- saucer
- measuring cup
- measuring spoons
- four small glass jars
- small piece of cloth to cover glass container
- warm towel
- cold-water bath (pan with ice in cold water)
- stirring spoon
- four pencils (long enough to lay across the tops of the four small glass containers)
- marking pen

Approximate Budget
$2 (most materials are common household items).

Timetable
20 minutes initial time; 30 minutes after several days; 20 minutes over the next 2 weeks.

Step-by-Step Instructions
1. To grow a seed crystal, heat a half a cup of water until it is almost at the boiling point and carefully pour it into a glass. Add 5 table-spoons of Epsom salt and stir mixture until all the salt dissolves.

How to Experiment Safely

You are using very hot water in this experiment. Ask an adult to help you when using the stove or hot plate.

Continue adding Epsom salt, stirring after each addition, until the solution is completely saturated. You will know you are at the saturation point when a small amount of Epsom salt sinks to the bottom no matter how hard you stir.

2. Pour the solution into a saucer and wait at least 24 hours until small crystals have grown in the saucer. This could take 2 or 3 days. Pour out any remaining liquid and choose the four largest crystals that are roughly the same size. These are your seed crystals.

3. Cut four pieces of dental floss about 6 inches long. Take each piece and tie one end around a pencil. Cut the piece of dental floss so the other end hangs slightly above the bottom of each jar.

4. Carefully tie a seed crystal to the loose end of each piece of dental floss.

Step 6: Hang a seed crystal in each solution by laying the pencil across the jars.

5. Heat 2 cups of water in the saucepan until it is almost boiling. Remove from heat and add ¾ cup of Epsom salt and stir. Contin-

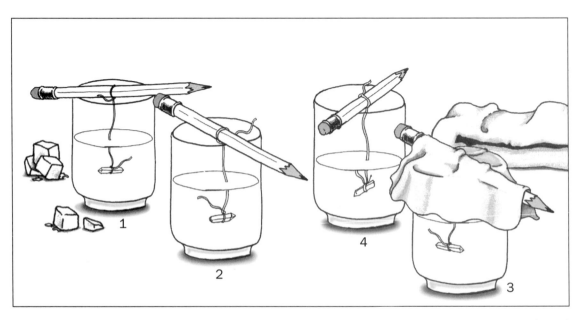

ue to stir while you add as much Epsom salt as you can—until no more will dissolve. When the solution is saturated, set the saucepan aside to cool for two minutes. Pour equal amounts of the solution into three glass jars.

6. In the fourth glass jar pour a roughly equal amount of plain warm water. Hang a seed crystal in each solution by laying the pencil across the jars.

7. Let Jar 1 completely cool and then place it in a cold-water bath. Leave Jar 2 at room temperature. Warm a towel in a clothes dryer, wrap it around Jar 3, and drape the piece of cloth over the top of

Troubleshooter's Guide

Below are some problems that may arise, some possible causes, and some ways to remedy the problems.

Problem: No crystals grew in one or more of the solutions.

Possible Cause: The solution may not have been saturated when the water was hot. You may not have stirred enough to dissolve the Epsom salt. Take out the seed crystal and pour the solution back into the saucepan. Reheat the solution, adding more of the Epsom salt and stirring well after each addition until you see bits of the Epsom salt fall to the bottom.

Possible Cause: The water may not have been hot enough to become completely saturated. It should not be at the boiling point, but it does need to be hot. Take out the seed crystal and pour the solution back into the saucepan. Reheat the solution, adding more of the Epsom salt and stirring well after each addition until it is saturated.

Problem: The crystals are cloudy.

Possible Cause: There may be impurities in the water or the jar. Examine the jar and, if it is dirty, try the experiment again with a clean jar. If the glass is clean, try repeating the experiment using distilled or purified water.

the jar before placing the jar in a warm area, like a cupboard near the stove. Leave Jar 4 at room temperature.

8. Every day place fresh ice in the cold-water bath for Jar 1, and reheat the towel for Jar 3. After about a week, compare the crystals.

Summary of Results

Compare the rate of crystal growth, using the control crystal in Jar 4 as your standard. Examine if there are small crystals on the side or the bottom of the jars. Estimate the size of each crystal on the string compared to the standard, or control crystal, that was sitting in the water. Graph your results, using the percentage of growth on the y-axis and the rate of cooling on the x-axis.

Change the Variables

You can change the variables in the experiment several ways. You can alter the crystal-growing substance and repeat the experiment. You can also change the temperature of the water to make the saturated solutions. Does anything happen if the crystals are grown on a piece of yarn as opposed to dental floss?

 # Design Your Own Experiment

How to Select a Topic Relating to this Concept

Crystals have a range of diverse physical and mechanical properties that you can explore in experiments. Explore your surroundings and make a list of all the materials made of crystals. An experiment with crystals could include exploring some of the traits crystallographers use to identify them, such as how a crystal reacts to light or its hardness.

Check the For More Information section and talk with your science teacher or librarian to learn more about crystals. As you consider possible experiments, make sure to discuss them with your science teacher or other adult before conducting them.

Steps in the Scientific Method

To do an original experiment, you need to plan carefully and think things through. Otherwise, you might not be sure what question you are answering, what you are or should be measuring, or what your findings prove or disprove.

Here are the steps in designing an experiment:

- State the purpose of—and the underlying question behind—the experiment you propose to do.
- Recognize the variables involved and select one that will help you answer the question at hand.
- State your hypothesis, an educated guess about the answer to your question.
- Decide how to change the variable you selected.
- Decide how to measure your results.

Recording Data and Summarizing the Results

Your data should include charts and graphs such as the one you did for these experiments. They should be clearly labeled and easy to read. You may also want to include photographs and drawings of your experimental setup and results, which will help others visualize the steps in the experiment.

If you are preparing an exhibit, you may want to display your results, such as any experimental setup you designed. If you have completed a nonexperimental project, explain clearly what your research question was and illustrate your findings.

Related Projects

Some experiments with crystals will depend on having crystals with different properties. You can examine the crystalline structures of everyday substances around you. Many rocks are crystals. You could identify the unique properties of crystalline rocks and group them according to their common properties. You could also take on a research project. You could examine what crystals are used in appliances, electronic devices, and tools, as well as what properties these crystals supply. Through interviews with professionals or library research, you could examine the work of cystallographers and determine the instruments and properties they use to identify crystals.

For More Information

Math Forum. http://mathforum.org/alejandre/workshops/chart.html (accessed August 24, 2003). ❖ Descriptions and examples of the seven basic crystal systems.

Rockhounds. http://www.rockhounds.com/rockshop/xtal (accessed August 24, 2003). ❖ Technical definitions of crystal systems in rocks.

Shedenhelm, W. R., and Joel E. Arem. *Discover Rocks & Minerals.* Lincolnwood, IL: Publications International, 1991. ❖ Basic facts on rocks and minerals with plenty of photographs.

Stangl, Jean. *Crystal and Crystal Gardens You Can Grow.* New York: Franklin Watts, 1990. ❖ Simple explanation of crystals with directions for growing different crystals.

Symes, R. F., and R. R. Harding. *Crystal & Gem.* New York: Alfred A. Knopf, 1991. ❖ Clear book with loads of illustrations on identifying and using various types of crystals.

Deoxyribonucleic acid (DNA)

Your hair color, a leaf's shape, a bird's wing: These diverse features all share one key inherited trait known as **deoxyribonucleic acid** or DNA. DNA is commonly called the building block of life, for it is the inherited substance that all characteristics build from. Passed down from generation to generation, DNA directs how an organism functions, develops, and appears. Every life form on Earth carries DNA. And unless you are an identical twin, your DNA is completely unique to you.

The findings of DNA have led to awesome advances in a wide range of fields, from medicine to crime solving. Researchers have used their knowledge of DNA to examine inherited diseases, produce medicines, study the relationships between species, and develop foods with desired characteristics. As the work to understand DNA continues, researchers hope that gaining knowledge about the molecule will help improve people's lives all over the world.

The transforming factor

DNA is a large molecule inside almost every cell in the body. In humans, DNA is found in the nucleus, the brain-center of the cell. Much like a cell, a nucleus is held together by a membrane or nuclear envelope. The DNA molecule coils in the nucleus so tightly that if all of the DNA in your body were unraveled and laid end to end, it would stretch from Earth to the Moon about 6,000 times!

In the late 1800s and early 1900s, scientists were working to discover what substance played a role in heredity. From early experiments and observations researchers knew parents passed their

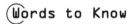

Words to Know

Amino acids:
The building blocks of proteins.

Base:
Substance that when dissolved in water is capable of reacting with an acid to form salts and release hydrogen ions; has a pH of more than 7.

Base pairs:
In DNA, the pairing of two nucleotides with each other: adenine (A) with thymine (T) and guanine (G) with cytosine (C).

Words to Know

Control experiment:
A setup that is identical to the experiment, but is not affected by the variable that acts on the experimental group.

Deoxyribonucleic acid (DNA):
Large, complex molecules found in the nuclei of cells that carry genetic information for an organism's development; double helix. (Pronounced DEE-ox-see-rye-bo-noo-klay-ick acid)

DNA replication:
The process by which one DNA strand unwinds and duplicates all its information, creating two new DNA strands that are identical to each other and to the original strand.

Double helix:
The shape taken by DNA (deoxyribonucleic acid) molecules in a nucleus.

characteristics onto their offspring. Then a 1928 experiment showed that there was some substance that transmitted infectiousness to non-infectious bacteria. This was called the "transforming factor," because it transformed the bacteria.

Scientists narrowed the possibilities of the transforming factor down to two substances: proteins or DNA. At this time, researchers knew that an organism's cells contained DNA. DNA is a simple molecule with relatively few chemical parts to it. They also knew each cell contained **proteins,** large molecules made of chemicals called **amino acids.** There are twenty amino acids that make up the hundreds of thousands of proteins in the human body. Lots of researchers argued that DNA was too simple a molecule to account for the vast diversity of life—from a weed to a human.

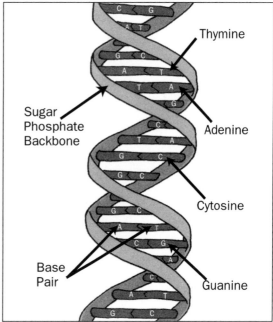

In 1943, American scientist Oswald Avery (1877–1955) and his colleagues conducted a groundbreaking experiment. First they took DNA from a disease-causing strain of a bacterium. Then they placed this DNA into a strain of the bacterium that did not cause disease, an inactive bacterium. They found the inactive bacterium turned into a disease-causing bacterium. Avery concluded that it was the DNA from the disease-causing strain that "transformed" the inactive form of the bacterium. Many in the scientific community were skeptical of this conclusion because they still believed DNA was too simple a substance. Then in 1952 biologists Alfred Hershey and Martha Chase conducted an experiment that conclusively proved DNA was the transforming factor, the molecule responsible for heredity.

Solving the structure

The 1950s were a big decade for DNA. While many researchers were working to prove exactly what DNA did, other scientists were racing to figure out how DNA was structured. In 1953 molecular biologists James D. Watson (1928–) and Francis Crick (1916–) solved the puzzle of DNA's double-helix molecular structure. Their discovery is recognized as one of the most important scientific findings of the twentieth century.

Prior to Watson and Crick's discovery, researchers knew that DNA was made up of units called **nucleotides.** There are four types of

LEFT:
American scientist Oswald Avery. (Courtesy of the Library of Congress.)

RIGHT:
Components of a DNA strand.

Words to Know

Enzyme:
Any of numerous complex proteins produced by living cells that act as catalysts, speeding up the rate of chemical reactions in living organisms.

Hypothesis:
An idea in the form of a statement that can be tested by observation and/or experiment.

Molecular biologists Francis Crick and James D. Watson were the first to map the structure of DNA, which was one of the most important scientific findings of the twentieth century.

Words to Know

Nucleotide:
The basic unit of a nucleic acid. It consists of a simple sugar, a phosphate group, and a nitrogen-containing base. (Pronounced noo-KLEE-uh-tide.)

Protein:
A complex chemical compound consisting of many amino acids attached to each other that are essential to the structure and functioning of all living cells.

Variable:
Something that can affect the results of an experiment.

nucleotides found in DNA, differing only in their nitrogen-containing **bases**: adenine (A), guanine (G), thymine (T), and cytosine (C). Each nucleotide consists of three components: a sugar deoxyribose, a phosphate group, and a nitrogen-containing base.

Watson and Crick used a type of X-ray image produced by British scientist Rosalind Franklin (1920–58) to develop their model of DNA's structure. They determined that DNA consists of long chains of repeating nucleotides, joined together and twisted around each other into a spiral shape known as a **double helix.** It has the appearance of a twisted ladder. The backbone of the ladder is made up of the nucleotides' sugar and phosphate molecules. The rungs of the two strands are formed by attached bases that are always complementary, A pairs with T (A-T) and G pairs C (G-C). These **base pairs** are held together with hydrogen bonds.

Since each nucleotide always pairs with the same complementary nucleotide, this explains how DNA replicates itself. During **DNA**

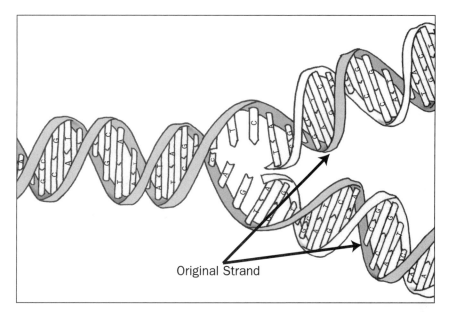

DNA replication: The DNA strand unwinds and complementary nucleotides bind together.

Original Strand

DNA

All living organisms carry DNA; its unique sequence determines individual characteristics.

replication, the DNA helix unzips. The exposed bases match up with complementary bases of nucleotides. The nucleotides bind together to form two new strands that are identical to the strand that separated.

Sequencing the alphabet

Everyone has the same four nucleotides, but it is the order of the nucleotides, the sequence, that determines DNA's instructions. Reading the sequence of the four bases, A, G, C, and T, is similar to reading the order of letters in words. Different combinations create different meanings. In some cases, just one letter out of place in a sequence can cause a person to have a completely distinct characteristic. In the disease sickle cell anemia, for example, a single base change from an A to a T changes the shape and function of red blood cells, causing blood to clog and anemia (a condition in which the blood cannot carry enough oxygen to body tissues).

Different species have varying amounts and sequences of DNA. Humans have about 3.2 billion base pairs in our DNA. Researchers have found no correlation between DNA length and the complexity of an organism. A species of wheat, for example, has roughly 16 billion base pairs, the fruit fly has 137 million, and a species of corn checks in at only slightly less than that of humans, at 3 billion.

As a general rule, the greater the similarity between DNA sequences, the more similar the organisms. In the human species, your DNA sequence is about 99.9 percent identical to every other person's. Your DNA sequence is even more similar to your family members. And although the DNA you share with other nonhuman species is significantly less, about 31 percent of the DNA traits in yeast are similar to humans and about 40 percent of the DNA traits in worms are similar.

Rice, yeast, the pufferfish (pictured), and the rat are among the organisms whose DNA sequences are known. (© Stephen Frink. Reproduced by permission of Corbis.)

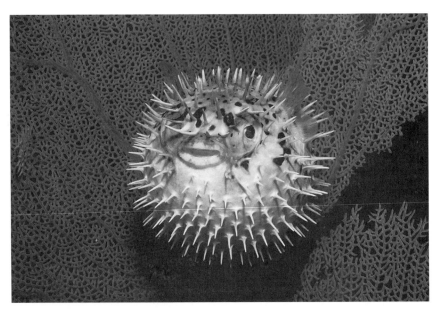

In the late 1900s, with the help of powerful technologies, researchers unraveled the sequences of many organisms. Rice, yeast, the pufferfish, and the rat are among the organisms whose DNA sequences are known. In 2001, researchers published a draft of the entire human DNA sequence. The advances in DNA continue at a rapid pace in the quest to learn the details of how this simple molecule functions.

Project 1
The Stuff of Life: Isolating DNA

Purpose/Hypothesis

DNA is present in all life. In this project, you will extract DNA to see what this molecule looks like.

DNA is twisted inside the cell nucleus. A cell's nucleus also contains proteins and other substances. To see the DNA, you will have to separate out the DNA from all the cell's other molecules (see Figure A). You will first liquefy the substance and separate the cells by blending it. Detergent or soap will break apart the cell's outer and inner membrane, in much the same way that soap loosens dirt and grease. The cell's membranes are made of a fatty substance that contain proteins. Detergent contains a substance that pulls apart the fats and proteins, freeing the DNA.

The DNA in the nucleus is wound up with proteins. To isolate the DNA from these proteins, you will use an **enzyme,** a protein that quickens a chemical reaction. Meat tenderizer contains enzymes that cut away the proteins.

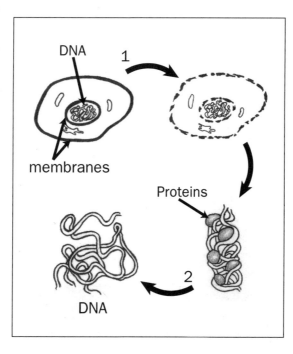

Figure A. Process of DNA isolation: (1) Detergent breaks up the cell's membranes; (2) enzymes cut away the protein to (3) isolate the DNA.

Adding alcohol will then allow you to see the DNA. DNA is not soluble in alcohol. DNA precipitates, or separates out of the solution, in alcohol, moving away from the watery part of the solution and rising towards the alcohol. Proteins and other parts of the cell will remain in the bottom watery layer.

Level of Difficulty

Moderate.

Materials Needed

- spinach
- knife
- salt
- coldwater
- blender
- refrigerator
- liquid soap with no conditioner
- chopstick or toothpick
- strainer or cheesecloth
- cup
- small glass jar
- meat tenderizer
- 91 percent isopropyl alcohol (available in drug stores) or 95 percent ethyl alcohol (slightly preferred; available from science supply companies)

Approximate Budget

$10.

Timetable

1 hour.

Step-by-Step Instructions

1. Take 1/2 cup of the spinach and place it in the blender. Add a large pinch of table salt and about 1/3 cup of cold water. Blend together for 10 seconds and pour the mixture into the cup.
2. Slowly pour the liquid out of the cup and into the glass jar through the cheesecloth or strainer. Fill the jar about one-quarter to one-half full.
3. Add about 2 teaspoons (10 milliliters) of liquid soap to the jar and stir slowly for 5 seconds.

How to Work Safely

Be sure to handle the knife carefully when cutting. If you get any alcohol on your hands, wash your hands immediately and make sure to keep them away from your eyes. Keep the container of alcohol away from open flames. Thoroughly wash the cup, jar, strainer, and chopstick after the experiment. Discard the mixture after you have studied and documented the results.

4. Let the mixture sit for 10 minutes.
5. Add a pinch of the meat tenderizer and stir the mixture gently. Do not stir too hard.
6. Slowly pour the alcohol down the side of the glass jar (jar should be at a slight tilt) until the jar is almost full.
7. Place the jar in the refrigerator for 5 minutes, then remove and wait another 5 minutes. The DNA should have risen to the top of the glass. Use a chopstick or toothpick to extract the spinach DNA.

Summary of Results

Write down what the DNA looks like. Your toothpickful of DNA contains millions of DNA strands clumped together. Since you were not using chemicals to extract a highly purified DNA, it also contains some proteins and other nucleic acids (ribonucleic acid or RNA) that were not separated. With the right equipment and materials in a laboratory, it is possible to extract pure DNA.

Step 6:
Slowly pour the alcohol down the side of the glass jar (jar should be at a slight tilt) until the jar is almost full.

Troubleshooter's Guide

Below are some problems that may arise during this experiment, some possible causes, and some ways to remedy the problems.

Problem: The DNA is broken into small bits. (DNA should be a long, white strand.)

Possible cause: You could have stirred too harshly when you added the enzymes or at different points throughout the experiment and broken the DNA strands. Try repeating the experiment, stirring gently every time.

Problem: You do not see any DNA. (DNA looks white and stringy.)

Possible cause: The cells may not have broken open when they were blended. Try repeating the experiment, blending the DNA until is liquidy.

Possible cause: If the soap had conditioner in it, it would not have broken open the fatty DNA cell membranes, and the DNA would not have gotten free. Make sure the soap does not have any conditioner.

Possible cause: You may not have allowed enough time for each step. Wait another 45 minutes for the DNA to rise into the alcohol layer. If you still do not see any DNA, try the experiment again, increasing the time slightly for each step.

Possible cause: You may not have had enough DNA from the source. Repeat the experiment, cutting the amount of water added to the DNA source in half before placing it in the blender.

Experiment 2
Comparing DNA: Does the DNA from different species have the same appearance?

Purpose/Hypothesis

The DNA molecule produces the unique characteristics for all life forms. DNA is composed of the same biochemical molecules in all species: four nucleotides and a sugar-phosphate backbone. Nucleotide sequences, which account for the distinctive characteristics, cannot be seen by the naked eye.

In this experiment you will compare if DNA appears the same in four different species. You will conduct the same DNA extraction process on each of the species and then examine its physical characteristics.

To extract DNA, you will have to separate out the DNA from all the cell's other molecules. You will first liquefy the substance and separate the cells by blending it. Detergent or soap will break apart the cell's outer and inner membrane, in much the same way that soap loosens dirt and grease. The cell's membranes are made of a fatty substance that contain proteins. Detergent contains a substance that pulls apart the fats and proteins, freeing the DNA.

The DNA in the nucleus is wound up with proteins. To isolate the DNA from these proteins, you will use an **enzyme,** a protein that quickens a chemical reaction. (See Figure A on page 159.) Meat tenderizer contains enzymes that cut away the proteins. Adding alcohol will then allow you to see the DNA. DNA is not soluble in alcohol. DNA precipitates or separates out of the solution in alcohol, moving away from the watery part of the solution and rising towards the alcohol. Proteins and other parts of the cell will remain in the bottom watery layer.

What Are the Variables?

Variables are anything that might affect the results of an experiment. Here are the main variables in this experiment:

- the DNA source

- the type of alcohol

- the type of detergent

- the temperature of the water

In other words, the variables in this experiment are everything that might affect the appearance of the DNA. If you change more than one variable at the same time, you will not be able to tell which variable had the most effect on the DNA.

To begin this experiment, make an educated guess about the outcome of the experiment based on your knowledge of DNA. This educated guess, or prediction, is your **hypothesis.** A hypothesis should explain these things:

- the topic of the experiment
- the **variable** you will change
- the variable you will measure
- what you expect to happen

A hypothesis should be brief, specific, and measurable. It must be something you can test through further investigation. Your experiment will prove or disprove whether your hypothesis is correct. Here is one possible hypothesis for this experiment: "DNA will have the same physical characteristics in all the species, with each species having a unique quantity of DNA."

Variables are anything you can change in an experiment. In this case, the variable you will change will be the DNA source. The variable you will measure will be the DNA itself and the quantity of the DNA.

Level of Difficulty
Difficult (this experiment is not technically difficult, but it requires careful attention to timing and each step).

Materials Needed
- four DNA sources: possible sources include banana, wheat germ, onion, kiwi, grapes, peas
- salt
- cold water
- knife
- blender
- refrigerator
- liquid soap or detergent with no conditioner
- four wooden sticks such as chopsticks or toothpicks
- strainer
- four small glass jars
- four cups
- marking pen
- masking tape
- meat tenderizer

- 91 percent isopropyl alcohol (available in drug stores) or 95 percent ethyl alcohol (slightly preferred; available from science supply companies)
- filter paper
- gram scale (optional)

Approximate Budget
$15.

Timetable
One-and-a-half hours to start; 15 minutes after a 3-day waiting period.

Step-by-Step Instructions
1. Cut about a 1/2 cup of one DNA source, such as a banana, and place it in the blender. Add a large pinch of table salt and about twice as much cold water as the source. Blend together for about 10 seconds and pour into a cup.
2. Repeat the procedure with the other DNA sources.
3. Label each glass jar. Pour each mixture from the cup into its marked glass through the cheesecloth or strainer. Make sure to wash the strainer and cup between pours. Fill the jars about one-quarter to one-half full.
4. Add 2 teaspoons (10 milliliters) of liquid soap to each jar and stir slowly for 5 seconds.
5. Let the mixtures sit for 10 minutes.
6. Add a pinch of the meat tenderizer to each glass and stir the mixtures gently. Do not stir too hard.

How to Experiment Safely
Be sure to handle the knife carefully when cutting. If you get any alcohol on your hands, wash your hands immediately and make sure to keep them away from your eyes. Keep the container of alcohol away from open flames. Thoroughly wash the cup, jar, strainer, and chopstick after the experiment. Discard the mixtures after you have studied and documented the results.

Step 9: Gently extract the DNA from each substance using a toothpick or chopstick.

7. Pour the alcohol down the sides of the glass jars until they are almost full.

8. Place the jars in the refrigerator for about 5 minutes and then remove them and wait another 5 minutes.

9. Use a chopstick or toothpick to gently extract the DNA from each substance and observe its characteristics.

10. Gently place the DNA on filter paper. (If you have a sensitive scale, weigh the filter paper.)

11. Place the filter paper aside and leave for 3 days or until it is completely dry. Note how much DNA each substance contained by comparing them to one another. On the scale, you can weigh the filter paper with the DNA. Subtract the weight of the filter paper from the total. Note how much the DNA from each source weighs.

Summary of Results

Examine your results and determine whether your original hypothesis was correct. Did the DNA react the same way in all the sources? Did the DNA appear the same from all the species? Draw, describe, or take pictures of the DNA, both when it is freshly extracted and when it is dried. (It may be helpful to view the extracted DNA under a microscope.) Write a description of each of the species' DNA and your conclusions.

Change the Variables

You can vary this experiment several ways.

• You can alter the DNA sources and observe the DNA from other plant and fruit sources. Whatever you choose, make sure the

Troubleshooter's Guide

Below are some problems that may arise during this experiment, some possible causes, and some ways to remedy the problems.

Problem: The DNA is broken.

Possible cause: You could have stirred too harshly when you added the enzymes or at different points throughout the protocol and broken the DNA strands. Try repeating the experiment, stirring gently every time.

Problem: There was no DNA.

Possible cause: The cells may not have broken open when they were blended. Try repeating the experiment, blending the DNA until is liquidy.

Possible cause: If the soap had conditioner in it, it would not have broken open the fatty DNA cell membranes and the DNA would not have gotten free. Make sure the soap did not have any conditioner.

Possible cause: You may not have allowed enough time for each step. Wait another 45 minutes for the DNA to precipitate into the alcohol layer. If you still do not see any DNA, try the experiment again, increasing the time slightly for each step.

Possible cause: You may not have had enough DNA from the source; some DNA sources contain more water than others. Repeat the experiment, cutting the amount of water added to the DNA source in half before placing it in the blender.

source is not too watery. Yeast, strawberries, and peas are three other good sources for this experiment.

- Using one DNA source, such as wheat germ, you can alter the type of soap or detergent.

- You can also change the amount of the soap used.

- You can change the alcohol. What happens to the DNA if you use a lesser concentration of alcohol, such as 70 percent rubbing alcohol?

Design Your Own Experiment

How to Select a Topic Relating to this Concept

The study of DNA is a relatively new topic of study for researchers. There are many intriguing questions and unknowns related to the topic that researchers are beginning to understand. How is the DNA of different species related? What are some ways that DNA sequences are manipulated, and how can this help treat or cure human disease?

Check the For More Information section and talk with your science teacher or librarian to start gathering information on any questions that interest you. You could also consider visiting companies in your local area that conduct DNA research.

Steps in the Scientific Method

To do an original experiment, you need to plan carefully and think things through. Otherwise, you might not be sure what question you are answering, what you are or should be measuring, or what your findings prove or disprove.

Here are the steps in designing an experiment:

- State the purpose of—and the underlying question behind—the experiment you propose to do.
- Recognize the variables involved and select one that will help you answer the question at hand.
- State your hypothesis, an educated guess about the answer to your question.
- Decide how to change the variable you selected.
- Decide how to measure your results.

Recording Data and Summarizing the Results

Your data should include charts and graphs such as the one you did for these experiments. They should be clearly labeled and easy to read. As DNA is difficult to visualize, you may also want to include photographs and drawings of your experimental setup and results. This will help others visualize the steps in the experiment.

If you are preparing an exhibit, you may want to display your results, such as any experimental setup you designed. If you have completed a nonexperimental project, explain clearly what your research question was and illustrate your findings.

Related Projects

Because the nucleotides or sequences of DNA are invisible to the naked eye, the majority of experiments with DNA will need special laboratory equipment. With the right equipment, you can compare the bands or fingerprints of DNA from different organisms. Called DNA fingerprinting, this is one technique that forensic scientists use to compare a suspect's DNA with the DNA found at a crime scene. Check the Resources section for companies that sell kits on DNA fingerprinting.

Using a DNA technique that combines bits of DNA from two different organisms is another possible project. Called DNA Transformation, the technique can transfer a desired trait to another organism. To perform transformation, you will need a kit, along with special equipment and adult supervision. Transformation kits are sold at many biological supply companies.

The topic of DNA also brings with it many ethical dilemmas. Transformation techniques have allowed researchers to cut-and-paste the DNA of two different species together. Should a person be forced to store his or her DNA in a computer databank if it will help solve crimes? If a DNA sequence predicts that a person may get a certain disease, does that person's insurance company have the right to know this information? You might focus on one ethical issue from differing viewpoints.

For More Information

DNA From the Beginning. http://www.dnaftb.org/dnaftb/ (accessed on August 24, 2003). ❖ An animated introduction on the basics of DNA, heredity, and genetics.

The Genes We Share with Yeast, Flies, Worms, and Mice. http://www.hhmi.org/genesweshare/ (accessed on August 24, 2003). ❖ Clear report from the Howard Hughes Medical Institute.

Groleau, Rick. "Journey into DNA." *Nova Online.* http://www.pbs.org/wgbh/nova/genome/dna.html (accessed on August 24, 2003). ❖ Interactive site on the basics of DNA and related issues.

Human Genome Project Information http://www.ornl.gov/hgmis (accessed on August 24, 2003). ❖ Updates and information on the sequencing of the human DNA.

Ridley, Matt. *Genome: The Autobiography of a Species in 23 Chapters.* New York: HarperColllins, 2000. ❖ Each chapter looks at one gene on a human's chromosome.

Shute, Nancy. "Haven't got a clue? Maybe DNA will do." *U.S. News,* July 24, 2000. http://www.usnews.com/usnews/doubleissue/mysteries/dna.htm (accessed on August 24, 2003). ❖ Article on how DNA analysis is being used to solve family mysteries and identify unknown people.

The Tech Museum of Innovation. http://www.thetech.org/exhibits/online/genome/overview.html (accessed on August 24, 2003). ❖ Online exhibit has interactive explanations and ethical scenarios.

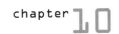

Flowers

The word flower often conjures up images of familiar blooms that enliven homes, such as roses and sunflowers. Yet flowers do far more than beautify the world. A **flower** is the reproductive structure of flowering plants, which are called **angiosperms.** Flowering plants include the familiar blooms as well as grasses, shrubs, and trees. The flowers on plants are widely diverse in size, shape, color, and scent. Flower sizes range from the *Wolffia,* which can fit through the eye of a sewing needle, to the Titan Arum, a cone-shaped flower that can tower 9 feet (2.7 meters). Some flowers resemble insects, and others sport brightly colored petals. Yet all flowers share the same key function: to make seeds to give rise to a new generation of the plant.

The evolution of flowers supplied many advantages for plant survival and thus, life on Earth. Flowers provide protection for seeds and a food source for animals. In return for food, the animals supply genetic variation to the flower. Mixing up the genetic material allowed flowers to develop new features that led to plants increasing in types and numbers. First appearing on Earth about 145 million years ago during the era of dinosaurs, today about 90 percent of plants are flowering plants.

The inside story

Flowers contain the plant's male and female parts for reproduction. The male part produces powdery grains called **pollen.** Each pollen grain contains male reproductive cells, called sperm cells. When pollen joins with the female part of the flower it is called **pollination.** The result is the development of a seed. There are four basic parts to most flowers: the stamen, pistil, petal, and sepal.

Words to Know

Angiosperm:
A flowering plant that has its seeds produced within an ovary.

Anther:
The male reproductive organs of the plant, located on the tip of a flower's stamen.

Control experiment:
A setup that is identical to the experiment, but is not affected by the variable that acts on the experimental group.

Cross-pollination:
The process by which pollen from one plant pollinates another plant of the same species.

Did You Know?

- Species of the Wolffia plant's flowers are so small that 250 of them can fit on a postage stamp.

- Cucumber flowers can change from male to bisexual to female. The last flowers on some cucumbers do not need to be pollinated to produce a fruit—they make the fruit on their own.

- A fig has its tiny flowers crammed inside the fruit. The pollen is carried to the figs by fig wasps that fit through an opening. Fig wasps are so tiny they fit through the eye of a needle.

- Scientists estimate that it takes about 10 pounds of nectar for honeybees to make 1 pound of honey. To gather this nectar, bees need to visit about 2 million flowers by traveling about 55,000 miles (88,000 kilometers), over twice the distance around the world, and carry about 37,000 loads of nectar back to the hive.

- Nearly all wild bananas and many cacti species are bat-pollinated.

- Hummingbirds have overcome the need to land when they feed on nectar because they beat their wings so fast: some hummingbirds can beat their wings up to 200 times per second.

- Scientists study ancient pollen for clues to our early ancestors' eating habits, forest biodiversity, the content of ancient ship cargoes, and the authenticity of archaeological finds.

- People have long used the scents from flowers as perfumes: Perfumers gather flowers, such as the rose, lily, and jasmine, when scents are at their peak and then extract their oils.

Words to Know

Filament:
In a flower, stalk of the stamen that bears the anther.

Flower:
The reproductive part of a flowering plant.

Hypothesis:
An idea in the form of a statement that can be tested by observation and/or experiment.

Imperfect flower:
Flowers that have only the male reproductive organ (stamen) or the female reproductive organs (pistil).

Nectar:
A sweet liquid found inside a flower which attracts pollinators.

Ovary:
In a plant, the base part of the pistil that bears ovules and develops into a fruit.

Ovule:
Structure within the ovary that develops into a seed after fertilization.

The male reproductive organ is called the **stamen.** The stamens are offshoots that grow in a circle around the blossom. A stamen is made up of the **anther** located at the top, which holds the pollen, and a **filament,** which is the thin stalk that supports the anther.

The female reproductive organ is called the **pistil.** The pistil has three major parts: the **stigma,** a sticky surface at the top that holds the

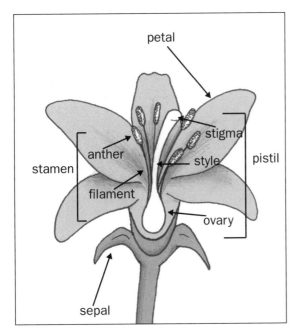

pollen; the **style,** the stem that holds the stigma upright; and the **ovary,** the structure located at the bottom of the stigma that produces **ovules,** the female reproductive cells or eggs.

The most recognizable part of a flower is its **petals.** Petals enclose the flower's sex organs. They can bloom in vibrant colors that attract animals to the flower. **Sepals** are the leaflike structures at the bottom of the petals that protect the flower bud before it opens. When the bud opens, the sepals fold back.

For pollination to occur the pollen must move from the anther of a stamen to the pistil's stigma. The sperm cells in the pollen move down a tube that forms from the style to the ovary. There, the sperm cells can fertilize the eggs in the ovule.

Not all flowers contain all parts. For example, grasses do not contain petals in their flowers. Some flowers produce either the male or female part, and others produce both. The flowers with both pistils and stamens are called **perfect flowers.** Examples of perfect flowers includes the rose, sweet pea, and lily. Flowers that have only the pistil or the stamen are called **imperfect flowers.** (The same plant, however, can contain both male and female flowers.)

An imperfect flower prevents a plant from **self-pollinating,** meaning when the pollen transfers from the male to female parts of a single flower or plant. This can occur simply by gravity causing the pollen to drop. Plants that self-pollinate have the exact same genetic material as the parent, causing them to have a decreased chance of survival if the environment changes. Even if flowers are capable of self-pollinating it is not the desired method of pollination. Flowers have evolved mechanisms to avoid self-pollination such as developing its stamens and pistils at different times, and having its pistil reach far above the stamen.

In **cross-pollination** pollen is transferred from one flower to another. Cross-pollination combines genetic material and generates greater diversity in the offspring. Plants are usually stronger and healthier over the long run than self-pollinators. While cross-pollination has genetic advantages, it also means that plants are more dependent on a way to have their pollen carried about.

Pollen on the move

In order for pollen to transfer from one flower to another, it must have a way to move. Some flowering plants depend upon the wind to blow its pollen onto another flower. Examples of wind-pollinated plants include pine trees, corn, and grasses. Plants that pollinate by wind—and sometimes splashes of rain—produce large quantities of light pollen, as a large percentage of the pollen will be wasted by not landing on its target spot. These flowers do not need the vibrant features that tempt pollinators (see below) and often have plain, small flowers.

The large majority of flowering plants depend upon animals to ferry the pollen from one flower to another. These pollen-carriers are called **pollinators.** Insects, birds, butterflies, and even bats are pollinators. Bees are among the most numerous and important pollinators.

Flowers first must attract pollinators by offering food, color, scents, and other temptations. A pollinator that comes into contact with the flower rubs against the anther, causing some pollen to stick to its body. When the pollinator then visits another flower of the same species, its pollen brushes or falls onto that flower's stigma. Animal-pollinated flowers produce less pollen than the wind-pollinators, as the animal carries the pollen directly to a flower.

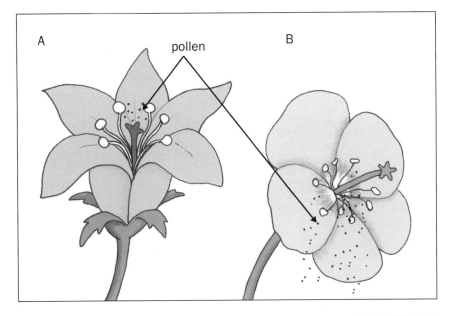

(A) In a self-pollinating flower, pollen falls from the anther to the stigma; (B) a flower can avoid self-pollination if its pistil reaches above the stamen.

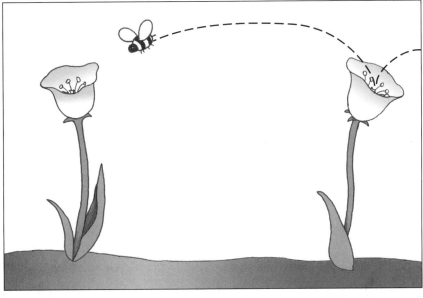

In cross-pollination, genetic material (pollen) is exchanged from one flower to another.

ⓦords to Know

Self-pollination:
The process in which pollen from one part of a plant fertilizes ovules on another part of the same plant.

Sepal:
The outermost part of a flower; typically leaflike and green.

Stamen:
Male reproductive organ of flowers that is composed of the anther and filament.

Allure of the wild

In the quest to lure pollinators, flowers have evolved several ingenious features. Many flowers offer food in the form of **nectar.** Nectar is a sweet liquid that provides nourishment for birds, bees, butterflies, and other animals. Nectar is located deep within the flower at the base of their petals. Petals often sport lines or dots that serve as a guide to the hidden nectar. In some flowers nectar accumulates in long pouches

Bees are among the most numerous and important pollinators. (© George D. Lepp/CORBIS. Reproduced by permission.)

Flowers have many ways of attracting pollinators. One way is nectar, a sweet liquid located deep within the flower that provides nourishment for birds, bees, butterflies, and other animals.

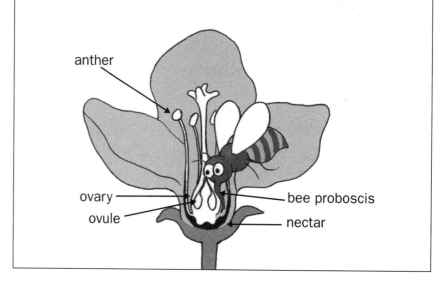

anther

ovary

ovule

bee proboscis

nectar

that is available to animals with long beaks or tongues. Some flowers time their production of nectar to coincide with the schedule of their desired pollinator. For example, night-blooming flowers increase their production of nectar at night so the scent attracts bats, moths, and other nocturnal pollinators.

Some plants have many different pollinators, while others are particular to just one type. A plant with many pollinators will have more organisms carrying its pollen, yet there is a greater chance the pollen will not make it to the same type flower. Having a pollinator who only likes one type of flower cuts down the amount of traveling pollen but ensures that the pollen will be delivered to a like flower. For example, the orchid *Angraecum sesquipedale* ensures that only a specific type of insect pollinates it by having its nectar located about 15.7 inches (400 millimeters) within the flower. The hawkmoth, which is an insect but is the size of a small bird, with its 12-inch (30-centimeter) proboscis is the only insect that can reach the nectar.

Animals can get other meals from flowers as well. Some flowers produce a second type of pollen that pollinators can eat. Oils on the flowers are food for some insects.

Flowers also attract pollinators with their petal colors and shapes. Animals all have unique color perception and are attracted to colors that they can spot. Flowers that appeal to birds are often red (some have evolved a landing area for the bird). Bees are attracted to blues, purples, and yellow pigments. Butterflies prefer to eat sitting down so they prefer flat, wide surfaces and bright colors. Bats need large, sturdy and pale-colored flowers to support their weight and show up in the darkness.

Scents—both sweet and foul—are another method of appealing to certain animals. The bee orchid, for example, resembles and smells like a bee. When male bees, tempted by its scent, attempt to mate with the flower they become covered with pollen and spread it to their next flower mate. Another orchid species, the Lady's Slipper, holds a fragrance in its pouch that has a wild attraction for flies. The flies

The pouch on a Lady's Slipper orchid, which contains the flower's pollen, has a fragrance that attracts pollinators to it. (Reproduced by permission of Field Mark Publications.)

climb around and inside the pouch, getting pollen stuck to them in the process.

Foul odors attract pollinators who feed on decaying matter. The smells are similar to those of the food that these insects and other animals eat. Along with laying claim to the world's largest flower, the Titan's flower is also the world's smelliest. Giving off an odor similar to rotting meat, the stench attracts beetles and flies that feed on or lay eggs in rotting flesh.

Some flowers have mechanisms that force a pollinator to stay for a prolonged visit. With flowers up to one foot across, the giant water lily of the Amazon has to work fast as it only blooms for two days. The flower attracts beetles during the day, then traps them inside when it closes for the night. Covered in pollen, the beetles are released when the flower opens at dusk of the following day. The Dutchman's pipe has a tube-shaped flower with a waxy surface. It emits a putrid smell that appeals to flies. When insects land they slip down the flower and are trapped by its thick hairs. The flies can lap up nectar while they get covered in pollen.

The appearance and smell of a flower provides clues as to its pollinator. In the following two experiments you will explore pollination and how a flower's features shape its pollinators.

Experiment 1
Self versus Cross: Will there be a difference in reproduction between self-pollinated and cross-pollinated plants of the same type?

Purpose/Hypothesis
Flowering plants can be cross-pollinators or self-pollinators. Botanists and flower developers cross-pollinate specific plants intentionally to produce a desired trait in the offspring, such as a specific color. The cross between two parent plants produces a hybrid.

In this experiment, you will both cross-pollinate and self-pollinate the same type of plant. Because of possible variations, you will use two plants for each trial. You will then wait for the plants to develop and observe any differences in the flowers and outcome.

What Are the Variables?

Variables are anything that might affect the results of an experiment. Here are the main variables in this experiment:

- the type of plant

- the source of pollen

- the environment (e.g., sunlight, wind, air temperature)

- the amount of water applied to the plant after pollination

  In other words, the variables in this experiment are everything that might affect pollination. If you change more than one variable at the same time, you will not be able to tell which variable had the most effect on plant reproduction.

Before you begin, make an educated guess about the outcome of this experiment based on your knowledge of flowers and pollination. This educated guess, or prediction, is your **hypothesis.** A hypothesis should explain these things:

- the topic of the experiment
- the **variable** you will change
- the variable you will measure
- what you expect to happen

A hypothesis should be brief, specific, and measurable. It must be something you can test through further investigation. Your experiment will prove or disprove whether your hypothesis is correct. Here is one possible hypothesis for this experiment: "The flowers that are cross-pollinated will produce seeds and the self-pollinated plant will not."

In this case, the variable you will change is the source of the pollen. The variable you will measure is the development of the flowers and seeds.

Conducting a **control experiment** will help you isolate each variable and measure the changes in the dependent variable. Only one variable will change between the control and the experimental setup, and that is the pollen a plant receives. For the control, you will place a plant in an isolated, indoor area to ensure it receives no pollen from another plant. At the end of the experiment you can compare the results of the control to the experimental plants.

Level of Difficulty
Moderate.

Materials Needed
- eight young flowering, cross-pollinating plants of one type, purchased before any flowers have grown (if not available as young plants, you can grow with seeds, potting soil, and pots. For a faster option, you can order Wisconsin Fast Plant seeds from Carolina Biological; see For More Information). Talk with an expert at a gardening store or conduct research to make sure that you have selected a plant that cross-pollinates. (In general, geraniums, corn, and cucumbers work well; avoid tomatoes, beans, and peas.)
- several cotton swabs
- several toothpicks
- tweezers
- marking pen
- magnifying glass (optional)

Approximate Budget
$20.

Timetable
Varies widely depending on plant; 30 minutes for pollination; about 10 minutes of regular observations for 6 to 14 weeks.

How to Experiment Safely
There are no safety hazards in this experiment. (If you have strong allergies to pollen you may want to check with an adult before conducting this experiment.

Step-by-Step Instructions

1. Conduct the experiment inside and away from other plants of the same species. There should be two plants in each trial: Label two plants "A," two plants "B," two plants "C," and two plants "D." The plants labeled "D" will be the Control. Set plants in distant locations from one another, such as in separate parts of a room, or even in separate rooms. Make sure each plant has equal light.

2. After the plants have formed blossoms and before the petals open, gently push aside the petals with a toothpick. On Plants A use the tweezers to remove all the stamens on each flower, leaving the stigma. Label the pot: "Female/Cross."

3. When all the plants have open flowers, (this should occur at roughly the same time) note whether the stigma stands below, equal, or higher to the anthers. You will need to pollinate, self-pollinate, and not pollinate the same number of flowers on each

Step 4: Gently rub the pollen grains from the stamen against the tip of the stigma.

Troubleshooter's Guide

Below is a problem that may arise during this experiment, some possible causes, and some ways to remedy the problem.

Problem: The plants did not produce seeds.

Possible cause: There can be several possible causes: The plant may have been exposed to too much heat, or it may not have had enough water or nutrients. Make sure you use a rich soil that contains nutrients, and follow the directions for the seed carefully. You may want to talk with a professional at a plant store.

Possible cause: You may not be able to see the seeds. The pistil should be enlarged, change shape, and become dry. When this happens, carefully look inside the pistil to see if there are seeds, then remove each seed carefully.

plant. Count the least number of flowers on one of the plants and use that as the guide. Gently snip off the remaining flower shoots that you will not need. For example, if one of the plants only has three flowers and the rest have over six, snip off the extras on the other plants so all plants have three flowers.

4. Rub a cotton swab against the stamens of Plants B. You should see pollen grains on the swab. You may want to use a magnifying glass. Gently rub those pollen grains against the tip of the stigmas on Plants A. Make sure you see the pollen grains on the stigma.

5. Repeat with a fresh swab for each transfer of pollen flowers.

6. Self-pollinate Plants C by taking a fresh swab and moving the pollen from the stamen to the stigma in each flower. Label plants: "Self-Pollinated."

7. At regular intervals, (depending on plant, could be every three days) note any changes in the pistil in Plants A, C, and D. Note what day the petals fall off and any changes in the sepals.

Summary of Results

As the flowers continue to develop, construct a chart with the similarities and differences among the plants. Note the pistil development and count the number of seeds in each pistil. Average the seeds for each of the two plants in each group. Compare the control to the self-pollinated plant. How did the groups of plants differ? How were they the same?

Change the Variables

To change the variable in this experiment you can change the type of plant. You can also conduct the same type of pollination on each plant, and alter the environmental conditions. You can also alter the nutrition of the plants by changing the soil content. Use a soil with few nutrients, and then add specific nutrients one by one to determine which nutrients affect seed production.

Experiment 2
Sweet Sight: Can changing a flower's nectar and color affect the pollinators lured to the flower?

Purpose/Hypothesis

Among the many characteristics a flower uses to attract pollinators are its color and nectar. There are some pollinators that respond to certain colors. For example, in general butterflies are attracted to bright reds and oranges; bees to blues and yellows; and beetles to many different colors. Nectar also varies among flowers in the amount of sugar it contains. Some pollinators are attracted to nectar that has about 20 to 25 percent sugar; other pollinators, such as bees, prefer a richer sugar content of about 50 percent.

In this experiment, you will determine if you can attract a certain type of pollinator based on the color and sugar-concentration of nectar. You can measure the results by noting the numbers and types of pollinators. Among the animals to look out for are ants, butterflies, bees, birds, and spiders. You will first apply a constant nectar content to three colors: yellow, blue, and white. After finding one color that attracts the most pollinators, you will then vary the nectar by placing an artificial nectar on the color.

Nectar is a syrupy-solution made up of several types of sugar, primarily sucrose, which is common table sugar. You will make varying concentrations of artificial nectar: a 20 percent sugar syrup and a 50 percent sugar syrup.

What Are the Variables?

Variables are anything that might affect the results of an experiment. Here are the main variables in this experiment:

- the shape of the bowl/cup
- the environment the cup is placed
- the weather conditions
- the time of observations
- the concentration of nectar
- the color of the flower

In other words, the variables in this experiment are everything that might affect the pollinators who approach the cups. If you change more than one variable at the same time, you will not be able to tell which variable had the most effect on attracting pollinators.

Before you begin, make an educated guess about the outcome of this experiment based on your knowledge of flowers and pollinators. This educated guess, or prediction, is your **hypothesis.** A hypothesis should explain these things:

- the topic of the experiment
- the **variable** you will change
- the variable you will measure
- what you expect to happen

A hypothesis should be brief, specific, and measurable. It must be something you can test through further investigation. Your experiment will prove or disprove whether your hypothesis is correct. Here is one possible hypothesis for this experiment: "There will be one combination of color and nectar that will attract the most of one type of pollinator: The yellow, high nectar concentration will lure the most bees."

In this case, the variables you will change, one at a time, are the color and then the concentration of the artificial nectar. The variable you will measure is the number and type of pollinators.

Conducting a control experiment will help you isolate each variable and measure the changes in the dependent variable. Only one variable will change between the control and your experiment. After determining the color that attracts the most of a certain type of pollinator, your control will change the concentration of nectar. For the control in this part of the experiment, you will use plain water instead of nectar. At the end of the experiment you can compare the experimental data to the control data.

Level of Difficulty
Moderate.

Materials Needed
- 3 cups sugar
- outside area with a high ledge area
- 2 nice days
- 6 cups water
- six clear plastic cups
- swatches of blue, yellow, and white felt: enough to fit in the plastic cups
- colored felt
- small rocks
- stirring spoon
- measuring cup
- marking pen

Approximate Budget
$5.

Timetable
1 hour for experiment setup; 1 hour each day for 2 days.

How to Experiment Safely
The artificial nectar should attract bees and other insects. Make sure to stand at least several feet away when making your observations. Do not disturb the bees or insects. Have an adult present when you handle the boiling water.

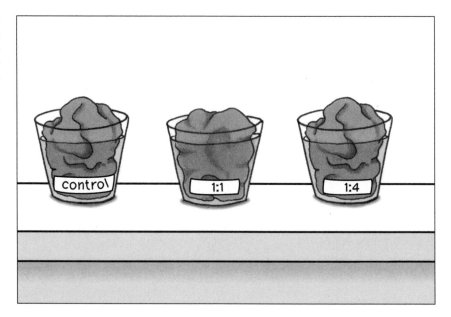

Step-by-Step Instructions

1. Day 1: Cut a swatch of the colored felts and scrunch each one into a clear cup. Place a small stone in the felt to weigh it down.

2. Set each of the cups in the same general area outside on a high ledge, at roughly 2 feet apart from one another. Choose two times of day to observe the colored cups for a 30-minute period each time: one time in the morning and one in the afternoon or early evening. You will need to observe at the same two times the following day. For each color, note the number and type of pollinators that visit the cup.

3. Day 2: Vary the nectar concentration. Use your data from the previous day to select one of the colors that attracted the most pollinators. Place a swatch of the selected color into each of three clear plastic cups.

4. Label the cups according to the ratio of sugar to water: "1:1," "1:4," and "Control." The Control will be plain water.

5. Boil the 6 cups of water. Pour 2 cups of sugar into a glass bowl labeled 1:1. Add 2 cups of boiled water and stir until all sugar has dissolved. Allow the artificial nectar to cool.

6. Pour 1/2 cup sugar into a glass bowl labeled 1:4. Add 2 cups of boiled water and stir until all sugar has dissolved. Allow to cool.

Troubleshooter's Guide

Below is a problem that may arise during this experiment, some possible causes, and some ways to remedy the problem.

Problem: There were too few pollinators to draw any conclusions.

Possible cause: Vary the time of day you are making your observations. You may also want to change the location to one with more plant growth and surrounding flowers.

7. Fill the 1:1 cup and the 1:4 cup with their designated artificial nectar. Fill the Control cup with 2 cups of cooled boiled water without any sugar. Place the cups outside on a ledge.

8. At the same two times of day as the previous day, observe the flowers for 30-minute periods and note the type and number of visitors to each cup.

Summary of Results

Examine your results for both the color and concentration. Graph the major pollinators number of visits by the color. Create another graph of the major pollinators number of visits by the nectar concentration. Could you attract one specific pollinator by altering the nectar and color? Conduct some research and determine what types of flowers this pollinator(s) visits the most frequently. How do the characteristics of these flowers compare to your experimental results?

Change the Variables

As it is the combination of many different factors that influence a flower's pollinators, you can vary this experiment in many ways to determine the relative effect of each characteristic.

- Change the shape of the setup by creating petals of different shapes, then using one concentration of nectar.
- Change the colors of the setup, using single colors and multiple colors
- Vary the scent of the setup, either by purchasing flower scents or by extracting scents from real flowers

- Change the environment to compare pollinators, such as in a wooded area, park, and backyard.

Design Your Own Experiment

How to Select a Topic Relating to this Concept

While flowers all have the same function, they are widely diverse in appearance. Many flowers, especially the self-pollinators, are so small and nondescript that you may not notice them. To gather ideas for a topic you can look at the many different types of flowers that grow in your area. Visit a greenhouse or a florist to observe species' shapes, colors, and scents. As flowers are unique to a geographic region, you may want to look up photographs and descriptions of flowers in different locations around the United States and the world. Examine how the flower's appearance shapes its role, if any, with possible pollinators.

Check the For More Information section and talk with your science teacher to learn more about flowers and pollination. You could also speak with a professional at a local greenhouse or nursery.

Steps in the Scientific Method

To conduct an original experiment, you need to plan carefully and think things through. Otherwise, you might not be sure what question you are answering, what you are or should be measuring, or what your findings prove or disprove.

Here are the steps in designing an experiment:

- State the purpose of—and the underlying question behind—the experiment you propose to do.
- Recognize the variables involved and select one that will help you answer the question at hand.
- State your hypothesis, an educated guess about the answer to your question.
- Decide how to change the variable you selected.
- Decide how to measure your results.

Recording Data and Summarizing the Results

Your data should include charts and graphs such as the one you did for these experiments. They should be clearly labeled and easy to read.

You may also want to include photographs and drawings of your experimental setup and results, which will help other people visualize the steps in the experiment.

If you are preparing an exhibit, you may want to display your results, such as any experimental setup you designed. You may also want to display any flowers that you studied. If you have completed a nonexperimental project, explain clearly what your research question was and illustrate your findings.

Related Projects

With the wide variety of flowers and their pollinators, there are numerous flower-related projects. You can use a magnifying glass to carefully dissect a flower, separating and labeling each of its parts. By doing this with several different types of flowers you can compare the flower parts. Flowers have several main attractants to pollinators: color, nectar, shape, and scent. You can examine the relationship between one or all of these with the pollinator. For example, you can examine the effect of flower scents on pollinators. You can look up techniques to capture the scent of a flower and then place the scents outside on the same substance.

Different species of flowers release pollen of varying appearance. You can collect and compare the pollen grains from several types of flowers. Look at how the grains from self-pollinators compares to cross-pollinators. You can also examine what types of pollinators are attracted to each of the pollen types. For a research paper, you can examine what the pollen grains offer the pollinator, such as protein, sugar, and shelter. Some flower species have evolved deceptive appearances and smells to entice pollinators that you could also observe and research. You could also look at the biology of pollination and map out the genetics of plant reproduction.

For More Information

Attenborough, David. *The Private Life of Plants: A Natural History of Plant Behaviour.* Princeton, NJ: Princeton University Press, 1995. ❖ These stories of plant life and survival feature plants from all over the world with full-color photographs.

Bailey, Jill. *Plants and Plant Life: Flowers & Fruits.* Danbury, CT: Grolier Educational, 2001. ❖ This volume of the series on plants covers reproduction.

Black, David, and Anthony Huxley. *Plants: The World of Science.* New York: Orbis Publishing, 1985. ❖ Contains comprehensive information on plants, with photographs.

Ganeri, Anita. *Plant Science.* New York: Dillon Press, 1993. ❖ Answers questions on basic plant characteristics and behavior.

Hopkin, Michael. "Flowers play rotten trick on flies: Insects fooled into fertilizing foul-smelling blooms." *Nature.* (December 12, 2002). http://www.nature.com/nsu/021209/021209-9.html (accessed on August 24, 2003) ❖ An article with photos and text about flowers that use smell to attract insects.

"Plants and Animals: Partners in Pollination." *Smithsonian Center for Education and Museum Studies.* http://educate.si.edu/resources/lessons/siyc/pollen/start.html (accessed on August 24, 2003) ❖ Covers various aspects of how animals help pollinate plants.

"Private Life of Plants: Flowering." *BBC Nature.* http://www.bbc.co.uk/nature/plants/plop/flowering.shtml (accessed on August 24, 2003) ❖ A short article on the pollination of flowering plants.

"Rice Anatomy." *Plant Biology Division of Biological Sciences, University of California, Davis.* http://www-plb.ucdavis.edu/labs/rost/Rice/reproduction/flower/flower.html (accessed on August 24, 2003) ❖ Shows the various reproductive components of rice flowers and how they interact.

Souza, D.M. *Freaky Flowers.* New York: Franklin Watts, 2002. ❖ Filled with photographs that show intriguing flowers from around the world.

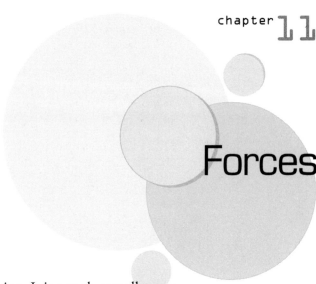

chapter 11

Forces

A **force** causes or changes an object's motion: It is a push or pull on an object. Forces have both a size and a direction. Forces also work in pairs: In order for a force to occur there must be an interaction between two objects. For example, when throwing a boomerang a person applies a force to the object that makes it move. Weightlifting exerts a force on the weight to pull it upward. These are forces that occur by physical contact between the two objects.

Yet forces also occur upon a person who is standing still. Forces are, in fact, occurring on everyone and everything on Earth, along with celestial objects. In these forces, two interacting objects exert a push or pull with no physical contact between them. An example of this force is **gravity.** Gravity is the force of attraction between any two objects in the universe.

Guiding principles

While there have been numerous contributors to people's knowledge of forces, English scientist Isaac Newton (1642–1727) formulated the laws of motion, the rules that explain how forces work. As he was working on the laws of motion, Newton also explained the effect of gravity throughout the universe. In 1687 Newton published his landmark work *Philosophiae Naturalis Principia Mathematica (Mathematical Principles of Natural Philosophy),* which gave people a new understanding of the universe and laid the foundation for the development of physics.

Newton developed three laws of motion to explain forces:

Words to Know

Acceleration:
The rate at which the velocity and/or direction of an object is changing with respect to time.

Centripetal force:
A force that pushes an object inward, which causes the object to move in a circular path.

Control experiment
A setup that is identical to the experiment, but is not affected by the variable that acts on the experimental group.

Words to Know

First law of motion (Newton's):
An object at rest or moving in a certain direction and speed will remain at rest or moving in the same motion and speed unless acted upon by a force.

Force:
A physical interaction (pushing or pulling) tending to change the state of motion (velocity) of an object.

Gravity:
Force of attraction between objects, the strength of which depends on the mass of each object and the distance between them.

Hypothesis:
An idea in the form of a statement that can be tested by observation and/or experiment.

Inertia:
The tendency of an object to continue in its state of motion.

First law of motion: With no force, an object at rest will stay at rest, and an object moving in a certain direction and speed will remain moving in that same path and **velocity.** Velocity is the speed of an object in a particular direction. This resistance of an object to change its motion is called **inertia.** The greater the mass of an object is, the more force is needed for the object to overcome its inertia. For example, a toy train moving around a track would require relatively little force to make it move compared with the push a real train would need.

Second law of motion: When a force acts upon an object it will accelerate. **Acceleration** is the rate of change in velocity. The acceleration of an object depends upon the size of the force and the mass of the object. The relationship between these variables in mathematical terms is: Force (F) = Mass of Object (m) x Acceleration of Object (a), or F = ma, which can also be written a = F/m. As the force increases, the acceleration will also increase. The more mass an object has, the lower the rate of acceleration.

An example of this law is evident when comparing the force need-ed to throw two objects, such as two balls. If Ball 1 has ten times the mass as Ball 2 and a pitcher throws the balls with equal force, then Ball 1 will accelerate at one-tenth the acceleration of the lighter ball. To make the two balls accelerate at the same rate, the pitcher will need to use ten times more force on Ball 1 than on Ball 2.

Newton's second law of motion: acceleration. For example, if someone throws two balls with equal force, the ball with the lower mass will have greater acceleration.

Third law of motion: For every action, there is an equal and oppo-site reaction. This law states that forces always work in pairs. When one force moving in a certain direction acts upon another force, then there must be a force of equal strength moving in the opposite direction.

There is usually more than one force at work. For example, when a boat is sitting still at the dock the force of gravity pulls with a downward force and the water responds with an equal and opposite upward force. A person who boards the boat and pushes it away from the dock exerts another force. The push starts the boat moving gradually away from the dock due to its inertia. Yet once moving, the boat will need that same amount of force to stop it. When the boat stops and the boater steps back onto the dock, that is another force. As the person steps off the boat with a push, the boat will move back in the opposite direction.

Round and round we go

Newton's laws explain both straight motion and circular motion. A force that causes an object to follow a circular path is called

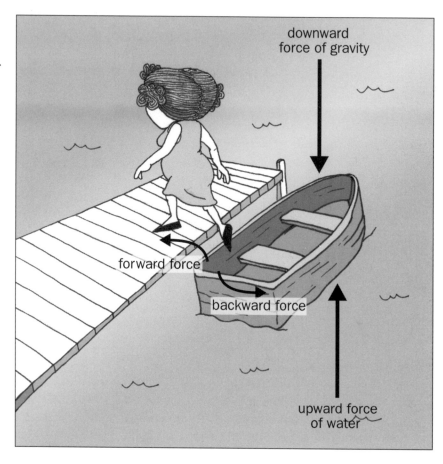

downward force of gravity

forward force

backward force

upward force of water

Newton's third law of motion: Forces always work in pairs. For example, when stepping off of a boat there are multiple forces at work.

centripetal force. The word centripetal comes from the Latin words *centrum* and *petere,* meaning center seeking. (This force is often confused with centrifugal force, meaning center fleeing. Centrifugal force is not considered a true force, as there is no force acting upon the object; it is only the tendency of the object to continue in a straight line. See Ocean chapter.) Anytime there is a circular movement around a central point, then centripetal force is at work.

Centripetal force is based on Newton's first law of motion that states an object will travel along a straight path with constant speed unless a force acts upon it. Thus, for a circular motion to occur, there must be a constant force pulling the object towards the center of the circle. This force is always directed inward. For a planet orbiting the Sun, the force is gravity; for a ball twirling on a string, the force is the tension in the string; for a loop in a roller coaster ride, the force is applied by the curved track.

In centripetal force, the inward force pulls the object or body away from its straight path to form a circular movement.

An object moving in a circle is constantly accelerating because it is continuously changing its direction. This is true even if the object is moving at a uniform speed. (Acceleration is a change in velocity and velocity is the speed of an object in a particular direction.) The amount of centripetal force needed to keep an object moving in a circular path depends upon its acceleration, along with its mass.

When the centripetal force is taken away, the object follows Newton's first and third laws: Its inertia causes the object to move in a straight line and the force by which it moves outward is equal in strength and opposite in direction.

Experiment 1
Newton's Laws in Action: How do water bottle rockets demonstrate Newton's laws of motion?

Purpose/Hypothesis
The laws of motion explain how force affects the movement of an object. Many objects such as trains, airplanes, and theme park rides demonstrate these laws. In this experiment, you will work with a water bottle rocket to observe Newton's laws. After constructing a basic launcher you will use a plastic two-liter bottle and water to mea-

sure the force required to lift the rocket. By adding water to the rocket, you will increase its mass.

A rocket exhibits all three of Newton's laws of motion. Newton's first law states that an object at rest will stay at rest, and an object in motion continues in motion. When the rocket is sitting on the launcher it is an object at rest. Once a force is applied to the rocket and it is in motion, it continues in motion. Newton's second law explains that when a force acts upon an object it causes the object to accelerate. This is seen when force—in this case, the pressure of the air pumped in the bottle by the tire pump—is exerted on the rocket. The rocket launches and accelerates in upward motion. Newton's third law refers to reactions, stating that for every action there is an equal and opposite reaction. When the rocket lifts, the air and water that filled the bottle are forced out of the spout in the opposite direction while propelling the rocket higher.

The rocket will be your object, either at rest or in motion. The force is the pressure of the air pumped inside the launcher. As the rocket propels forward, the water will escape and cause the mass to change.

Before you begin, make an educated guess about the outcome of this experiment based on your knowledge of rockets and Newton's laws of motion. This educated guess, or prediction, is your **hypothesis.** A hypothesis should explain these things:

- the topic of the experiment
- the **variable** you will change
- the variable you will measure
- what you expect to happen

A hypothesis should be brief, specific, and measurable. It must be something you can test through further investigation. Your experiment will prove or disprove whether your hypothesis is correct. Here is one possible hypothesis for this experiment: "The greater the amount of water in the rocket (bottle), the more air pressure (force) is required for launching."

In this case, the variable you will change is the mass (the amount of water in the rocket). The variable you will measure is the force (the air pressure in the rocket) required for liftoff.

Level of Difficulty

Difficult.

A rocket exhibits all three of Newton's laws of motion. (1) When the rocket is sitting on the launcher it is an object at rest. (2) Once a force is applied to the rocket and it is in motion, it continues in motion. (3) When the rocket lifts, propellants in the rocket are forced out in the opposite direction while propelling the rocket higher. (Reproduced by permission of AP/Wide World.)

What Are the Variables?

Variables are anything that might affect the results of an experiment. Here are the main variables in this experiment:

- the amount of water in the bottle
- the air pressure in the bottle
- the tightness of the seal between bottle and launcher
- thickness of the bottle
- preciseness of gauge on tire pump

In other words, the variables in this experiment are everything that might affect the mass of the rocket and the force applied by the compressed air inside. If you change more than one variable, you will not be able to tell which variable impacted the rocket liftoff.

Materials Needed

To build launcher:

- 5 feet (1.5 meters) of 3/4-inch CPVC pipe (available in the plumbing section of home improvement or hardware stores. It is generally a yellowish color and is sold in 10-foot (3-meter) lengths. Use a saw or PVC cutters to cut).
- 7 inches (18 centimeters) of 1/2-inch CPVC pipe
- T-joint fitting with 3/4-inch ends and a 1/2-inch center for CPVC pipe
- 45-degree elbow with 3/4-inch ends for CPVC pipe
- 90-degree elbow with 3/4-inch ends for CPVC pipe
- two end caps for 3/4-inch CPVC pipe
- PVC primer (minimal amount)
- PVC glue/cement (minimal amount)
- roll of masking tape (1/2- or 3/4-inch wide)
- 2 inches (5 centimeters) of 5/8-inch inner diameter clear vinyl tubing. (Available at hardware or home improvement store.)
- tire valve stem (Ask at a local tire store and explain it's for a science experiment; it may be possible to get a donation.)

- saw or PVC cutting tool
- drill
- paring knife
- expandable pipe wrench; it needs to have the capacity to hold the 3/4-inch cap
- scrap wood block
- safety goggles
- protractor

For launch:
- water
- bike tire pump with pressure gauge. Make sure it is a full-size pump. Small pumps that fit in a backpack may not create enough force.
- measuring cup
- 2-liter plastic soda bottle
- permanent marker
- paper towels or a drying rag
- tape measure
- open space
- partner and adult present when using tools

Approximate Budget
$18 (not counting the bicycle pump).

Timetable
1 hour to build; 30 minutes to dry; 30 minutes for experiment.

How to Experiment Safely
This is an involved experiment. It should be constructed and performed with the assistance of another person. Have an adult present when working with the drill and saw or similar cutting device. Wear safety goggles during construction. It is important to work in a well-ventilated area when working with PVC cement. The rocket should be launched in a large open area. Do not attempt to catch the rocket. It is also important to only use plastic bottles and not glass bottles.

Step-by-Step Instructions

To build the launcher:

1. From the 5-foot (1.5-meter) piece of the 3/4-inch pipe cut two 6-inch (15-centimeter) pieces and one 2-inch (5-centimeter) piece. The remaining piece should be approximately 46 inches (117 centimeters) long.

2. One person will clamp one of the 3/4-inch end caps with the wrench. Rest the cap on the scrap wood block to avoid drilling through the workspace. Have the helper drill a hole in the center of the PVC cap. The hole needs to be large enough for the tire stem to come part way through, approximately 1/4 inch. Check to ensure the tire valve is able to be pushed partway through the hole. It may be necessary to trim away part of the rubber around the valve stem. This may be done with a paring knife.

3. Glue the end cap to the 2-inch length of pipe: Push the valve stem partway through the 2-inch (5-centimeter) tube. Apply primer to the outside of the 2-inch (5-centimeter) pipe, the inside of the end cap, and a small amount to the base of the valve stem. Next, apply the glue over the primer. (Note: PVC glue dries very quickly and makes a lasting bond. Once the two pieces of CPVC touch, you have only a few seconds before they are connected forever.)

Steps 2 to 4 and Steps 7 to 11: Constructing the launcher.

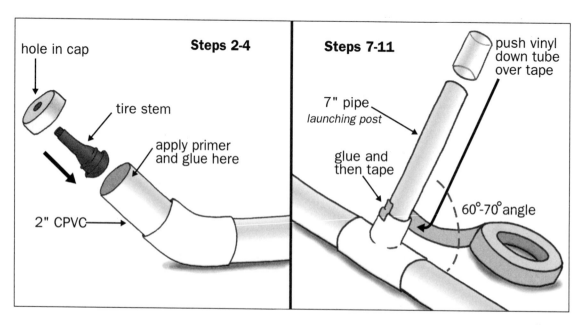

hole in cap

Steps 2-4

tire stem

apply primer and glue here

2" CPVC

Steps 7-11

push vinyl down tube over tape

7" pipe
launching post

glue and then tape

60°-70° angle

4. Hold the valve stem partway out of the 2-inch (5-centimeter) piece of pipe and place it through the hole on the end cap. The valve stem should stick out of the hole in the cap. Pull firmly and slightly twist the valve stem, making sure it is secure. Wipe away excess glue.

5. Connect the 46-inch (117-centimeter) piece of pipe to the 2-inch (5-centimeter) piece with the 45-degree elbow. Apply the primer and glue to the inside of the elbow and the outside of the long piece. Insert the pipe into the elbow. Next, apply to the other side of the elbow and the outside of the 2-inch piece. Firmly press the elbow on the 2-inch piece of pipe. Wipe away excess glue. Set aside to dry.

6. Cut a 7-inch (18-centimeter) length of the 1/2-inch pipe. This will become your launching post.

7. Connect the launching post to the T-joint fitting. Glue the two 3/4-inch CPVC pieces to the ends of the T-joint fitting. First apply the primer, then the glue again to the inside of the connector and the outside of the pipe. The 7-inch piece of 1/2-inch CPVC is then glued into the empty hole of the T-joint fitting.

8. Tape masking tape around the connection of the 1/2 in PCVC post and the T. It will be necessary to make several wraps and tapering the tape slightly (about an inch or two) up the post. Next, push the 2-inch piece of clear vinyl tubing down the tube and over the tape. Use an extra piece of the 3/4-inch PCVC to assist in pushing the tubing down snugly over the tape. The tape and tubing will create a stopper for the bottle to fit on.

9. Using your bottle, test to see if the tape and tubing will create a tight seal. If the seal is not tight, remove the tubing and add more tape.

10. Glue the 90-degree elbow to the long piece made in the first 5 steps.

11. Use your protractor to glue the T post to the 90-degree elbow. The post should create between a 70-degree and 60-degree angle with the ground, pointing away from the valve stem end of the launcher. Do not angle the post less than 45 degrees.

12. Allow launcher to sit about 30 minutes to dry.

To Launch:

1. In an open area, fill the 2-liter bottle with 2 cups (about 0.5 liter) of water.

Data for Rocket Launch (averages)

	Pressure/Force	Distance
2 cups water		
3 cups water		
4 cups water		

TOP:
Steps 3 and 4: Pump the tire pump to fill the bottle with air. Keep pumping at a slow and steady pace until the rocket launches.

BOTTOM:
Step 5: Data chart for rocket launch.

2. Place the launch post in the bottle and push for a snug fit. Mark this spot with a permanent marker. (It works best to turn the launcher slightly on its side, and gently "roll" it back to its standing position with the bottle on top. This way the water will not come out of the bottle.)

3. Attach the tire pump to the valve nozzle.

Troubleshooter's Guide

Below is a problem that may arise during this experiment, a possible cause, and a way to remedy the problem.

Problem: The rocket will not take off.

Possible cause: Make sure your seal is tight. Wipe the stopper off after each launch. Check the tire pump to determine if it is attached appropriately. The pump may be too weak to perform the launch.

4. Pump the tire pump to fill the bottle with air. Keep pumping at a slow and steady pace until the rocket launches. The helper should note the gauge and record the pressure required for liftoff.
5. Repeat launch for two more trials, noting the force (air pressure) and distance for each trial.
6. Fill the 2-liter bottle with 3 cups (about 0.75 liter) of water.
7. Repeat Steps 2 through 5.
8. Fill the 2-liter bottle with 4 cups (about 1.0 liter) of water.
9. Repeat Steps 2 through 5.

Summary of Results

Examine your results to determine which amount of water required the greatest amount of force for liftoff? Was your hypothesis correct? Hypothesize what would happen if you changed the bottle size, and maintained the water amount. What would occur if a cone top and wings were attached to the rocket? Write a brief summary of the experiment and your analysis.

Change the Variables

There are several ways you can modify the experiment by changing the variables. You can change the sizes of the bottle and maintain the water amount. Another approach could include using various bottle sizes and filling each bottle to half of capacity, rather than a uniform water amount. If you have access to a football field, you could perform the experiment on the field and attempt to measure the distance of each launch. It may be beneficial to prop the launcher on a block of wood to create more of an angle (do not go less than 45 degrees).

experiment
CENTRAL

Experiment 2
Centripetal Action: What is the relationship between distance and force in circular motion?

Purpose/Hypothesis

Centripetal force is any force that acts on an object at a right angle to its path of motion. The constant right angle force results in the object moving in a circular path. In this experiment, you will examine how altering the force and radius will affect the acceleration of an object. **Radius** is the distance from the center to the outer point of a circle. The object's mass will stay the same.

A piece of string will have a mass attached to one end and washers creating the force attached to the other end. You will first alter the radius, and then alter the force. For a more accurate measure of how many times the mass completes a circle or revolution, you will count how many times it revolves in 30 seconds. That number will then be divided by 30 to give its revolutions per second. Another way to increase accuracy is to complete three trials of each experimental trial.

Comparing the results to a **control experiment** will help you isolate each variable and measure the changes in the dependent variable. In this experiment there will be two variables that you will change, one at a time. Only one variable will change between the control and the experimental setup each time. In the first part, the distance will change when the radius increases. In the second part, the force will change. At the end of the experiment you can compare each of the results to the standard experiment.

Before you begin, make an educated guess about the outcome of this experiment based on your knowledge of centripetal force. This educated guess, or prediction, is your **hypothesis.** A hypothesis should explain these things:

- the topic of the experiment
- the **variable** you will change
- the variable you will measure
- what you expect to happen

A hypothesis should be brief, specific, and measurable. It must be something you can test through further investigation. Your experiment will prove or disprove whether your hypothesis is correct. Here is one pos-

What Are the Variables?

Variables are anything that might affect the results of an experiment. Here are the main variables in this experiment:

- the force
- the radius
- the mass

In other words, the variables in this experiment are everything that might affect the acceleration of the mass. If you change more than one variable at the same time, you will not be able to tell which variable had the most effect on centripetal force.

sible hypothesis for this experiment: "The greater the force, the greater the acceleration; the greater the radius; the lower the acceleration."

In this case, the variable you will change is the force and the distance, one at a time. The variable you will measure is the acceleration of the mass.

Level of Difficulty
Easy to Moderate.

Materials Needed
- spool of thread with narrow hole
- ruler
- ten metal washers of equal size
- 3 feet (90 centimeters) of string
- masking tape
- watch with second hand
- bobbin, small spool of thread, rubber stopper or other lightweight object that can be easily tied
- helper

Approximate Budget
$2.

Timetable
30 minutes.

How to Experiment Safely

Be careful when swinging the mass and check to ensure the knot is tight. Make sure you are working in an open area.

Step-by-Step Instructions

1. Slide the string in the large spool of thread and move the spool up 2 feet (0.6 meters).
2. On the long side of the string, attach four metal washers (this is the force) to the end and secure with a knot.
3. Tie the bobbin or rubber stopper to the end of the short side of the string. This is the mass.
4. Wind a piece of tape about 1 inch (2.5 centimeters) below the spool to make sure it does not slide down and change the radius. Mark the string at the point above the tape.
5. Hold the washers with one hand and begin to swing the mass until it is moving parallel to the floor. Practice swinging at a steady rate.
6. While you are swinging, have your helper time 30 seconds and count the number of revolutions the bobbin makes.

Steps 5 and 6: Count the number of revolutions of the mass in 30 seconds.

7. Repeat Step 6 two more times so that you have three trials. This is your standard experiment.

8. Remove the tape and slide the spool down 1 foot (0.3 meters) towards the washers. Reattach the tape about 1 inch (2.5 centimeters) below the spool.

9. Again, time the number of revolu-

Troubleshooter's Guide

Below is a problem that may arise during this experiment, a possible cause, and a way to remedy the problem.

Problem: The radius looked like it was changing.

Possible cause: The paperclip might have slid loose. Use a tight paperclip and make sure it is attached firmly, then repeat the experiment.

tions in a 30-second period, then repeat for two more trials. Note the results.

10. Return the spool to its beginning position, reattaching the tape at the marked point on the string.

11. Double the number of washers to eight. Support the washers until you have a steady swing and then have your helper time 30 seconds while you count the revolutions. Repeat two more times and note the results.

Summary of Results

Determine the time for each revolution per second by dividing the total revolutions by 30. Once you have the revolutions per second for each trial, average the three trials. Make a chart of your data. Compare how long it took to complete a full circle when the radius lengthened. How much force would it take to have the revolutions of different radiuses be the same. Look at how the increased force compares with the acceleration of the lesser force? What would happen to the acceleration if you halved the force? Hypothesize how the force and/or radius would need to change if the mass was doubled and you wanted to keep the acceleration equal.

Change the Variables

You can continue to experiment on changing the variables in this experiment in new ways and new combinations. Try to halve the force and halve the radius. Look at what occurs if the radius is tripled and the force remains constant. You can also change the mass of the object, making it lighter or heavier. Make sure you secure the mass tightly to the string and try to work in an open area.

Design Your Own Experiment

How to Select a Topic Relating to this Concept

Force is a broad topic that has many possible experiments. To gather ideas on force, you can observe how force is applied in daily life. Look at sporting events and playground rides to see the application of Newton's laws and centripetal force. You could also research how celestial bodies in the universe apply centripetal force.

Check the For More Information section and talk with your science or physics teacher to learn more about force.

Steps in the Scientific Method

To conduct an original experiment, you need to plan carefully and think things through. Otherwise, you might not be sure what question you are answering, what you are or should be measuring, or what your findings prove or disprove.

Here are the steps in designing an experiment:

- State the purpose of—and the underlying question behind—the experiment you propose to do.
- Recognize the variables involved and select one that will help you answer the question at hand.

A planet orbits a sunlike star. Astronomers depend on the principles of centripetal force to help them predict orbits and revolutions. (© AFP/CORBIS. Reproduced by permission.)

- State your hypothesis, an educated guess about the answer to your question.
- Decide how to change the variable you selected.
- Decide how to measure your results.

Recording Data and Summarizing the Results

Your data could include charts and graphs to display your data. If included, they should be clearly labeled and easy to read. You may also want to include photographs and drawings of your experimental setup and results, which will help other people visualize the steps in the experiment.

If you are preparing an exhibit, you may want to display your results, such as any experimental setup you designed. If you have completed a nonexperimental project, explain clearly what your research question was and illustrate your findings.

Related Projects

There are many possible projects related to force. You could construct simple machines to experiment with the amount of force required for work. These projects could explore how force varies with distance and mass. Astronomers depend on the principles of centripetal force to help them predict orbits and revolutions. You could examine how the planets, suns, and moons each have their own unique orbits due to the principles behind centripetal force. You could also explore the force of gravity with everyday objects.

For More Information

Christianson, Gale E. *Isaac Newton and the Scientific Revolution.* New York: Oxford University Press, 1998. ❖ The personal life story of Newton and his work.

Clark, John O. E. *Physics Matters!* Danbury, CT: Grolier Education, 2001. ❖ Provides a clear explanation of the science of physics with pictures and applications.

"Newton's Laws of Motion." *NASA Glenn Research Center.* http://www.grc.nasa.gov/WWW/K-12/airplane/newton.html (accessed on August 24, 2003) ❖ Explanations and illustrations of Newton's laws of motion presented with different details for different grade levels.

"Skateboard Science." *The Exploratorium.* http://www.exploratorium.edu/skateboarding (accessed on August 24, 2003) ❖ A look at the science of skateboarding and how it relates to centripetal force.

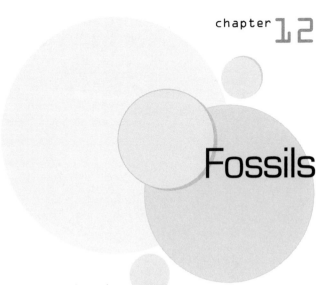

chapter 12

Fossils

From dinosaurs to prehistoric humans, fossils provide a glimpse into Earth's past events, environment, and life forms. **Fossils** are the remains or traces of ancient organisms. Fossils can range in age from a mere ten thousand years to several billion years old. They can be microscopic or hundreds of feet long. From the Latin word *fossilis,* meaning something dug up, fossils are found on every continent. Scientists who study fossils are called **paleontologists.**

Studying fossils has revealed a wealth of data about Earth's 4.6 billion-year-old history, including its past geography, weather, animals, plants, biodiversity, and how life has changed over time. Fossils can provide information on past environmental conditions. Different types of plants, for example, require specific temperature, acidity, and amounts of water to live. By studying fossils, scientists can also determine an ancient animal's age, health, eating habits, and movements. Unearthing 3.5 billion-year-old bacteria fossils led to theories on when life began and how it impacted the development of future life. Other fossil evidence shows how continents have shifted over time. Fossils can also create an understanding of modern Earth and how people can best preserve the planet.

Until about two centuries ago, fossils were mysterious objects that cultures explained in varying ways. Some theorized that fossils were weapons left behind from the gods; others believed they were the seeds of adult animals, or the remains of animals that did not make it onto Noah's ark. In the 1800s, scientists began turning up fossils of strange animals by the thousands: the giant reptilian *ichthyosaur,* the

Words to Know

Absolute dating:
The age of an object correlated to a specific fixed time, as established by some precise dating method.

Cast:
In paleontology, the fossil formed when a mold is later filled in by mud or mineral matter.

Coprolites:
The fossilized droppings of animals.

Control experiment
A setup that is identical to the experiment, but is not affected by the variable that acts on the experimental group.

Did You Know?

- The fossil record shows a lot of extinct species: Scientists theorize that of all the species that ever lived on Earth, over 90 percent of them are now extinct.

- Most of the dinosaur skeletons shown in museums are lightweight replicas of the original fossils to prevent damage and to keep the originals available for study.

- History is filled with important fossils discovered by amateurs. In 1990, amateur fossil hunter Sue Hendrickson discovered the largest, most complete, and best-preserved *Tyrannosaurus rex*—it was 67 million years old and had a 5-foot-long (1.5-meter-long) skull.

- In 2002 the oldest known skull related to humans was uncovered in Africa, a six-to-seven-million-year-old relic of our past.

- In 2001 researchers found the largest, most complete fossil of a cockroach—it was about the size of a mouse and lived 55 million years before the first dinosaurs.

- Along with fossil dung, scientists also study fossil vomit. In 2002 scientists discovered what they estimate is the world's oldest fossilized vomit, believed to be from a 160-million-year-old marine reptile!

Words to Know

Fossil:
The remains, trace, or impressions of a living organism that inhabited Earth more than ten thousand years ago.

Fossil record:
The documentation of fossils placed in relationship to one another; a key source to understand the evolution of life on Earth.

Hypothesis:
An idea in the form of a statement that can be tested by observation and/or experiment.

Mold:
In paleontology, the fossil formed when acidic water dissolves a shell or bone around which sand or mud has already hardened.

Paleontologist:
Scientist who studies the life of past geological periods as known from fossil remains.

40-foot-long *Megalosaurus,* and teeth from the immense plant-eating *Iguanodon.* People began to understand what fossils were and, in the late 1800s, fossil hunting began in earnest.

Ancient rock formations

The vast majority of living organisms live, die, and decay without leaving behind any physical trace of their existence. Paleontologists estimate that only about 1 to 2 percent of all life forms ever become fossils. In order for a fossil to form, a number of conditions must occur simultaneously. Where an organism settles after death and its surroundings are the main factors that determine fossil formation.

experiment
CENTRAL

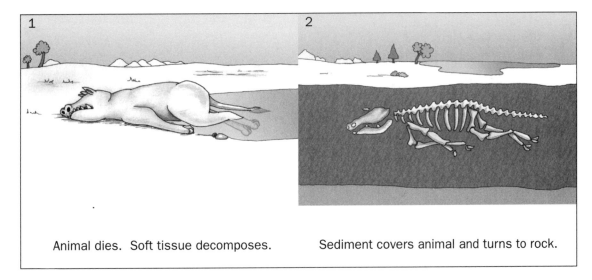

| 1 | 2 |
| Animal dies. Soft tissue decomposes. | Sediment covers animal and turns to rock. |

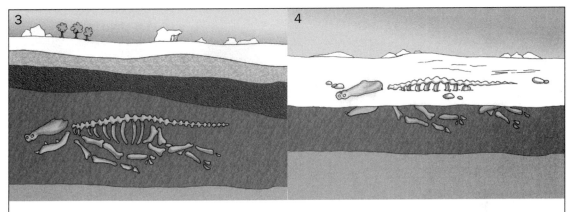

| 3 | 4 |
| Bones are replaced by minerals. New layers of rock form over millions of years. | Shifting in Earth causes bones to come to the surface. |

Fossils occur in rocks. The majority of fossils are found in a type of rock called **sedimentary rock.** Sedimentary rock forms when **sediment** particles—such as mud, sand, and gravel—settle and form rock. The sediments build up in layers. Thus, the oldest rocks normally lie on the bottom layer and the youngest at the top. Sedimentary rock is the type of rock most exposed at Earth's surface. Shale, limestone, and sandstone are examples of sedimentary rock.

One common fossilization process, called **permineralization,** creates a three-dimensional replica of the remains when minerals replace some or all of the organic matter. The first step in permineralization is

TOP:
Turning bone into rock: the fossilization process of permineralization.

BOTTOM:
Permineralization continues. When the organic matter is completely replaced by minerals it is called petrifaction.

for a dead organism to become buried in sediment quickly, before it is eaten or decomposed by other organisms. Over the next several hundred thousand years, layers of sediments cover the dead organism.

The quicker a dead organism is covered with layers of sediment the greater its chance of being preserved. How quickly sediment covers a dead life form also determines the degree of preservation. Organisms are made up of soft parts, such as skin and tissue, which decompose quickly. Animals will eat them, microorganisms will break them down, and weather will erode them. In general, these parts decompose before they are protected by sediments, leaving only the hard parts of the dead organism, such as teeth, bones, and shells.

As the sediment turns into rock, minerals and water from the rock seep into the remains. Slowly, these minerals fill in the open pore spaces of the organism's remains. When the organic matter is completely replaced by minerals it is called **petrifaction.** The result is a duplicate of the structure made of rock. Petrifaction commonly occurs in wood. One of the largest examples of petrifaction is at the Petrified Forest National Park in Arizona, which holds acres of 200-million-year-old logs that have turned to stone.

Even after a fossil is formed, a set of circumstances still must occur before it can be found. Shifting landmasses, weather eruptions, and natural disasters can destroy the fossil. The rock must also move towards a top layer of Earth in order for it to be exposed. This may occur over millions of years as the rock is pushed to the surface, or human activity can expose it.

Forming other fossils

Another type of fossil occurs when no part of the organism's body remains. A fossil **mold** is an imprint of a bone, shell, or other hard body part. A mold forms when the dead organism settles in sediment and then decays, leaving an outline of its shape. If the mold fills with minerals it is called a **cast.** The rock cast has the same outer three-dimensional shape as the organism. Paleontologists often create casts of fossil molds by filling them with liquids, such as plaster, that harden.

Body parts of ancient plants, insects, spiders, and other small animals are also found preserved in tree resin. Fossils form when one of these creatures becomes trapped inside the sticky resin, which hardens to become a substance called amber. These life forms are often preserved with incredible detail. Some are so well preserved that scientists

Words to Know

Permineralization:
A form of preservation in which mineral matter has filled in the inner and outer spaces of the cell.

Petrifaction:
Process of turning organic material into rock by the replacement of that material with minerals.

Radioisotope dating:
A technique used to date fossils, based on the decay rate of known radioactive elements.

Relative age:
The age of an object expressed in relation to another like object, such as earlier or later.

Sediment
Sand, silt, clay, rock, gravel, mud, or other matter that has been transported by flowing water.

have attempted to extract the organism's genetic material, the deoxyribonucleic acid (DNA) molecule.

Fossils that are not part of the animal or plant are called **trace fossils.** Examples of trace fossils include footprints, tunnels, and dung. Trace fossils provide evidence of the organism's physical characteristics, eating habits, and activities. Examining fossilized droppings or dung, called **coprolites,** can supply evidence of where an animal lived and what it ate. A footprint can reveal an animal's weight, size, and whether it hopped, sprinted, or walked.

Because an animal sets down many hundreds of thousands of traces during its lifetime, but leaves only one body, paleontologists find trace fossils far more frequently than body fossils.

The dating game

In order to piece together a timeline of life on Earth, scientists need to understand a fossil's age and how it relates to others. This information

The imprint of a 200-million-year-old fossilized plant discovered in 2002. (Reproduced by permission of AP/Wide World.)

Words to Know

Sedimentary rock:
Rock formed from compressed and solidified layers of organic or inorganic matter.

Variable:
Something that can affect the results of an experiment.

for all fossils is documented in the **fossil record,** a key source in understanding how species have evolved. Some organisms dominate the fossil record more than others because of certain physical characteristics. For example, fossils of animals without bones or shells are far more rare than those with hard parts. Marine animals are preserved more readily than land animals because they are more likely to be preserved in soft sediment. This is one reason why estimating the existence span of a species, its first appearance until its extinction, is one of the most challenging parts of the fossil record.

One way to date a fossil is to determine its **relative age,** or how old it is in relation to other fossils or rocks. Unless the rock layers were overturned, fossils found in lower rock layers would be older than those found in upper layers. Fossilized rock with similar features and different locations are compared and placed relative to each other in the fossil record.

The fossil record traces organisms through Earth's history.

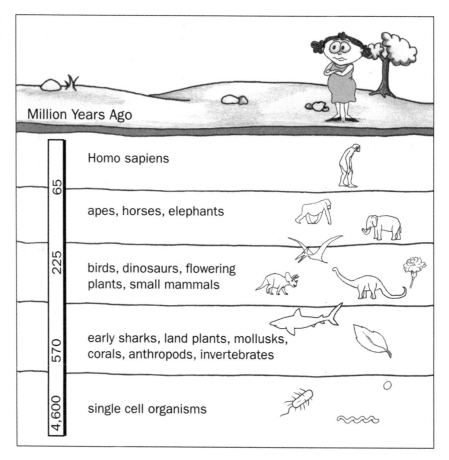

Million Years Ago

65	Homo sapiens
225	apes, horses, elephants
570	birds, dinosaurs, flowering plants, small mammals
4,600	early sharks, land plants, mollusks, corals, anthropods, invertebrates
	single cell organisms

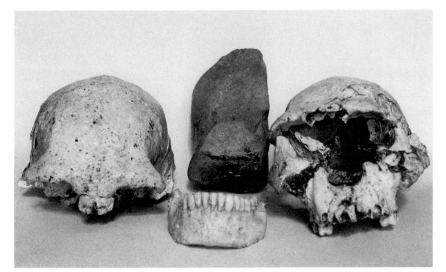

Discovered in the European nation of Georgia and dated by scientists at 1.7 million years, these partial human-like skulls are the oldest human ancestral fossils ever found outside of Africa. (Reproduced by permission of AP/Wide World.)

Absolute dating is a more precise approach that determines how many years old the fossil is from the current year. These methods were developed in the twentieth century with the findings of the known rate of decay of certain radioactive elements. Each element decays at its own constant and unique rate. **Radioisotope dating** techniques measure the amount of a certain element in nearby rocks to date the fossil.

While relatively precise, absolute dating provides only an approximate date for the organism, accurate to hundreds of thousands of years. One type of absolute dating method examines the amount of the element carbon 14 found in the rock. All plant and animal life absorb carbon 14, and its rate of decomposition is known. This method is useful on material that is less than about 50,000 years old, which includes many human remains but excludes most fossils. For older fossils, scientists measure the amount of other radioactive elements left in rock, such as potassium, thorium, and uranium.

Experiment 1
Making an Impression: In which soil environment does a fossil most easily form?

Purpose/Hypothesis

Paleontologists have found fossils on every continent, yet some areas contain more fossils than others. One of the key factors leading to fossil formation is the type of sediment or material in which a dead organism settles. (Most organisms settle where they die; in some cases a river, wind, or animals can carry the organism to another location.) Scientist use fossils to study and determine the lifestyles and adaptations of plants and animals. The more details found in a fossil, the more information the scientists gain.

In this experiment, you will determine how the soil makeup of different geographical areas impacts the number of fossil casts formed. You will make three fossil casts in three soils of varying moisture content. One of the soils will be dry sand. Sand is made up of large particles and does not hold moisture. A second type of soil will be a mixture between sand and moist topsoil, which is made up of smaller soil particles that retain water. The third soil will be a wet topsoil.

These soils will be the foundation layer for a plaster of paris cast. Using one object, a shell, you will first press the organism into each soil to equal depths. The plaster of paris will form a cast from this mold. This cast will be the fossil.

To begin this experiment, make an educated guess about the outcome of the experiment based upon your knowledge of fossils and sediment. This educated guess, or prediction, is your **hypothesis.** A hypothesis should explain these things:

- the topic of the experiment
- the **variable** you will change
- the variable you will measure
- what you expect to happen

A hypothesis should be brief, specific, and measurable. It must be something you can test through further investigation. Your experiment will prove or disprove whether your hypothesis is correct. Here is one possible hypothesis for this experiment: "The moist soil will make the best fossil impression; the dry material will not be firm enough to cause a fossil to form."

Once you have gathered your soil bases you need to make your impressions. It is best to use a seashell with distinguishing qualities such as scallops, ridges, and possibly an erosion hole or chip.

The variable you will change will be the soil. The variable you will measure will be the general shape and amount of detail of the impression. The item you use to make the impression should stay the same.

What Are the Variables?

Variables are anything that might affect the results of an experiment. Here are the main variables in this experiment:

- the soil makeup

- the consistency of the plaster of paris

- the object/organism

- the depth the object is pressed

In other words, the variables in this experiment are everything that might affect the ability of the object to make an impression. If you change more than one variable at the same time, you will not be able to tell which variable had the most effect on the impression.

Level of Difficulty

Easy to Moderate.

Materials Needed

- plaster of paris (available at craft stores)
- shell, preferably one with identifiable features such as a hole, chip, or alternate mark
- three small disposable containers, such as a butter dish, large enough to fit the shell
- water
- disposable spoons
- measuring spoon
- ruler
- straw
- tweezers
- marking pen
- bowl
- 3 cups (0.75 liters) of sand (available at garden store)
- 3 cups (0.75 liters) of moist, organic topsoil (available at garden store)

Approximate Budget

$5 to $10.

Timetable

1 hour for the experiment; overnight for the plaster of paris to harden.

Step-by-Step Instructions

1. Make a sketch of your shell, noting the width, depth, and any identifiable features.
2. In a bowl, mix 1 cup (about 0.25 liters) of moist topsoil with 1 cup (about 0.25 liters) of sand. This is the moist soil.
3. Mix 2 cups (about 0.5 liters) of topsoil with 8 tablespoons (about 120 milliliters) water. This is the wet soil.
4. Label each container with the type of soil and place each soil type into the appropriate container. The soil should be at least 2 inches (5 centimeters) deep. Even out the surface of the soil.

Step 6: Push the straw down until the mark on the straw is level with the soil.

experiment
CENTRAL

How to Experiment Safely
Be careful when removing your fossil casts; plastic containers may break.

5. Use the ruler to mark a line on the straw at 0.8 inches (2 centimeters).
6. Place your shell in the soil with the ridges facing down. Gently place the straw in the center of the shell. Push the straw down with your pointer finger until the mark on the straw is level with the soil.
7. Using tweezers, carefully remove your shell.
8. Wash and dry the shell. Repeat Step 6 for the other two soil samples.
9. Mix enough plaster of paris to make a 1-inch-deep (2.5-centimeters) layer in each container. The plaster should be the consistency of thick pudding.
10. Pour a layer of plaster of paris into each container.
11. Allow plaster to harden overnight.
12. Remove your fossil casts by slipping a butter knife or similar thin object in the side between the soil, fossil, and container. It may be necessary to break the plastic containers.
13. Make sketches of each cast. (If a digital camera or polaroid is available, you could take pictures.) Include any measurements of width and depth you are able to determine from your fossil cast.

Summary of Results
Review the sketches of the casts compared to that of the shell. Which soil type is best for making fossils? What qualities did you compare to determine the best soil? Note on the sketch or photograph where any information can be observed on the fossil. For example, a shell may have a hole in one point that can indicate erosion. What type(s) of environments do you feel are most suitable for fossils to form? From your conclusions, how would the environment impact the study of species through fossils?

Change the Variables
To change the variable in this experiment, you could use different objects to make the cast. Try both heavier and lighter objects. You

could also change the soil type, creating a wet mud soil and comparing that to the dry sand. Another way to alter the experiment is to vary the thickness of the soil layer.

Experiment 2
Fossil Formation: What are the physical characteristics of an organism that make the best fossils?

Purpose/Hypothesis

Organisms vary from the microscopic and jelly-bodied to the mammoth and skeletal. The physical characteristics of the organism and its environment are two key factors in forming a fossil. Dating back about 3,500 million years, the fossil record does not represent all types of organisms equally. Paleontologists theorize that many groups of animals and plants have left no fossil remains. There are some types of organisms that are more dominant in the record than others. There are some organisms that have hard parts, some with only soft parts, and many with both. Examples of hard parts include bones, teeth, and wood; examples of soft parts include skin, muscle, and internal organs.

In this experiment, you will examine how an organism's characteristics determine the fossil remains left behind. You will create a fossil mold out of four different types of organisms or parts from organisms.

You will begin by preparing a clay base for each of the items you are going to fossilize. Clay is a soft, moist substance similar to the watery sediment that preserves many fossils. You will first select four organisms to observe from four different categories: an exoskeleton, meaning skeletal bones on the outside; an endoskeleton, meaning an internal skeleton; an organism without a skeleton; and a plant. Examples of these four categories are a shell (exoskeleton), chicken bone (endoskeleton), feather (lacking a skeleton), and a leaf (plant).

Each organism has physical characteristics that you can note before forming its imprint. Characteristics include if the organism has hard or soft parts, its shape, width, height, and any distinguishing features. To form an imprint you will drop a heavy book from the same height to make sure you use the same amount of pressure for each organism. After making an imprint of each organism, you can then compare the characteristics of the organism and the fossil imprint it makes.

Before you begin, make an educated guess about the outcome of this experiment based on your knowledge of fossilization. This educated guess, or prediction, is your **hypothesis**. A hypothesis should explain these things:

- the topic of the experiment
- the **variable** you will change

What Are the Variables?

Variables are anything that might affect the results of an experiment. Here are the main variables in this experiment:

- the hardness of the organism

- the definable shape of the organism

- the flexibility of the organism

- force applied to make mold

- placement of the object on clay base

In other words, the variables in this experiment are everything that might affect the organism's imprint. If you change more than one variable at the same time, you will not be able to tell which variable had the most effect on the physical characteristics of each organism's mold.

- the variable you will measure
- what you expect to happen

A hypothesis should be brief, specific, and measurable. It must be something you can test through further investigation. Your experiment will prove or disprove whether your hypothesis is correct. Here is one possible hypothesis for this experiment: "The feather will produce a poor fossil that is difficult to identify because it has no specific shape or form; the chicken bone will produce the best fossil imprint."

In this case, the variable you will change is the organism. The variable you will measure is the physical characteristics of the mold created by the organism.

Level of Difficulty
Moderate.

Materials Needed
- modeling clay
- plant (leaf, fern)
- chicken bone, or another small bone
- shell (or other object to represent an endoskeleton)
- feather (or other object lacking a skeleton)
- heavy book
- ruler
- pencils
- magnifying lens
- wax paper
- tape
- four pieces of cardboard

Approximate Budget
$8.

Timetable
60 to 90 minutes.

Step-by-Step Instructions
1. Create a data chart, listing the organisms across the top columns and the observable characteristics down the sides. Make the chart boxes large enough to illustrate your observation and include descriptive words.

experiment
CENTRAL

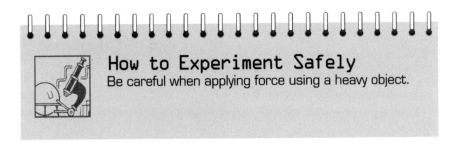

2. Feel each organism prior to making the fossil mold and note whether it is hard, soft, or both.

3. Draw a sketch of your organism. Measure the height and width and include in the sketch.

4. Cover each piece of cardboard with a sheet of wax paper, and then create four clay bases. Make the bases of equal size and thickness. The base should be about twice as high as the highest organisms,

Step 1: Data chart for Experiment 2.

	shell	bone	feather	fern
hard/softness of organism				
sketch of organism's shape				
sketch of mold's shape				
features of organism				
features of mold				
height & width of organism				
height & width of mold				

and be at least 1 inch (2.5 centimeter) larger in diameter than the largest object.

5. Gently place the first organism in the center of the first clay base. Do not apply pressure.

6. Place the clay base against a wall (or any flat, vertical object) and tape the ruler against the wall perpendicular to the base. Hold the book about 2 inches (5 centimeters) above the clay base with the organism on it, and drop the book. The height of the book above the organism does not have to be exactly 2 inches (5 centimeters); however, whatever the height is, use that same height for all organisms.

7. Remove the book and gently remove the organism.

8. Repeat Steps 5 through 7 for each organism.

9. Use the ruler to reexamine the same physical characteristics that you noted for the organism and note the results on your chart. Use the magnifying glass to observe any distinguishing features in the mold.

Step 6: Drop a heavy object from the same height onto each organism.

Troubleshooter's Guide

Below is a problem that may arise during this experiment, a possible cause, and a way to remedy the problem.

Problem: There was no imprint on any or most of the objects.

Possible cause: You may not have used enough force to press down on the object. Repeat the experiment, using a heavier book or raising the book to a higher measurement on the ruler.

Summary of Results

Examine your chart. Which qualities are the most varied among your organisms? Which mold provides the most accurate information? How does the detail of the mold relate to whether the organism is hard or soft? What are some other characteristics on the organism that the mold does not convey? Hypothesize what would occur to each material if you used a lighter book. Analyze what would happen to each organism if it was turned over and the imprint was made of the other side. Write a brief summary of the experiment and your analysis.

Change the Variables

There are several ways you can modify the experiment by changing the variables. You can change the organisms you use. Try several different samples from the same class; for example, in the plants you could use a flower, a leaf, and a cactus. You can also alter the substance that sets the imprint formation. You could try dough made of a mixture of used coffee grounds, cold coffee, flour, and salt. How would this moist base impact your experiment? Another way to alter the variable is to change the force used to press down on the object in the clay.

Design Your Own Experiment

How to Select a Topic Relating to this Concept

Fossils open a window into Earth's life, geography, and environment that can reach back billions of years. To think of fossil-related pro-

Paleontologists excavating a fossil bed in Utah, circa 1984. (© James L. Amos/CORBIS. Reproduced by permission.)

jects, you can make a list of ancient events and people you have learned about and consider how fossils could have been used to gather the data.

Check the For More Information section and talk with your science teacher to learn more about fossils. You can also gather ideas for topics by visiting a natural history museum or science museum.

Steps in the Scientific Method

To conduct an original experiment, you need to plan carefully and think things through. Otherwise, you might not be sure what question you are answering, what you are or should be measuring, or what your findings prove or disprove.

Here are the steps in designing an experiment:

- State the purpose of—and the underlying question behind—the experiment you propose to do.
- Recognize the variables involved and select one that will help you answer the question at hand.
- State your hypothesis, an educated guess about the answer to your question.
- Decide how to change the variable you selected.
- Decide how to measure your results.

Recording Data and Summarizing the Results

In any experiment you conduct, you should look for ways to clearly convey your data. Your data should include charts and drawings such as the one you did for these experiments. They should be clearly labeled and easy to read. You may also want to include photographs and drawings of your experimental setup and results, which will help other people visualize the steps in the experiment.

If you are preparing an exhibit, you may want to display your results, such as any experimental setup you designed. If you have completed a nonexperimental project, explain clearly what your research question was and illustrate your findings.

Related Projects

There are many project ideas that relate to fossils. If there is a museum or university in the area in which you can see fossils, you can compare the different types of preservation, including petrifaction and fossils preserved in amber (these are sold by several companies). For a research project, you could explore the environmental conditions of areas that are rich with fossils, both in the United States and other parts of the world. You can explore fossil molds and imprints by examining how the environment or other factors play a part in the fossilization process.

How paleontologists collect fossils is another area of study. Identifying and collecting fossils is a meticulous process that requires many skills. There are many organizations and companies that offer fossil hunts, complete with lessons on how to locate, unearth, and identify fossils. Dinosaurs are a popular topic for documentaries and movies. You can examine these films to look at how the filmmakers reached their representation of these creatures, how much of it was artistic freedom, and what was taken from the fossil record. For example, do paleontologists know that dinosaurs were certain colors? How do the more modern representations of dinosaurs differ from those made in the mid-1900s?

For More Information

Clarke, Tom. "Oldest fossil footprints on land: Animals may have beaten upright plants to land." *Nature.* http://www.nature.com/nsu/020429/020429-2.html (accessed on August 25, 2003) ❖ Description of a recent fossil discovery that may prove animals, not plants, were the first form of life to venture out of the ocean onto land.

"Dino-Era Vomit Fossil Found in England." *National Geographic News,* (February 12, 2002). http://news.nationalgeographic.com/news/2002/02/0212_020212_

dinovomit.html (accessed on August 25, 2003). ❖ Story on fossil vomit discovery, with lots of links to other dinosaur news stories and sites.

Kittinger, Jo S. *Stories in Stone: The World of Animal Fossils.* New York: Franklin Watts, 1998. ❖ Photographs accompany information on various types of fossils and how they help people understand life on Earth.

"Largest fossil cockroach found." *BBC News.* http://news.bbc.co.uk/2/hi/science/nature/1640807.stm (accessed on August 25, 2003). ❖ Information about the fossil of an ancient cockroach that was as big as a mouse.

"Museum of Paleontology." *University of California, Berkeley.* http://www.ucmp.berkeley.edu/index.html (accessed on August 25, 2003). ❖ Information on many aspects of studying fossils.

"Rocks and Layers." *U.S. Geological Survey.* http://pubs.usgs.gov/gip/fossils/rocks-layers.html (accessed on August 25, 2003). ❖ Brief description of where fossils are found in rocks.

Trueit, Trudi Strain. *Fossils.* New York: Franklin Watts, 2003. ❖ What fossils look like, and how paleontologists use them to understand Earth.

"Walking with Dinosaurs: How Do We Know?" *BBC News.* http://www.bbc.co.uk/dinosaurs/howdoweknow/ (accessed on August 25, 2003). ❖ Clear explanations about dinosaur fossils.

chapter 13

Fungi

As a way of organizing living things, scientists have created five main classifications called **kingdoms** (some scientists use more than five). Each kingdom breaks down into smaller and smaller classifications. Plants and animals, for example, are two of these kingdoms. **Fungi** form another kingdom.

There are thousands of types of fungi. They are both single-celled and multicelled; living on land and in water. They include the microscopic, such as yeasts, and the relatively mammoth, such as mushrooms. Scoop up a single teaspoon of topsoil and you will find about 120,000 fungi. As of 2003, the largest living organism on Earth is a fungus, dubbed the humongous fungus, which extends about 3.5 miles (5.6 kilometers).

Fungi play a vital role in Earth's cycle of life. They decompose or break down dead bugs and plant material, such as leaves, converting their components into elements that living organisms can reuse. They are an essential source of food for plants and animals. Many plants depend on fungi for their nutrients. Fungi also have had a profound effect on human life. Take a look at a moldy fruit and you are observing a type of fungi that has transformed modern medicine. People eat fungi and use them to manufacture bread, wine, and flavorings. Fungi can also cause plant and animal diseases. In humans, dandruff and athlete's foot are two widespread examples of disease caused by fungi.

It's a plant... It's an animal... It's a...

People once classified fungi as part of the plant kingdom. Years later they thought these creatures were part of the animal kingdom. As sci-

Words to Know

Antibiotic:
A substance produced by or derived from certain fungi and other organisms, that can destroy or inhibit the growth of other microorganisms.

Control experiment
A setup that is identical to the experiment, but is not affected by the variable that acts on the experimental group.

Eukaryotic:
Multicellular organism whose cells contain distinct nuclei, which contain the genetic material. (Pronounced yoo-KAR-ee-ah-tic)

Did You Know?

- The fungi *Phytophthora infestans* caused Ireland's great potato famine of the 1800s, which rapidly spread through crops and caused widespread famine.

- Hieroglyphics suggest that ancient Egyptians were using yeast to produce alcoholic beverages and to leaven bread over 5,000 years ago.

- The word pencil comes from the mold *penicillium,* a Latin name given for its brushlike shape. The name fit because early pencils were a small brush used by artists.

- In 2003, scientists completed unraveling the genome of a bread mold, an organism that researchers have long studied. The mold has approximately 10,000 genes—only about a third fewer than that of humans.

- Lichens come in an array of colors and were among history's early dye sources. In modern day lichens are still used to color some fine wools and other materials.

Fungi are one of the five kingdoms that scientists use to classify living organisms.

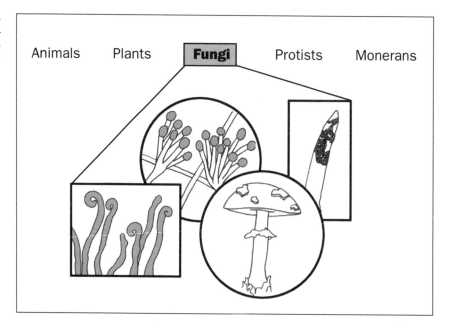

Animals   Plants   **Fungi**   Protists   Monerans

Some fungi are decomposers, breaking down dead organic matter as they draw nutrients from it. A fungus that grows on fallen leaves is an example of a decomposer. (© Gary Braasch/ CORBIS. Reproduced by permission.)

Fungi that grow on living animals and plants are called parasites. Fruit that has mold on it is an example of a plant fungal parasite. (Copyright © Kelly A. Quin. Reproduced by permission of Kelly A. Quin.)

entists learned more about this varied group of life, they found all fungi share characteristics that make them a unique kingdom.

Fungi are **eukaryotic** (pronounced yoo-KAR-ee-ah-tic) organisms, meaning that their DNA or genetic material is enclosed in a **nucleus.** A nucleus is the round or oval structure inside a cell that is surrounded by a protective envelope. Fungi need air, food, and water to live. They thrive in moist, warm environments, such as the underside of a rock or the space between a person's toes. Most types of fungi do not depend on sunlight for energy, as plants do. Because of this, they thrive in dark areas, such as caves and in soil.

Fungi do not manufacture their own food. To grow, fungi draw nutrients from the materials on which they live. Some fungi are decomposers, breaking down dead organic matter as they draw nutrients from it. A fungus that grows on a rotting tree or fallen leaves is an example of a decomposer.

Fungi that grow on living animals and plants are called **parasites.** Parasites take the materials from the creature, or host, sometimes harming the organism in the process. A fungus that lives on a plant's roots, for example, receives its food from the plant. Ringworm is an example of a human fungal parasite. Fruit that has mold on it, called a blight, is an example of a plant fungal parasite.

One unique type of fungi is the lichen. Commonly found on rocks, trees, and buildings, lichens are composed of fungi living in partnership with one or more other types of organism. One common lichen unites fungi with green algae. In this lichen, algae produce food for the fungi and fungi provide an outer layer of protection for the algae.

There are microscopic single-celled fungi, but the majority of fungi are more complex. Multicelled fungi string their cells together in long, threadlike strands called **hyphae** (pronounced HIGH-fee). The hyphae produce chemicals that break down the complex nutrients of its food source into simpler forms. These nutrients are absorbed through the walls of the hyphae, and flow between their cells. In search of food, hyphae spread outwards underneath the visible part of the fungi. The tangled mass of hyphae forms a network called a **mycelium.** Myceliums range in size from clumps of mold to systems that stretch for miles (kilometers). A fungus's mycelium can expand quickly, adding up to a kilometer of new hyphae per day.

Reproducing styles

Most fungi reproduce by releasing tiny particles called **spores.** Usually composed of a single cell, spores are smaller than dust particles and float through the air. A spore contains all the chemicals needed to make its fungus. Wind and water are the two main ways spores spread. Animals can also carry the spores. For example, the stinkhorn fungi produce an odor that attracts flies and beetles, which then carry the spores away.

Words to Know

Fermentation:
A chemical reaction in which enzymes break down complex organic compounds (for example, carbohydrates and sugars) into simpler ones (for example, ethyl alcohol).

Fungi:
Kingdom of various single-celled or multicellular organisms, including mushrooms, molds, yeasts, and mildews, that do not manufacture their own food.

Hypha:
Slender, cottony filaments making up the body of multicellular fungi. (Plural: hyphae)

Hypothesis:
An idea in the form of a statement that can be tested by observation and/or experiment.

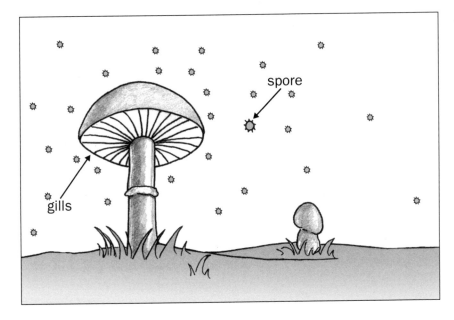

The tangled mass of hyphae forms a network called a mycelium.

mycelium

hyphae

Most fungi reproduce by releasing spores that float through the air and grow when they find the right environment.

spore

gills

Spores can end up everywhere—they are in the air, on clothes, plants, and skin. When the spore encounters the right conditions it will grow and develop into the individual fungus.

Fungi can also reproduce by growing and extending their hyphae. Hyphae grow as new cells form at the tips, creating ever-longer chains of cells. Many yeasts reproduce by **budding.** In budding, a parent

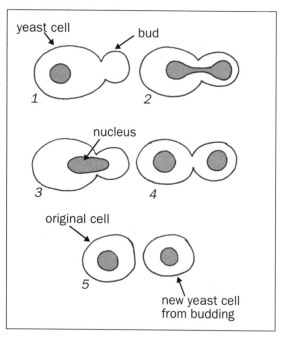

yeast pushes out its cell to form a bud. In time, the bud pinches off and a new yeast cell is produced.

Popular fungi

Fungi can cause diseases in plants and animals. Yet there are many types of fungi that humans commonly use, from tasty treats to medicines.

Mold: Mold is a type of fungi. It was a few of these stray mold spores that altered the treatment of bacterial diseases throughout the world. In 1928, British bacteriologist Alexander Fleming (1881–1955) was growing the *staphylococcus* bacteria in his laboratory for study. Bacteria are a type of microscopic organism, some of which can cause disease (see Bacteria chapter for more information). At that time, bacterial infections were sweeping throughout the world and killing millions of people.

One day Fleming accidentally left a dish of bacteria uncovered on his lab bench before he took a vacation. When he returned Fleming noticed the dish was crowded with bacterial growth except for one clear area where a patch of mold was growing. The mold had produced a substance that stopped bacteria from growing. Fleming named the substance penicillin, after the *Penicillium* mold.

Years later during World War II (1939–1945) scientists Howard Florey and Ernst Chain continued Fleming's work. Bacterial infections were common in the war and were causing many soldiers to die. The scientists found penicillin effective against a wide range of harmful bacteria and they began to mass-produce it. Penicillin became the first **antibiotic.** Antibiotics weaken or destroy bacteria and other organisms that cause diseases. The success of penicillin led to the developments of many other antibiotics, such as streptomycin, that stop the spread of disease.

Mushrooms: Mushrooms are one of the most familiar types of fungi. They can grow in damp soil and rotting wood. Although some mushrooms are edible to humans, many of these fungi contain harmful poisons. Eating even a small bite of some types, such as the white destroying angel mushroom, can kill a healthy adult.

The common mushrooms found in grocery stores produce their spores from gills located under their umbrella-like cap. A single mushroom can produce about two billion spores. The main part of the mushroom, its hyphae, lives underground. Cup-shaped mushrooms are part of another fungi group and they carry their spores in tiny pouches. Types of these mushrooms are rare and highly valued, For example, truffles are delicacies that belong to this group. Truffles live completely underground. Truffle hunters use highly trained pigs and dogs to sniff out their location.

Yeast: Yeasts are single-celled fungi that belong to the same group as the truffles. These cells look like little round or oval blobs under a microscope. Clusters of yeast create a white powdery appearance. They are commonly found on leaves, flowers, soil, and fruits.

Bakers have long made use of a natural process in yeast called **fermentation.** Yeasts eat a form of sugar or starch. In fermentation, yeasts break down the sugars and starches into carbon dioxide gas and alcohol. The carbon dioxide gas bubbles, causing an expansion or rising of the material around it. People use yeast to make bread rise, and produce the alcohol in beer and wine.

In the following two experiments, you will explore how yeast both breaks down food and in what environment it grows best. For an experiment on food spoilage and the fungi mold, see the Spoilage chapter.

Words to Know

Kingdom:
One of the five classifications in the widely accepted classification system that designates all living organisms into animals, plants, fungi, protists, and monerans.

Mycelium:
In fungi, the mass of threadlike, branching hyphae.

Nucleus:
Membrane-enclosed structure within a cell that contains the cell's genetic material and controls its growth and reproduction. (Plural: nuclei.)

Spore:
A small, usually one-celled, reproductive body that is capable of growing into a new organism.

Variable:
Something that can affect the results of an experiment.

Experiment 1
Decomposers: Food source for a common fungi

Purpose/Hypothesis

Decomposition is a critical part of Earth's cycle of life. In this experiment you will examine how fungi affect decomposition. You will use a banana as the food source for the fungi. This fruit provides a moist environment and other conditions that promote yeast growth. For the fungi you will use dry yeast that is used in cooking. The yeast becomes activated when it is given a source of moisture. You will place the yeast on a banana and then observe how it affects the fruit. Changes to the fruit can include changes in color, breaks in the skin, and odor.

Before you begin, make an educated guess about the outcome of this experiment based on your knowledge of fungi and decomposition. This educated guess, or prediction, is your **hypothesis.** A hypothesis should explain these things:

- the topic of the experiment
- the **variable** you will change
- the variable you will measure
- what you expect to happen

 ## What Are the Variables?

Variables are anything that might affect the results of an experiment. Here are the main variables in this experiment:

- the food source (fruit)
- the type of fungi
- environmental conditions, such as temperature and humidity
- exposure to air

In other words, the variables in this experiment are everything that might affect the decomposition of the fruit. If you change more than one variable at the same time, you will not be able to tell which variable had the most effect on the decomposition.

A hypothesis should be brief, specific, and measurable. It must be something you can test through further investigation. Your experiment will prove or disprove whether your hypothesis is correct. Here is one possible hypothesis for this experiment: "Yeast will cause the banana to decompose more rapidly than it would without the yeast."

In this case, the variable you will change is the addition of yeast to the banana. The variable you will measure is the description of the banana.

Conducting a control experiment will help you isolate each variable and measure the changes in the dependent variable. Only one variable will change between the control and your experiment. For your control in this experiment you will use a plain banana. At the end of the experiment you can compare the control and the experimental results.

Level of Difficulty
Easy.

Materials Needed
- dry yeast, about 1 tablespoon
- one banana
- two self-sealing plastic bags or plastic bags with twisty ties
- knife
- marking pen

Approximate Budget
$3

Timetable
15 minutes setup; 5 minutes daily for about a week.

Step-by-Step Instructions
1. Peel the banana and slice two pieces. (You may want to cut it in half first lengthwise.)

How to Experiment Safely
Be careful when handling the knife. Do not taste or ingest any food in this experiment.

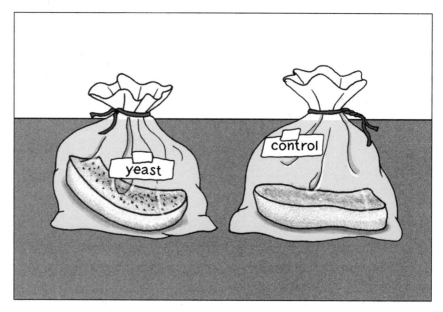

Step 5: Seal or tie both bags and leave in a warm place.

2. Place a slice of banana inside each plastic bag.
3. Sprinkle dry yeast on one slice.
4. Label the bag with the yeast "Yeast" and the bag without the yeast "Control."
5. Seal or tie both bags shut and leave them in a warm place.
6. Observe the bags daily for one week. Each day write a brief description of how each banana appears. On the final day, note the difference, if any, between the two banana pieces. Observe changes in color, breaks in the skin, odors, and physical changes in the shape, size, or consistency (hard, soft, mushy) of the fruit.

Summary of Results

Look at the description of your results. Which banana slice shows the most and fastest decomposition? Was your hypothesis correct?

Change the Variables

There are several ways to change the variables in this experiment. You can alter the fungi's food source by using another fruit, fruit skin, or other item. Make sure the food source contains some moisture to activate the yeast. You can also use another type of fungi. If necessary, you can purchase a specific fungi from a biological supply company. Another way is to change the environment of the fruit, such as by placing one piece in a dark area and one in a bright area.

experiment
CENTRAL

Experiment 2
Living Conditions: What is the ideal temperature for yeast growth?

Purpose/Hypothesis

People have long taken advantage of the natural fermentation process of yeasts to produce foods, including alcohol and risen bread. (Ancient cultures' use of fermentation is one of the earliest uses of biotechnology, which applies living organisms for human use.) Bakers commonly use the *Saccharomyces cerevisiae* yeast to produce carbon dioxide, which causes bread to rise.

In this experiment you will examine in which conditions yeasts best live and grow. Yeasts kept in the most suitable living conditions will be the most active; those kept in less suitable conditions will not be as active. You will pour equal amounts of yeast into similar bottles and provide the yeast with water and a food source, sugar. Each bottle of yeast will be given a different growth environment: one warm and one cold. You will compare them to a third bottle kept at room temperature.

You will measure the activity of the yeast by measuring the amount of carbon dioxide the yeast releases. You can do this in two ways. To measure the carbon dioxide, you will seal the opening of the bottle with an empty balloon. The carbon dioxide gas produced will cause the balloon to inflate. Every twenty minutes you will measure the amount of gas produced by measuring the circumference of the balloon. Another way to measure the carbon dioxide is to measure the

What Are the Variables?

Variables are anything that might affect the results of an experiment. Here are the main variables in this experiment:

- temperature
- type of fungi (the yeast)
- quantity of the fungi
- type of food source (the sugar)
- quantity of the food source

In other words, the variables in this experiment are everything that might affect the amount of carbon dioxide produced from the yeast. If you change more than one variable at the same time, you will not be able to tell which variable had the most effect on the yeast's growth.

acidity of the yeast solution. Carbon dioxide mixes with water in the yeast solution to form a weak acid, called carbonic acid. The more carbon dioxide produced, the more acidic the solution. You will use acid/base indicator strips to check the level of acidity after you remove the balloon.

Before you begin, make an educated guess about the outcome of this experiment based on your knowledge of fungi. This educated guess, or prediction, is your **hypothesis.** A hypothesis should explain these things:

- the topic of the experiment
- the **variable** you will change
- the variable you will measure
- what you expect to happen

A hypothesis should be brief, specific, and measurable. It must be something you can test through further investigation. Your experiment will prove or disprove whether your hypothesis is correct. Here is one possible hypothesis for this experiment: "The yeast given the warmest environment will grow the most rapidly and produce the most carbon dioxide gas; the yeast in the coldest environment will grow the least rapidly and produce the least gas."

In this case, the variable you will change is the temperature of the yeast's environment. The variable you will measure is the amount of carbon dioxide produced.

Conducting a control experiment will help you isolate each variable and measure the changes in the dependent variable. Only one variable will change between the control and your experiment. The control you will use for this experiment is a room temperature environment (water) for the yeast. Before you introduce the yeast to its environment, you will measure the acidity of the plain sugar-water to have a control for the acidity level. At the end of the experiment you can compare the control results with the experimental results.

Level of Difficulty
Moderate.

Materials Needed
- three identical small glass or plastic bottles with narrow mouths
- three balloons
- three packets of dry yeast (not rapid-rising)
- about nine teaspoons of sugar
- string
- tape
- ice cubes
- hot water
- three cups
- two clear bowls or rectangular containers, at least half the bottles' height
- tape measure
- acid/base indicator strips
- measuring cup, with spout preferably
- measuring spoons
- funnel (optional)
- thermometer or temperature gauge, should range from 65–115 degrees Fahrenheit (18–46 degrees Celsius) (optional)
- marking pen

Approximate Budget
$8

How to Experiment Safely

Have an adult present when handling hot water. Do not taste or ingest any of the solutions in the experiment.

Timetable

1 hour allowing water to sit; 1 hour and 45 minutes for experiment.

Step-by-Step Instructions

1. To get room temperature water: In three separate cups, measure ¾ cup water. The water should not be hot or cold to the touch. Allow the water to sit for about one hour to reach room temperature. If you have a thermometer, the water should be at about 68–73.4 degrees Fahrenheit (20–23 degrees Celsius).

2. While waiting, label one bottle "Hot," one bottle "Cold," and one bottle "Control."

3. Add 3 teaspoons of sugar to each cup and mix thoroughly.

4. Dip an indicator strip briefly in one of the sugar–water solutions. Compare the indicator color to the color chart. An acid should turn the indicator red, a base should turn the indicator blue. Note the results.

5. Pour the sugar-water into the three bottles. You may need a funnel for this. Clean the cups for later use.

6. Prepare a warm-water bath and a cold-water bath. For the warm-water bath, fill one of the two clear bowls or rectangular containers with warm water from the kitchen sink faucet. Let the water run until it gets fairly warm to the touch, but not scalding hot (about 104–113 degrees Fahrenheit [40–45 degrees Celsius]). For the cold-water bath fill the other bowl or container with cold water from the kitchen sink faucet and add ice cubes until the water gets cool to the touch (about 41–59 degrees Fahrenheit [5–15 degrees Celsius]).

7. Add one packet of dry yeast to each of the three bottles.

8. Securely place a balloon over the top of each bottle opening. Tape each balloon to the bottle to ensure no gas can escape.

9. Swirl each bottle gently to mix the contents.

10. Place the bottle labeled "Hot" in the warm-water bath. Place the bottle labeled "Cold" in the cold-water bath. You may need to secure the bottles down with string and tape so that they sit firmly in the water and do not bob.

11. After 20 minutes, measure the circumference of each balloon. When you wrap the tape measure around the balloon make a small mark on the balloon with the pen above the measure to mark the spot. Note the results in a data chart (see page 246).

12. Check to make sure the warm water is still warm. If it has cooled significantly, scoop some out and replace with fresh warm water. Add ice cubes to the cold water, if necessary

13. Continue measuring the balloons in 20-minute intervals until the balloons no longer expand. It should take about 60 minutes or more.

14. Remove the balloon from the "Cold" bottle and pour some of its contents into a clean cup. Dip an indicator strip briefly in the

Step 10: Place yeast in hot, cold, and room temperature environments.

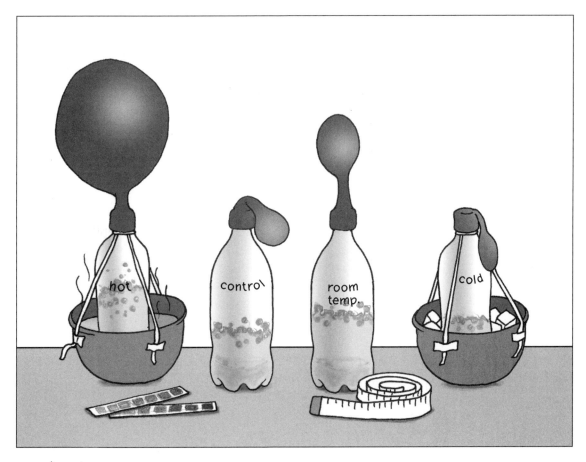

	Circumference			Acid/Base/Neutral
	20	40	60	
hot				
cold				
room temperature				
control/no yeast				

Step 11: Note the circumferences of the balloons and acidity of the solutions in a data chart.

solution. Compare the indicator color to the color chart and note the results.

15. Repeat Step 14 for the bottles labeled "Hot" and "Control," making sure to pour the contents into a clean cup each time. Note the results of each indicator strip.

Troubleshooter's Guide

Below are some problems that may arise during this experiment, some possible causes, and some ways to remedy the problems.

Problem: No balloons expanded and there was no indication of acidity in the solutions in the bottles labeled "Hot" and "Cold."

Possible cause: You may have used yeast that was no longer active. Check the expiration date of your yeast and, if necessary, purchase more. Repeat the experiment using this yeast.

Problem: The balloon on the bottle labeled "Hot" did not expand.

Possible cause: You may have used water that was too hot, causing the yeast to die instantly. Repeat the experiment, using warm water.

Summary of Results

Examine the data chart and graph the results of the circumference for each environmental condition. Label the measurements on one axis and the time on another. How does the balloon circumference of the yeast grown in a room temperature environment compare to that of the yeast grown in the cold-water and warm-water bath? Which bottle showed the greatest increase in balloon circumference? Which bottle was the most acidic? What do the results of the indicator convey about the growth of the yeast in each environment? Can you construct a hypothesis about the environmental conditions for all fungi from these results? Write a brief summary explaining your results and any conclusions you can draw from them.

Change the Variables

There are several ways to change the variable in this experiment. You can alter the type of fungi. You can change different environmental conditions, such as the light level on the yeast. By using varying concentrations of acidic foods, such as lemon juice or vinegar instead of sugar water, you can alter the acidity level of the yeast.

 Design Your Own Experiment

How to Select a Topic Relating to this Concept

From the microscopic to the mammoth, fungi are a wide and diverse kingdom of life. There are numerous projects related to fungi, from basic observation to exploring their living requirements. You could also explore fungi's profound effect on Earth's life cycle and human life.

Check the For More Information section and talk with your science teacher to learn more about fungi. While some fungi may appear edible, remember to never eat any mushroom or other fungus you find unless you have had it identified by an expert in fungi. The mushroom may be poisonous or you could be allergic to it.

Steps in the Scientific Method

To conduct an original experiment, you need to plan carefully and think things through. Otherwise, you might not be sure what question you are answering, what you are or should be measuring, or what your findings prove or disprove.

Here are the steps in designing an experiment:

- State the purpose of—and the underlying question behind—the experiment you propose to do.
- Recognize the variables involved and select one that will help you answer the question at hand.
- State your hypothesis, an educated guess about the answer to your question.
- Decide how to change the variable you selected.
- Decide how to measure your results.

Recording Data and Summarizing the Results

Your data should include charts and drawings such as the one you did for these experiments. They should be clearly labeled and easy to read. You may also want to include photographs and drawings of any fungi you worked with, the experimental setup, and results, which will help other people visualize the experiment.

If you are preparing an exhibit, you may want to display your results, such as any experimental setup you designed. You may also want to include specimens, in a closed container, so that others can observe what you studied. If you have completed a nonexperimental project, explain clearly what your research question was and illustrate your findings.

Related Projects

Fungi are a broad kingdom filled with many possible experiments at hand because fungi grow on such a wide variety of sources. Different materials will grow different fungi. You could conduct a project on the differences among one group of fungi, such as molds. Most molds grow well on materials such as bread, used coffee-grounds, fruits, or other food items that are moist with no preservatives. (See Spoilage chapter.) You could isolate and grow the same type of fungi on a variety of food sources. Or you can keep the food source constant and grow different types of fungi on it.

You could also perform a project on the reproduction of fungi. Examine the spores of fungi and the different methods fungi use to reproduce. For a research project, you could look at how fungi have had an effect on humans, in both positive and negative ways. You could look at how food manufacturers protect food against certain types of fungi and how fungi are a natural part of many foods.

experiment
CENTRAL

For More Information

Darling, Kathy. *There's a Zoo on You!* Brookfield, CT: The Millbrook Press, 2000. ❖ A look at fungi, bacteria, viruses, and other microbes that affect humans.

Fogel, Robert. "Fun Facts About Fungi." *University of Michigan.* http://www.herb.lsa.umich.edu/kidpage/Puffspor.htm (accessed on August 25, 2003). ❖ Fun facts and information on fungi.

Ho, David. "Alexander Fleming." *Time.com.* http://www.time.com/time/time100/scientist/profile/fleming.html (accessed on August 25, 2003). ❖ A profile of Alexander Fleming, who was one of the principal discoverers of the antibiotic penicillin.

"Humongous Fungus A New Kind Of Individual." *ScienceDaily.* http://www.science daily.com/releases/2003/03/030327074535.htm (accessed on August 25, 2003). ❖ A giant underground fungus is killing trees in Oregon.

"LichenLand: Fun with Lichens." *Oregon State University.* http://mgd.nacse.org/hyperSQL/lichenland/ (accessed on August 25, 2003). ❖ Discover the world of lichens.

"The Microbial World." *University of Edinburgh.* http://helios.bto.ed.ac.uk/bto/microbes/fungalwe.htm (accessed on August 25, 2003). ❖ Detailed information on fungi with lots of pictures.

Nardo, Don. *Germs.* San Diego, CA: KidHaven Press, 2002. ❖ Basic explanation of microbes.

Pascoe, Elaine. *Fungi.* New York: PowerKids Press, 2003. ❖ Simple introduction to fungi with many pictures.

Silverstein, Robert, Alvin, and Virginia. *Fungi.* New York: Twenty-first Century Books, 1996. ❖ Clear details on the fungi kingdom.

Volk, Tom. "Tom Volk's Fungi." *University of Wisconsin–La Crosse.* http://botit.botany.wisc.edu/toms_fungi/ (accessed on August 25, 2003). ❖ Information on fungi with links, pictures, and answers to frequently asked questions.

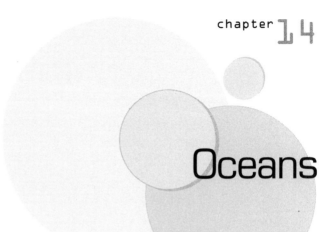

chapter 14

Oceans

If you were to look down at Earth from space you would see a planet that was covered in blue. That is because oceans cover almost three-quarters of the Earth's surface and contain about 97 percent of the planet's water supply. Life on Earth began in the ocean almost three-and-a-half million years ago and life could not exist without a healthy ocean environment. Today, the oceans are home to an incredibly variety of creatures, from the largest animal that ever lived, the blue whale, to microscopic organisms that can live in boiling waters.

People depend on the oceans in many ways. Oceans have an important effect on weather patterns. They are essential for transportation, for both economic and military purposes. Many people throughout the world rely on the ocean for food and their livelihood. People also use the oil and minerals that come from beneath the ocean floor.

The first voyage planned specifically to study the oceans was a British expedition that set out in 1872. In the twentieth century, interest in the oceans grew enormously. A new field evolved for **oceanographers** or people who study the ocean. Technological development allowed oceanographers to travel further and longer into the ocean depths. The discovery of previously unknown species and minerals in the ocean sparked further excitement and, today, the ocean is considered the last unexplored frontier.

A handful of seawater

Earth's oceans are all connected to one another. Until the year 2000, there were four recognized oceans: the Pacific, Atlantic, Indian, and

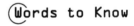

Words to Know

Bioluminescence:
The chemical phenomenon in which an organism can produce its own light.

Control experiment
A setup that is identical to the experiment, but is not affected by the variable that acts on the experimental group.

Convection current:
Also called density-driven current, a cycle of warm water rising and cooler water sinking.

Crest
The highest point of a wave.

Did You Know?

- In 1995 researchers found the deepest ocean water near the Mariana Islands in the Pacific, where the water is over 36,000 feet (11,000 meters) deep. If Mount Everest were placed on the ocean floor at that point, the summit would be 1 mile (1.6 kilometers) under water.

- The giant squid (*Architeuthis*) is the largest invertebrate that has ever existed on Earth, yet as of 2003 no human has ever seen one alive in its ocean habitat. Giant squids can grow up to 70 feet (21.3 meters) long and have eyes the size of dinner plates.

- Salinity in Israel's Dead Sea is the highest in the world. It is about ten times more salt than ocean water, and bacteria are the only life that can survive there.

- If the ocean's total salt content were dried, it would cover the continents to a depth of 5 feet (1.5 meters).

- Located off the United States' Northeast coast, the Bay of Fundy has the highest tides in the world. Tides there can reach up to 40 to 50 feet (12 to 15 meters), the height of the average four-story building.

Words to Know

Currents:
The horizontal and vertical circulation of ocean waters.

Density:
The mass of a substance compared to its volume.

Gravity:
Force of attraction between objects, the strength of which depends on the mass of each object and the distance between them.

Hypothesis:
An idea in the form of a statement that can be tested by observation and/or experiment.

Oceanographer:
A person who studies the chemistry of the oceans, as well as their currents, marine life, and the ocean floor.

Salinity:
A measure of the amount of dissolved salt in seawater.

Arctic. In 2000 the International Hydrographic Organization, the organization responsible for setting the oceans' boundaries, recognized a new ocean, the Southern Ocean, encircling Antarctica.

The main chemicals in ocean water are sodium and chlorine combined as sodium chloride, better known as ordinary table salt. Ocean waters also contain smaller amounts of many other chemicals. Salt, along with the other substances, flows into oceans from smaller bodies of water. Salt is a mineral that is found in soil and rocks. As river water flows, it picks up small amounts of salts from the rocks and soil. The rivers carry it into the ocean where it remains.

The **salinity,** or salt content, of ocean water varies across the oceans. Oceanographers report salinity in parts per thousand. On average, ocean salinity is thirty-five parts per thousand. That means there are 35 pounds of salt for every 1,000 pounds of water, or 3.5 percent salt.

Changing properties

On average, the ocean extends about 2.3 miles (3.7 kilometers) downwards from the surface. Seawater has different properties depending on its depth, from the surface to the ocean floor. As the water deepens, its pressure increases. The water near the ocean's surface has very little water pressing down on it and so the water pressure is low. On the bottom of the ocean, the weight of all the water above presses down and the water pressure is high. At the deepest point in the ocean, the pressure is more than 8 tons per square inch (1.1 metric tons per square centimeter)— equal to one person trying to support fifty jumbo jets.

Sunlight gives the surface water warmth. On average, sunlight extends down to a depth of about 650 feet (250 meters). Water near the ocean floor gets no sunlight and is cold and dark. Both temperature and salinity affect the **density** of the water. Density is how much mass a certain volume of water contains. Molecules in warm water have more energy to move about. They spread farther apart, which results in less mass in a certain volume and therefore less density. Molecules in cold water have less energy and stay close together, resulting in a more mass in a certain volume and greater density. Water that is heavier or denser than the water around it sinks, while water that is less dense rises.

Differences in density cause seawater to form layers in a process called **stratification.** A liquid will float on a liquid less dense than itself, such as oil on water. The layers formed in ocean waters can be incredibly stable and last for thousands of years.

Concentrations of seawater minerals

SALT	Chlorine	55.04%
	Sodium	30.61%
	Sulfate	7.69%
	Magnesium	3.69%
	Calcium	1.16%
	Potassium	1.1%

Remaining elements .71% (these include manganese, lead, gold, silver, iron, and zinc)

The main chemicals in ocean water are sodium and chlorine combined as sodium chloride, better known as ordinary table salt.

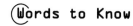

Words to Know

Stratification:
Layers according to density; applies to fluids.

Tides:
The cyclic rise and fall of seawater.

Trough:
The lowest point of a wave. (Pronounced trawf.)

Upwelling:
The process by which lower-level, nutrient-rich waters rise upward to the ocean's surface.

Variable:
Something that can affect the results of an experiment.

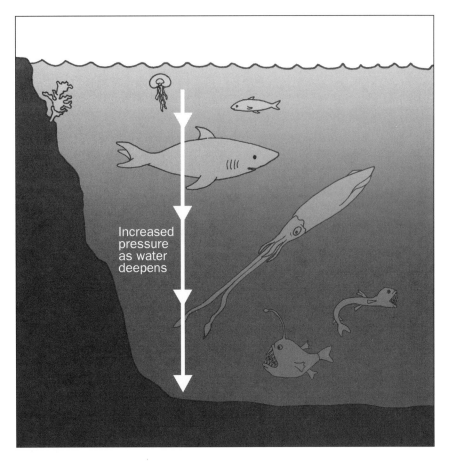

Seawater has different properties depending on its depth from the surface to the ocean floor. As the water deepens, its pressure increases.

Increased pressure as water deepens

Rising and falling

Currents are large streams of water flowing through the ocean. Currents occur in all bodies of salt water and can be caused by wind, salinity, heat content, the characteristics of the ocean's bottom, and Earth's rotation. Currents in the top layer of the ocean are called **surface currents** and these are mainly caused by steady winds. Surface currents flow clockwise north of the equator and counterclockwise (in the opposite direction) south of the equator. The Gulf Stream runs along the east coast of the United States and is one of the strongest and warmest currents known. In some places it may travel more than 60 miles in a day. The currents carry the Sun's heat from warmer regions to cooler areas, bringing mild weather to places that would otherwise be much cooler.

Currents also flow up and down within the water. These currents occur due to changes in seawater temperature and density and are called

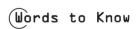

Words to Know

Wave:
The rise and fall of the ocean water.

Wavelength:
The distance between one peak of a wave and the next corresponding peak.

experiment
CENTRAL

convection currents or density-driven currents. When warm surface water loses some of its heat to the air, the surface water becomes cooler and denser and starts to sink. This forces some of the water at lower levels to rise to form an up-and-down current. Deep ocean currents are important to marine life. Water at the ocean surface takes in oxygen from the air. Convection currents carry the oxygen down to the animals and plants that live in the bottom ocean regions. Minerals along the bottom of the floor are carried up to the sunlight layer, where animals use them. This process of lower-level, nutrient-rich waters rising upward to the ocean's surface is called **upwelling.**

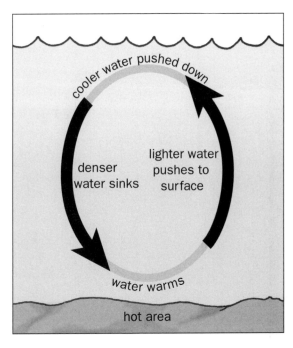

Convection currents are caused when waters of different temperatures and densities meet.

cooler water pushed down

denser water sinks

lighter water pushes to surface

water warms

hot area

The waters in the ocean are constantly in motion. When wind blows over the ocean's surface, it tries to pick up some of the water and creates **waves.** Waves are movements of water that rise and fall. The size of the wave depends on the wind's power. Gentle breezes form tiny ripples along the surface; strong winds can create large waves. Even though it looks like waves push the water forward, the water actually moves very little. When a wave arrives it lifts the water particles up and forward. As the wave passes, each particle falls and flows backwards underwater to return to its starting point. That is why a bottle, or anything else, floating in the ocean will remain in roughly the same place as the waves pass.

The highest point the waves reach is called the **crest.** The lowest point is called the **trough.** The distance from one crest to the next is the **wavelength.**

Tides are periodic rises and falls of large bodies of water. English mathematician and physicist Isaac Newton (1642–1727) was the first

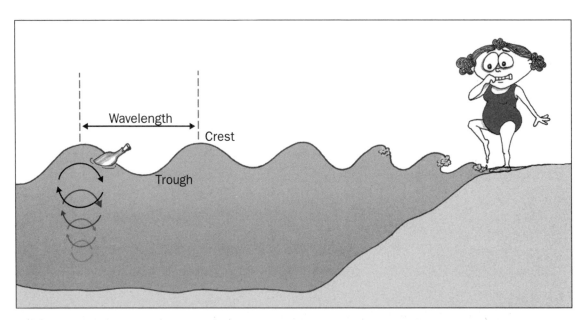

Wavelength

Crest

Trough

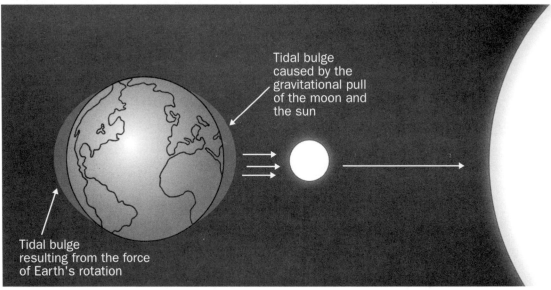

Tidal bulge caused by the gravitational pull of the moon and the sun

Tidal bulge resulting from the force of Earth's rotation

TOP:
Even though it may appear as though waves move the water forward, water moves in a circular motion.

BOTTOM:
Tides are caused primarily by the gravitational pull of the Moon on Earth, and by the rotation of Earth.

person to explain tides scientifically with his understanding of **gravity.** Gravity is a force of attraction between any two masses, such as the Sun and Earth.

Tides are caused primarily by the gravitational pull of the Moon on Earth, and by the rotation of Earth. The tug of gravity from the Sun also affects the tides, but it has about half of the Moon's force. The gravitational attraction causes the oceans to bulge out in the direction of the

Moon. Another bulge occurs on the opposite side of the Earth due to the water being thrown outward by the planet's spin. These are high tides. The areas between the tidal bulges experience low tide. (For a more detailed explanation of tides see the Rotation and Orbits chapter.)

The tide is low along this Washington State beach. (Photography by Cindy Clendenon. Reproduced by permission.)

Sea life

The oceans are filled with all types of amazing and bizarre-looking creatures. Although the Sun's light only reaches a small layer of the seawater, the majority of animals and plants live in the top sunlight regions. Microscopic organisms called plankton are the main food supply in the ocean. They live at or near the surface of the water and many produce oxygen, much of which escapes into the air for humans to breathe.

In the lower ocean regions, deep-sea creatures have developed unique adaptations to survive in the dim, high-pressure, cold waters. Many deep-water fish are **bioluminescent** or they make their own light. The anglerfish uses a lighted "lure" on the top of its head to attract prey. The flashlight fish carries bioluminescent bacteria in pouches under its eyes that it can flash on and off at will to capture prey

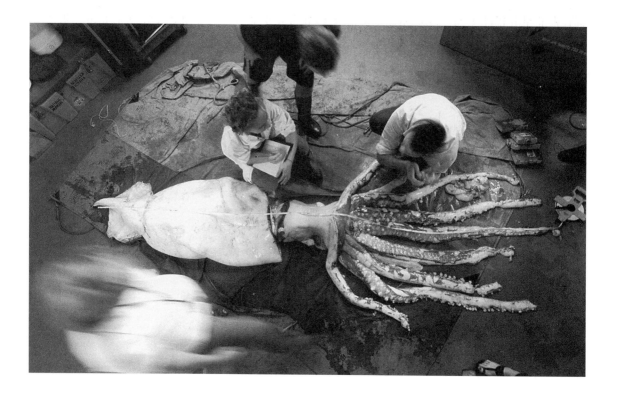

A giant squid netted from the waters near Melbourne, Australia, in February 2001. Measuring 12 feet (4 meters) long, it is estimated its feeding tentacles would likely bring the size to 36 feet (12 meters). (Reproduced by permission of AP/Wide World.)

or find a mate. A shrimp heaves bioluminescent vomit onto an attacking fish, perhaps to blind the attacker and allow the shrimp to escape.

Other deep-sea fish have expandable stomachs that can hold a fish much larger than themselves—a useful talent with the lack of food on the ocean floor. Fanglike teeth, hinged skulls, and large mouths are all traits that help these fish catch food. Some creatures attach themselves to the ocean floor, such as giant tube worms that can grow more than 10 feet (3 meters) long. In the 1970s, researchers discovered these worms, along with bacteria and giant clams, living in bubbling hot water with temperatures up to 650°F (350°C) spurting out from beneath the ocean floor.

Experiment 1
Stratification: How does the salinity in ocean water cause it to form layers?

Purpose/Hypothesis

Layers of seawater with different densities can lead to stratification that can last for centuries. Anyone who has gone into the ocean and felt distinct layers of cold meeting the warm water has experienced the effect of stratification. Temperature and salinity are the two key factors determining density and, thus, ocean stratification. High salinity makes the water denser than low salinity, and cold water is denser than warm water. The denser the water relative to the water around it, the lower that water sinks.

In this experiment you will examine how salinity affects stratification. You will make two saltwater solutions of different salinity concentrations: a 40 percent salinity solution and a 20 percent salinity solution. To visually observe the different densities, you will dye the water blue and place an object in the saltwater that is denser than fresh water—a small potato. You will then carefully place fresh water above the salt water and observe what happens.

Before you begin, make an educated guess about the outcome of this experiment based on your knowledge of density and stratification. This educated guess, or prediction, is your **hypothesis.** A hypothesis should explain these things:

- the topic of the experiment
- the **variable** you will change
- the variable you will measure
- what you expect to happen

A hypothesis should be brief, specific, and measurable. It must be something you can test through further investigation. Your experiment will prove or disprove whether your hypothesis is correct. Here is one possible hypothesis for this experiment: "Water that is higher in salinity is denser than water of lower salinity; the greater the difference between the densities, the more defined the stratification."

In this case, the variable you will change is the percentage of salt in the water. The variable you will measure is the density of the water.

Conducting a control experiment will help you isolate each variable and measure the changes in the dependent variable. Only one variable will change between the control experiment and your experiment. For your control in this experiment you will use a jar of fresh water. At the end of the experiment you can compare the control and the experimental results.

Note: When making a solid/liquid solution, it is standard to use weight/weight (grams/grams) or weight/volume (grams/milliliters).

What Are the Variables?

Variables are anything that might affect the results of an experiment. Here are the main variables in this experiment:

- the temperature of the water
- the type of salt
- the quantity of salt
- the item placed in the water

In other words, the variables in this experiment are everything that might affect the stratification of the water. If you change more than one variable at the same time, you will not be able to tell which variable had the most effect on stratification.

With water, 1 gram of water equals 1 milliliter. In this experiment, teaspoons and tablespoons are used to measure the solid.

Level of Difficulty

Easy to Moderate.

Materials Needed

- water
- three glass jars (mayonnaise jars work well)
- container to hold water
- salt
- three small red potatoes
- measuring cup
- measuring spoons
- baster
- blue or red food coloring
- marking pen
- masking tape

Approximate Budget

$5.

Timetable

15 minutes for the initial setup; about 2 hours waiting time.

How to Experiment Safely
Have an adult present when handling hot water.

Step-by-Step Instructions

1. Use the masking tape to label each glass jar: "Control," "40 percent salinity," and "20 percent salinity."
2. Pour 3 cups (700 milliliters) of hot water in each jar.
3. In the jar labeled "40 percent salinity," add 8 tablespoons of salt. Stir vigorously.
4. In the jar labeled "20 percent salinity," add 4 tablespoons of salt. Stir vigorously.

Step 8: Dribble the water along the inside of the jar so that it does not mix up the solution.

40% salt

experiment
CENTRAL

5. Add several drops of food coloring to the solution in each jar and stir.

6. Using one of the measuring spoons, carefully place a potato in each jar.

7. Allow the water to cool to room temperature. The jars should be about half full. If necessary, pour out some of the water at this point.

8. Fill up a container with plain water. Use the baster to carefully add this water to each jar until the jar is almost full. Dribble the water along the inside of the jar so that it does not mix up the solution. (See illustration on page 261.)

9. Set the jars aside for 15 minutes and observe.

Summary of Results

Write down or draw the results of the experiment. Was your hypothesis correct? Was there a difference in the stratification between the higher salinity water and the water of lower salinity? How does each compare to the control experiment? What does this tell you about the seawater where stratification occurs that lasts for hundreds or thousands of years? Name some reasons why stratification might occur for a short period of time. In the ocean both salinity and temperature affect density. As you write up your conclusions, hypothesize how changing the temperature of the salt water would affect the results.

Troubleshooter's Guide

Below is a problem that may arise during this experiment, some possible causes, and some ways to remedy the problem.

Problem: The water does not stratify and the potato sinks.

Possible cause: Your tap water could have minerals in it, which would make it less dense. Try conducting the experiment again with purified water.

Possible cause: You may not have thoroughly mixed the salt into the water. Try the experiment again, making sure to mix until the water is clear.

Change the Variables

In this experiment you can change the variables in several ways. You can alter the temperature of the water, mimicking the ocean conditions by using water of the same salinity and making the bottom layer cold and the top layer warm. You could make the salt water on the bottom warm and the fresh water cold. You can also use objects of differing densities to observe the relative density of the water.

Experiment 2
Currents: Water behavior in density-driven currents

Purpose/Hypothesis

One way that seawater moves vertically is when a mass of water changes densities. These convection or density-driven currents occur at a slower rate than surface currents. Density-driven currents occur when water becomes less dense and begins to rise, or water becomes more dense and begins to sink. Either way, the moving water pushes the water below or above it to take its place.

Density in ocean water is caused by both its salinity and temperature. This experiment focuses on how temperature differences help form density-driven currents. You will add liquids of different temperatures to various temperatures of water, and observe the behavior of the water. Dyes will allow you to observe the different temperature waters.

Before you begin, make an educated guess about the outcome of this experiment based on your knowledge of density-driven currents. This educated guess, or prediction, is your **hypothesis**. A hypothesis should explain these things:

- the topic of the experiment
- the **variable** you will change
- the variable you will measure
- what you expect to happen

A hypothesis should be brief, specific, and measurable. It must be something you can test through further investigation. Your experiment will prove or disprove whether your hypothesis is correct. Here is one possible hypothesis for this experiment: "Colder water is denser than warmer water and will sink, while the relatively warmer water will rise."

What Are the Variables?

Variables are anything that might affect the results of an experiment. Here are the main variables in this experiment:

- the temperature of the water

- the water contents

- the quantity of hot or cold water placed in each jar

- the quantity of the base water

In other words, the variables in this experiment are everything that might affect the movement of the water. If you change more than one variable at the same time, you will not be able to tell which variable had the most effect on water's density.

In this case, the variable you will change is the temperature of the water. The variable you will measure is the movement of the water.

Conducting a control experiment will help you isolate each variable and measure the changes in the dependent variable. Only one variable will change between the control experiment and your experiment. For the control in this experiment, the temperature of the added liquid will be the same as the water already in the control jar.

Level of Difficulty

Easy.

Materials Needed

- water
- three glass jars
- red and blue food coloring
- two cups for mixing
- three pieces of white paper or cardstock
- tea strainer or tongs
- eyedropper or medicine dropper
- ice-cube tray or small plastic cup

How to Experiment Safely
Have an adult present when handling hot water. Either throw away the medicine or eyedropper or ask an adult to help you rinse out and sterilize the dropper before putting it away.

Approximate Budget
$4.

Timetable
15 minutes for the experiment; about 1 hour waiting time.

Step-by-Step Instructions
1. Use the masking tape to label each jar: "Control," "Hot," and "Cold."
2. Add several drops of blue dye to enough water to make two small, blue, ice cubes. Freeze.
3. When the blue water has frozen into ice, fill the "Cold" jar about two-thirds full with ice-cold water.
4. Fill the "Hot" jar about two-thirds full with hot water. Cover the jar to prevent the heat from escaping.
5. Fill the "Control" jar with room-temperature water.
6. Fold the three pieces of paper or cardstock in half and place one in back of each jar. This will help you observe the experiment.
7. Let the water sit until completely still, about a minute.
8. While the water is sitting, add a small amount of red dye to about a quarter of a cup of hot water in a separate mixing cup.
9. Use the tea strainer or tongs to hold one of the blue ice cubes and gently place it in the middle of the "Hot" jar.
10. Use the eyedropper to release a small amount of the red-colored hot water in the middle of the cold water in the "Cold" jar.
11. Note the results.
12. In the "Control" jar, which has room-temperature water, gently place the second blue ice cube on the top of the water. Next, use the dropper to place a small amount of the hot, red-colored water deep in the water. Record the results.

Step 9: Use the tea strainer or tongs to hold one of the blue ice cubes and gently place it in the middle of the hot water in the "Hot" jar.

13. For the control experiment, empty either the "Cold" jar or the "Hot" jar and refill with room-temperature water (allow the empty jar to return to room temperature before refilling). Use the dropper to place a small amount of room-temperature blue dye and room-temperature red dye in the water (rinse the dropper after placing the first color). Record the results.

Summary of Results

Examine the results of your experiment and draw the movement of the water. Compare the results of the control to what you observed in the "Control" jar. How does what you observed relate to upwelling? In the ocean, both temperature and salinity affect the density of water; thus, both have an effect on density-driven currents. From what you have learned about seawater and density, write a paragraph on how adding salt to the dyed waters would affect the results.

Troubleshooter's Guide

Below is a problem that may arise during this experiment, some possible causes, and some ways to remedy the problem.

Problem: The dyed water mixes into the jar's water so quickly it is difficult to observe its movements.

Possible cause: You may have dropped or placed too much of the cold and/or hot water in the jar. Try the experiment again, using a smaller blue ice cube and only one large drop of the red water.

Problem: The results from the room-temperature water jar were the same as that of the Cold jar or Hot jar.

Possible cause: The water in the jars may not have enough temperature variation between them. To make sure both the Control jar and the room-temperature jar have room-temperature water, allow lukewarm water to sit out for at least two to four hours. If you have a thermometer, it should be approximately 70 to 73 degrees Fahrenheit (21 to 23 degrees Celsius). Make sure the hot water is hot; 140 to 149 degrees Fahrenheit (60 to 65 degrees Celsius).

Change the Variables

To change the variables in this experiment you can alter the content of the water by adding salt or other substances found in the ocean. You can also alter where the dyed water is placed in the jars. If a larger container was used you can vary the temperature of part of the water by using a heat lamp or heating the water from underneath.

Design Your Own Experiment

How to Select a Topic Relating to this Concept

The ocean is an immense subject with many possible projects that can branch from it. You could examine the properties of oceans and ocean life. You could also look at how oceans impact people's lives. With oceanographers using incredible technological tools in their work, the study of the oceans is another possible topic to explore.

Check the For More Information section and talk with your science teacher to learn more about oceans. You can also gather ideas from following ocean explorers, who often show life footage or descriptions of their expeditions on the Internet. People who live near an ocean could consider taking a field trip to collect samples, look at sea life, or observe the ocean. If you do take a field trip, make sure to discuss your trip with an adult.

Steps in the Scientific Method

To conduct an original experiment, you need to plan carefully and think things through. Otherwise, you might not be sure what question you are answering, what you are or should be measuring, or what your findings prove or disprove.

Here are the steps in designing an experiment:

- State the purpose of—and the underlying question behind—the experiment you propose to do.
- Recognize the variables involved and select one that will help you answer the question at hand.
- State your hypothesis, an educated guess about the answer to your question.
- Decide how to change the variable you selected.
- Decide how to measure your results.

Recording Data and Summarizing the Results

Your data should include charts and drawings such as the one you did for these experiments. They should be clearly labeled and easy to read. You may also want to include photographs and drawings of your experimental setup and results, which will help other people visualize the steps in the experiment.

If you are preparing an exhibit, you may want to display your results, such as any experimental setup you designed. If you have completed a nonexperimental project, explain clearly what your research question was and illustrate your findings.

Related Projects

Many of the findings about oceans are relatively recent and you can draw on this new information that oceanographers are discovering.

experiment
CENTRAL

The ocean is filled with life, from bacteria to fish to plants. You can explore the varied types of life and look at what lives in different parts of the ocean. Bioluminescence is one of the many adaptations that ocean creatures have developed. You can purchase bioluminescent organisms and observe their characteristics. Ocean plants differ from land plants in several ways. You can purchase an ocean plant and examine its characteristics. You could conduct a research project and study how the oceans support life suitable to that particular environment.

You could also examine the physical properties of oceans. Waves and tides are two basic properties of oceans. You can create a small body of water in your bathtub or large container to examine the movements of waves. Place an object on the wave to examine if waves carry an object. Tides are dependent on geographic location and time of year. You can gather data on the Internet or reference books to predict the high and low tides of oceans around the world. Researching how scientists take the salt out of the ocean is another possible project.

For More Information

Berger, Gilda, and Melvin Berger. *What Makes an Ocean Wave?* New York: Scholastic, 2001. ❖ Question-and-answer format about oceans and ocean life.

The Bioluminescence Web Page. http://www.lifesci.ucsb.edu/~biolum/ (accessed on August 25, 2003). ❖ Research data and graphics of bioluminescent ocean creatures.

"Deep Ocean Creatures." *Extreme Science.* http://www.extremescience.com/Deepest Fish.htm (accessed on August 25, 2003.) ❖ Nice pictures and facts on deep ocean creatures.

"Dive and Discover: Expeditions to the Seafloor." *Woods Hole Oceanographic Institute.* http://www.divediscover.whoi.edu (accessed on August 25, 2003). ❖ Follow ocean expeditions in this interactive web site.

Fleisher, Paul. *Our Oceans: Experiments and Activities in Marine Science.* Brookfield, CT: The Millbrook Press, 1995. ❖ Information on the physics and chemistry of the ocean with basic experiment ideas.

Oceana. http://www.oceana.org (accessed on August 25, 2003). ❖ The "Beneath the Surface" area has lots of ocean information, live pictures, and interactive maps.

"Ocean in Motion." *Office of Naval Research.* http://www.onr.navy.mil/focus/ocean/motion/tides1.htm (accessed on August 25, 2003). ❖ Brief explanation and animation of the tides.

Pulley, Sayre, and April Pulley. *Ocean.* Brookfield, CT: The Millbrook Press, 1997. ❖ Description of the physical features, life, and use of the ocean.

"Sea Dwellers." *Secrets of the Ocean Realm.* http://www.pbs.org/oceanrealm/sea dwellers/index.html (accessed on August 25, 2003) ❖ Pictures of life in the ocean.

"Water on the Move: The Ebbs and Flows of the Sea." *Museum of Science.* http://www.mos.org/oceans/motion/tides.html (accessed on August 25, 2003). ❖ From a museum ocean exhibit, includes real-time tide data.

sources for science supplies

The following is a selected list of sources that stock science supplies. Your science teacher and local library are also good sources of information regarding how and where to locate supplies for a science project. Always consult with a parent or teacher before ordering supplies.

American Science and Surplus
P.O. Box 1030
Skokie, IL 60076
(847) 647-0011
Internet: http://sciplus.com

Anchor Optical Surplus
4124 Edscorp Bldg.
Barrington, NJ 08007
(856) 573-6865
Internet: http://www.anchoroptical.com

Carolina Biological Supply Co.
2700 York Road
Burlington, NC 27215-3398
(800) 334-5551
Internet: http://www.carolina.com/

Edvcotek
Box 34123
Bethesda, MD 20827-1232
(800) 338-6835
Internet: http://www.edvotek.com

sources for science supplies

Fisher Science Education
Internet: https://www1.fishersci.com/education/index.jsp

Flinn Scientific Inc.
P.O. Box 219
Batavia, IL 60510
(800) 452-1261
Internet: http://www.flinnsci.com

Sargent-Welch/VWR Scientific Products Science Education
P.O. Box 5229
Buffalo Grove, IL 60089-5229
(800) 727-4368
Internet: http://www.sargentwelch.com

The Science Fair
140 College Square
Newark, DE 19711-5447
(302) 453-1817
Internet: http://thesciencefair.com

Science Stuff
7801 N. Lamar Blvd. #E-190
Austin, TX 78752-1016
(800) 795-7315
Internet: http://www.sciencestuff.com

budget index

Chapter name in brackets, followed by experiment name; *italic* type indicates volume number, followed by page number; **boldface** volume numbers indicate main entries in *Experiment Central*, Volumes 5 and 6.

Under $5

experiment
CENTRAL

$5–$10

budget index

$11–$15

experiment
CENTRAL

$16–$20

experiment
CENTRAL

$26–$30

$31–$35

level of difficulty index

Easy

Easy means that the average student should easily be able to complete the tasks outlined in the project/experiment, and that the time spent on the project is not overly restrictive.

Chapter name in brackets, followed by experiment name; *italic* type indicates volume number, followed by page number; **boldface** volume numbers indicate main entries in *Experiment Central*, Volumes 5 and 6.

Easy/Moderate

Easy/Moderate means that the average student should have little trouble completing the tasks outlined in the project/experiment, and that the time spent on the project is not overly restrictive.

**level of
difficulty
index**

experiment
CENTRAL

Moderate

Moderate means that the average student should find tasks outlined in the
project/experiment challenging but not difficult, and that the time spent
on the project/experiment may be more extensive.

**level of
difficulty
index**

Moderate/Difficult

Moderate/Difficult means that the average student should find tasks outlined in the project/experiment challenging, and that the time spent on the project/experiment may be more extensive.

Difficult

Difficult means that the average student will probably find the tasks outlined in the project/experiment mentally and/or physically challenging, and that the time spent on the project/experiment will be more extensive.

timetable index

Chapter name in brackets, followed by experiment name; *italic* type indicates volume number, followed by page number; **boldface** volume numbers indicate main entries in *Experiment Central*, Volumes 5 and 6.

1 hour

2 hours

2 days

3 days

6 days

3 to 4 weeks

6 weeks

6 to 14 weeks

general subject index

This index cumulates entries from the six-volume *Experiment Central* series. *Italic* type indicates volume number; **boldface** type indicates entries in Volumes 5 and 6; (ill.) indicates illustration or photograph.

general subject index

general subject index

experiment
CENTRAL

general subject index

experiment
CENTRAL

Proteins *5:* 154
Protists *3:* 388
Proton *6:* 273, 276
Protons *2:* 203, 461; *4:* 615
Protozoan *1:* 52; *3:* 387
Pufferfish *5:* 158 (ill.)
Pulleys *6:* 392–93
Pupa *2:* 341

R

Radiation *2:* 205, 360
Radicule *2:* 265
Radioisotope dating *5:* 214, 217
Radiosonde balloons *4:* 759
Radio wave *2:* 326
Radon *5:* 18, 21, 23
Rain *1:* 1–18; *4:* 729, 732 (ill.)
Rainforest *1:* 35, 38, 38 (ill.)
Ramp *6:* 390, 390 (ill.), 392
Rancidity *6:* 450–52
Reactants *1:* 61, 77
Reactions *2:* 217
Reaumur, Rene Antoine de *2:* 217
Recommended Daily Allowance
    (RDA) *6:* 505, 511–12
Recycling *1:* 109; *5:* 26; *6:* 331, 332
    (ill.)
Red Sea *3:* 543
Redshift *6:* 434–35, 434 (ill.)
Reduction *3:* 461
Reflection *2:* 358; *3:* 431
Reflector telescope *6:* 432–33, 432
    (ill.), 435
Refraction *3:* 431
Refractor telescope *6:* 432–33, 432
    (ill.), 436
Relative age *5:* 214, 216
Relative density *1:* 124, 125 (ill.)
Rennin *2:* 219
Resistance *2:* 188
Respiration *1:* 139, 265; *3:* 493
Resultant *4:* 633, 634 (ill.)
Retina *3:* 431
Retinal *6:* 507
Ribosomes *5:* 42
Richter, Charles F. *1:* 161, 162 (ill.)

Richter scale *1:* 161
Rivers *4:* 713–27
Rock *3:* 527–39
Rocket launch *5:* 197 (ill.)
Rocks *6:* 408, 411
    breakdown of into soil *6:* 409 (ill.)
    fossils in *5:* 213 (ill.)
Roller coaster *3:* 518
Root hairs *6:* 309, 311 (ill.), 312
Roots *2:* 264 (ill.)
Rotation and orbits *6:* 347–67
Rubies *5:* 135
Runoff *2:* 307; *6:* 290, 294, 294 (ill.)
Rust *1:* 62 (ill.), 462 (ill.), 469 (ill.)

S

Safe Water Drinking Act *5:* 26
Salinity *1:* 141; *3:* 541–55; *5:* 252–53
Saliva *5:* 104
Salmonellosis *5:* 45
Salting *6:* 450
Sand particles *6:* 411, 411 (ill.)
Sapphires *5:* 135
Satellite image *4:* 761 (ill.)
Satellites *2:* 279 (ill.)
Saturated *4:* 729
Saturated solutions *5:* 139, 140 (ill.)
Scars (tree trunk) *1:* 20
Scientific method *3:* 557–73
Screws *6:* 392–93
Scurvy *3:* 419; *6:* 506, 507
Sea caves *5:* 82, 83 (ill.)
Seasons *6:* 351
Seawater pressure *5:* 254 (ill.)
Second class lever *6:* 395
Second Law of Motion *5:* 192, 194
Sediment *5:* 213–14
Sedimentary rock *3:* 529; *5:* 213, 213
    (ill.), 217
Sedimentation *2:* 316
Seed crystal *5:* 139, 141
Seedlings *2:* 263, 263 (ill.)
Seismic belt *3:* 528
Seismic waves *1:* 159
Seismograph *1:* 161; *4:* 686
Seismology *1:* 161